KT-427-913

AN INTELLECTUAL HISTORY OF BRITISH SOCIAL POLICY

Idealism versus non-idealism

John Offer

First published in Great Britain in January 2006 by

The Policy Press
University of Bristol
Fourth Floor
Beacon House
Queen's Road
Bristol BS8 1QU
UK

Tel +44 (0)117 331 4054
Fax +44 (0)117 331 4093
e-mail tpp-info@bristol.ac.uk
www.policypress.org.uk

© John Offer 2006

British Library Cataloguing in Publication Data
A catalogue record for this book is available from the British Library.

Library of Congress Cataloging-in-Publication Data
A catalog record for this book has been requested.

ISBN-10 1 86134 530 5 hardcover
ISBN-13 978 1 86134 530 1

A paperback version of this book is also available

John Offer is Professor of Social Theory and Policy at the University of
Ulster, Coleraine, Northern Ireland.

The right of John Offer to be identified as the author of this work has been
asserted by him in accordance with the 1988 Copyright, Designs and Patents
Act.

All rights reserved: no part of this publication may be reproduced, stored in a
retrieval system, or transmitted in any form or by any means, electronic,
mechanical, photocopying, recording, or otherwise without the prior
permission of The Policy Press.

The statements and opinions contained within this publication are solely
those of the author and not of The University of Bristol or The Policy Press.
The University of Bristol and The Policy Press disclaim responsibility for any
injury to persons or property resulting from any material published in this
publication.

The Policy Press works to counter discrimination on grounds of gender, race,
disability, age and sexuality.

Cover design by Qube Design Associates, Bristol.
Front cover: © Stanley Spencer Gallery, Cookham, Berkshire, UK.
Printed and bound in Great Britain by Hobbs the Printers, Southampton.

Contents

Acknowledgements

Earlier versions of some sections of some chapters in the study have appeared elsewhere: sections from the first and last chapters as "'Virtue", "citizen character" and "social environment": social theory and agency in social policy since 1830', in *Journal of Social Policy* (Offer, 2006); from Chapters Two and Three as 'Spencer's future of welfare' and 'Free agent or "conscious automaton"? Contrasting interpretations of the individual in Spencer's writings on social and moral life', in *Sociological Review* (Offer, 1999c and 2003a, respectively); from Chapter Four as 'Dead theorists and older people', in *Sociology* (Offer, 2004); from Chapter Six as 'Idealist thought, social policy and the rediscovery of informal care', in the *British Journal of Sociology* (Offer, 1999a); and from Chapter Seven as 'Idealism versus non-idealism: new light on social policy and voluntary action in Britain since 1880', in *Voluntas* (Offer, 2003b). I am grateful to the publishers of these journals for permission to reproduce the material here. I am grateful too to the anonymous referees of these journals and of The Policy Press for their valuable comments, and also to participants who discussed issues with me at the three Social Policy Association conferences and other conferences where even earlier versions were launched, especially Tim Gray. I have benefited hugely from frequent discussions of many of the topics covered with Bob Pinker and John-Paul McGauran, and with two of my friends and long-suffering colleagues in Social Policy at Coleraine, Derek Birrell and Drew Hamilton. Janet Mackle helped to ensure that the book was completed. For what follows, however, the responsibility is mine.

I must record my sincere gratitude to the British Academy for three awards of financial assistance which facilitated research at the University of London Library and the British Library of Political Science. The results are reported in part in Chapters Four, Five and Eight. I am also deeply grateful to Liz McNeill, who has prepared the final typescript with patience and care.

Foreword

Professor Offer's scholarly account of the intellectual history of British social policy is structured around three interconnected themes of enquiry. He begins with a reappraisal of the theoretical contribution of Herbert Spencer and the non-idealistic character of his philosophy of welfare. He goes on to compare the key tenets of non-idealistic and idealistic theories of welfare and the influence they have had on the development of social policies. Lastly, he focuses attention on what we now call 'informal care' and Spencer described as the practice of 'positive private beneficence'. He explains why Spencer attached such significance to this form of social provision in his own philosophy of welfare.

Spencer was the only British sociologist of the nineteenth century to achieve a position of international authority and influence. His evolutionary theory of social development was intellectually grounded in a wide range of academic disciplines, including philosophy and the social and natural sciences. His philosophy of welfare was derived from his evolutionary theory which postulated that the progress of successful social adaptation occurred through the inheritance of acquired characteristics. In this respect, his theory was distinctively pre-Darwinian. It was Spencer, not Darwin, who coined the term 'survival of the fittest' in his interpretation of the history of human progress as an unremitting struggle for survival. The key to successful adaptation in this struggle was the development of human character, and, notably, the will to become self-determined and self-supporting in all matters relating to personal welfare.

Character, however, could only develop gradually over time on the basis of personal experience and in conformity with the laws of social evolution. It could not be changed quickly or 'artificially' by idealistically driven welfare agencies providing help to those who were failing to adapt successfully in the struggle for survival. In this respect, both statutory poor relief and non-statutory philanthropy were bound to fail. The taxes and donations they raised penalised the thrifty. The assistance they provided unjustly rewarded the maladaptive and feckless.

In Spencer's view, the sole task of government should be the administration of justice which was synonymous with altruism. Justice, as altruism, required that everyone should be free to do whatever they wanted, provided that they did not infringe the equal freedom of anyone else.

Spencer's second principle of altruism was expressed in his concept of 'positive private beneficence'. He thought that it was better to rely on 'parental affection, the regard of relatives and the spontaneous kindness of friends' than on formal social services in meeting welfare needs. Private beneficence strengthened the bonds of social solidarity and in no way impeded the evolutionary progress of social adaptation. Idealists who believed that it was possible to transform human character and create a better society through the agencies of social policy were bound to fail because such interventions violated the laws of social evolution.

Nevertheless, from the 1860s onwards, it was the idealist paradigm of social welfare that came to dominate the debate about the ends and means of British social policy and to direct the ways in which it subsequently developed. In the late 1860s, a small group of idealist philosophers and social reformers founded the Charity Organisation Society as a first step towards reorganising British philanthropy on 'scientific' lines.

The Society was committed to three main objectives – enforcing the deterrent principles of the 1834 Poor Law Amendment Act, encouraging self-help among the poorest members of society and applying the scientific principles of social casework in the assessment of their needs and moral character. Although the Society believed that there was a role for government in the fields of education, child care and prison reform it was implacably opposed to the extension of all other forms of statutory social provision.

The leading members of the Society included such luminaries as T. H. Green, Bernard and Helen Bosanquet and C. S. Loch. They were all idealists insofar as they shared an organic view of society and a belief that proactive and interventive social policies – directed primarily through the agencies of charitable organisations – had a vitally important role to play in the enhancement of moral and material welfare. For all of them, the ultimate test of the goodness of a social institution was whether or not it contributed to the development of moral character and encouraged the growing of an ethic of public service directed towards enhancing 'the common good'. Such ideals could not be realised by relying solely on the haphazard and unregulated dictates of 'positive private beneficence'. The deserving poor, at least, would always need the guidance and supervision of trained social workers.

The social idealists of the Charity Organisation Society offered a credible philosophical alternative to the hedonistic doctrines of Benthamite utilitarianism and classical political economy as well as the evolutionary determinism of Spencer's sociology. Throughout the period between the 1870s and the years prior to the outbreak of the First World War they were relatively successful in opposing the growth of statutory social services and in advocating greater reliance on the voluntary sector. Nevertheless, as Offer goes on the describe, their ascendancy was eventually challenged and superseded by a new generation of equally idealistic social theorists and reformers who believed that the goals of social policy could best be realised by greater reliance on statutory forms of intervention.

Like many other social policy scholars, Offer identifies the years just prior to the First World War as the period in which the institutional foundations of the British welfare state were laid down. It is, however, a central tenet in his thesis that almost all of the social policy thinkers who supported these reforms were also idealist in outlook, irrespective of their political convictions. This was certainly the case with regard to 'new liberals' like Hobhouse and Hobson and Fabian socialists like the Webbs. They may have disagreed with the Bosanquets about the respective roles of statutory and non-statutory intervention in social policy matters but they shared the same views about society as an organic entity and the same conviction that interventive social policies had a vitally important role to play in the improvement of moral character and the enhancement of welfare. In these respects they added a distinctively pro-statist and collective dimension to the ongoing traditions of idealist social thought.

But Offer goes on to suggest that these pro-statist and collectivist welfare theories have continued to be a dominant influence and source of ideas in the discipline of social policy down to the present day. He traces their subsequent development from the 1920s onwards through the writings of Tawney, Beveridge, Titmuss and other eminent social policy analysts. And he concludes that there is much in New Labour's approach to social policy issues that appears to be 'a reiteration of idealist modes of social thought'.

Offer finds it more difficult to identify any leading advocates of a non-idealist approach to social policy issues. He might have had greater success if he had included the disciplines of political science and economics in his field of enquiry. It is, however, difficult to subscribe to a Spencerian non-idealist theory of social welfare without, at the same time, accepting the basic tenets of his evolutionary theory.

Nevertheless, as Offer suggests, it is possible to detect 'the persistence of non-idealist thought in policy well into the twentieth century' albeit 'concealed ... below the Plimsoll line'. He goes on to identify two major gaps in the idealist approach to the study of welfare institutions. First, the leading scholars who wrote within this tradition invested so much trust in the capabilities of formally organised social services that they seriously neglected the whole field of informal social care. Second, they attached too much importance to the views of policy experts (including their own) and those of service providers and gave too little attention to those of ordinary people as service users.

In recent years, a small but growing number of social policy scholars have drawn attention to these omissions and sought to rectify them. Whether or not they should be classed as 'non-idealists' remains open to debate. Nevertheless, in their different ways, they have undoubtedly added a populist dimension to the study of social policy and, in so doing, have also challenged the idealist assumptions of those collectivist policy analysts and reformers who still believe that governments and experts always know best.

Offer concludes that, despite his uncompromising objections to all forms of interventive social policy, Spencer wrote with much insight and compassion about the dynamics of informal care and what he termed 'the principle of positive private beneficence'. Having belatedly rediscovered the importance of informal social care, the time may well have come for social policy thinkers and policy makers to rediscover what Spencer had to say on the subject. The publication of this original and challenging study by Professor Offer gives them an excellent opportunity to do so.

Robert Pinker
Emeritus Professor of Social Administration
London School of Economics and Political Science
August 2005

Introduction

It will be helpful to say something at the outset about how this book came to be written. Some time ago I had formed an interest in Herbert Spencer, and soon realised that his ideas on how liberty, the enforcement of justice, and the growth of altruism in general might advance welfare, developed in the second half of the nineteenth century, were not at all well understood in historical and theoretical studies of social policy. A reluctance to take Spencer seriously on such matters was to a degree excusable. His name was principally associated with the 'survival of the fittest', 'social Darwinism' and 'individualism', as it happens far from adequate or straightforward representations. None resonated positively in orthodox social policy circles.

However, unfamiliarity with Spencer concealed his innovative attention to the reality and potential of informal care, understood as 'private beneficence'. This state of affairs was ironic: by the late 1970s academics and policy makers involved in social policy and social work studies were, in a volte-face after customarily shunning informal care, waking up to it as a phenomenon needing research, and careful consideration in the framing of policies. My own research into informal care at the time (Cecil, Offer and St Leger, 1987) coupled with an interest in the analysis of Spencer's thought, led me to reflect on what sort of connection there might be between the neglect of Spencer and of informal care for so long in social policy discourse. It was clear at the time that liberal philosophies of welfare provision had not been in favour – the subject of social policy (or social administration as it was then more often known) – had apparently jettisoned them as inappropriate, or proven failures. It was also clear that taking seriously people's needs and preferences as they themselves defined them was to embrace liberal perspectives and pluralist values, not top-down command and unitary values (a perspective developed in two forthright articles by Antony Flew, 1983 and 1985 and which I surveyed in *Social workers, the community and social interaction* (Offer, 1999b)). Perhaps in some way the blossoming preoccupation with informal care in social policy studies was evidence of a 'paradigm shift', of an underlying disciplinary mind-set losing its hold. It seemed possible that such a mind-set had served both to eclipse from continued consideration the kind of liberal perspectives represented to my understanding by Spencer and to steer research and the process of making and implementing social policy itself away from informal care. But it was not yet clear how to identify the mind-set.

To fit the bill some broad feature or features needed to be discerned, in some substantial way shared by otherwise different sets of ideas. No one set could be involved. Fabian socialism, for instance, did not fit the historical record as the sole cause of Spencer's eclipse. Nor did it seem likely that party political change of government held the key; there had of course been Conservative governments before 1979 but these were not noted for a concern with informal care, and interest in informal care was in fact growing in a period when Labour was, just, in power though not promoting it.

The search was on for a body of mutating but nevertheless identifiable ingredients of social theory that had dominated thought about social policy from the last quarter of the nineteenth century to the 1970s – the dates are inevitably approximate – and which also meshed in reasonably well with the more generally politically dominant ideas over the same time span. It would need two crucial characteristics: to have expressed telling reservations over 'enabling' or 'empowering' informal care as objects of government action, and to offer an alternative to the kind of liberal social theory Spencer seemed to represent.

The search might easily have been entirely misguided – and might still be adjudged so. Perhaps my key generalisations were not sustainable, with no commonalities across such schools of thought conventionally accepted as disparate as 'christian socialism', 'Fabian socialism', and 'new liberalism', never mind feminist approaches as they gathered strength. Nevertheless the enterprise seemed to reflect concerns which others had run up against. In 1990 Norman Barry had suggested that 'one of the most decisive elements in contemporary thought is the assimilation of the idea of welfare to the state… However, this association is neither analytically compelling nor an accurate historical picture. Economists and social philosophers have indicated that there is a variety of sources of well-being' (Barry, 1990, p viii). I tried, therefore, without success, to weaken my confidence in them against the historical record of social policy itself, the development of social policy as a discipline and intellectual history. Perhaps I was placing too much emphasis on changes in social theory as a factor in change at the expense of wider social or economic pressures. This may indeed be so. However, I readily accept though do not explore here the fact that such pressures may be behind the shifts in theoretical orientation which I was attempting to pinpoint. More to the point, though, it seemed that in the absence of some shifts in social theory any economic or social pressures impinging on governments or policies would have led to outcomes different from what in practice occurred. In the field of 'community care', instead of policies designed to support 'carers', the direction of policy might have been to expand further already existing alternatives, or reductions in provision with no pluralist initiatives. Theory simply mattered.

Early on it became clear that a fundamental relevant distinction to be made in social theories was between, first, those theories that adopted a 'hands off' approach to achieving a 'good society', leaving it to be gained, if at all, *indirectly*, that is to say, through the outcomes of, left to their own decisions, whatever choices people make, and, second, those theories that argued that the 'good society' (or some synonymous expression) was to be attained by *directly* seeking to secure it. In the first kind of theory the prevention and rectification of 'unjust' aggressions on individuals, perhaps by the state itself, and the provision of financial support, where necessary, rather than the provision of services in terms of, say, professional intervention in one's lifestyle, were the routes forward that most readily suggested themselves. In the second kind of theory some vision of an attainable future and more moral state of affairs structured the kind of provision to be made available to people, and also the conditions, perhaps relating to their behaviour, surrounding their availability, so pushing them in a particular direction in their conduct. This was a distinction rarely dwelt upon in social policy studies and the possible potential of the first kind of theory was obscured. However, the distinction seemed to me to be the energy source which drove two compelling and radical books by Bob Pinker, *Social theory and social policy* of 1971 and *The idea of welfare* of 1979.

Spencer's fiercest critics from the 1870s onwards were philosophers, particularly at Oxford and in Scotland, known as Idealists, or sometimes Neo-Hegelians. Idealists contrasted what they called Spencer's 'atomic' individualism with their 'ethical' individualism. Individuals were so constituted as to be part of a moral unit, society, and a society could, and should, be guided towards spiritual advance by rulers in tune with the 'general will' of that society. Idealist thought at this time has for long been counted as influential in social policy up to the First World War. Thomas Hill Green, Bernard Bosanquet and Henry Jones are familiar names, particularly as idealist thought has recently attracted a process of reassessment (Vincent, 1984; Nicholson. 1990; Boucher and Vincent, 1993; and Boucher, 1997). Idealists are frequently credited with influencing the Charity Organisation Society, the Settlement Movement, the majority report on the Poor Laws of 1909 and the 'new liberalism' associated with Asquith's and Lloyd George's early twentieth-century governments. But then the trail usually goes cold. No link is made to the Fabians, or to the Webbs in particular. Idealists at work in much more recent times such as A.D. Lindsay and John Macmurray are quietly passed over. In a way this is not surprising because idealists' fundamental positions on philosophical questions to do with perception, the material world, and the nature of truth and meaning, were treated to punishing criticism from professional philosophers in the early twentieth century (notably by G.E. Moore and Bertrand Russell). Idealism lost considerable philosophical respectability, though it retained a niche position in 'social' philosophy.

In an important article of 1992, José Harris has advanced a case against a 'narrow' definition of idealist social thought associated simply with professional philosophy. Exponents of it were in at the birth of social science departments, social work education and adult education schemes, championing their growth and shaping their curricula. For Harris, key aspects of idealist social thought are present in the Webbs' writings on social policy, and idealist thought continued to mould social policy and theory well beyond the time span usually allotted to it. Idealist thought, argues Harris, was cultivated in muffled forms by Richard Titmuss. Titmuss had not been an undergraduate and so not exposed to idealist thought at the point at which most 'younger' idealists were. He was though impressed by R.H. Tawney's writings: Tawney himself had an idealist background.

What was next required was an examination of idealist social thought, defined broadly, to determine the relative importance it accorded to formal sources of assistance, both statutory and voluntary, compared with the assistance provided by relatives and neighbours. Complementary examinations of the nature and extent of idealist thought in Titmuss' writings, and of his views on informal care compared with other sources, were also required. Since it was already widely and reliably understood that social policy studies as a field was undergoing a transformation by the time Titmuss died in 1974, the change could, it was hoped, be presented in a theoretically rich context. At that time, though, it was a matter of serious dispute whether the change should be towards a greater reliance on Marxist perspectives associated with class conflict or towards a reappraisal of the importance and potential of sources of welfare in addition to the state. Titmuss had done a great deal to shape the teaching agendas and research priorities of departments of social administration after the Second World War, focused as they were on the legislation of the 1940s in the United Kingdom, which launched what is so often represented as a simple unity when called the 'welfare state', the theoretical diversity it embodied notwithstanding. With his blueprint for the subject being discarded, the inference that idealist frames of reference were imploding became available: there were new, or, as I prefer to refer to them, formerly eclipsed topics for teaching and research such as informal care basking in the sunlight on which idealist thought had drawn down the blinds. The shift seemed to have chimed in with reservations about idealist thought more generally in politics.

In short, then, this book draws and justifies a basic distinction between idealist and non-idealist social theories, and charts some of the divergent prescriptions about the objectives and scope of 'social policy' that they have begotten. It seeks to construct and substantiate an argument about the properties of the theories in question and the priorities apparent in both social policy studies and social policy itself over time.

My hope is to bring some novel and persuasive clarity both to the interpretation of the changes under review and to the assumptions behind some contemporary policy debates. In other words, the study should help towards an understanding of how we have come to think about social policy today in the way that we do. A related important aim is to plant Spencer much more firmly in the foreground than is usually the case. More space is devoted to Spencer than might be expected and I have tried to justify why this should be so as the discussion of his contribution and influence unfolds. Throughout the book, it should be noted, 'non-idealist' is used deliberately in preference to 'materialist', which might imply approval of idealist judgements on their opponents.

Given the objectives stated, the book is not intended to provide a comprehensive narrative of either the history of social policy or of the ideas situated therein. It has a more limited analytical concern with divergent ideas and images of welfare which is born out of a conviction that from the history of ideas in the field of social policy, past and present, springs genuine enlightenment for today. Dead theorists and 'old' theories, untended and mouldering in the graveyard that is the 'general background' afterthought on a reading list, is an intellectual outrage; they deserve their rightful status as intrinsic to the process of understanding our present 'problems' and our ways of making sense of the world. 'The welfare story', Lees has remarked, 'is not a whiggish saga of progress toward the sunny land of egalitarian social citizenship. To the contrary it is a tale shaped by the shifting winds of particular economic and social worlds. History and politics give it shape, and culture gives it meaning' (1998, p 353).

Something needs to be said about the use of 'social thought' in this book. First I have used it deliberately in preference to 'moral thought' or 'political thought'. Moral and political thought, or theory, both tend to rely on theories of social life but are more than such theories in seeking explicitly to furnish normative guidance. That is to say, they draw on one or other model of what a society is and the powers of individuals in it and then seek to develop a theory of, say, social justice, by which the performance of institutions may be judged. A focus on 'social thought', or 'social theory', is thus appropriate. Nevertheless, it means that social theories are more likely to be found conjoined with moral and political theories than developed in a free-standing manner. A further difficulty is how 'social thought' and 'social theory' stand in relation to 'sociological thought' and 'sociological theory'. At first sight it often seems that 'social' is used where 'sociological' might seem most appropriate. Percy Cohen's *Modern social theory* of 1968 was a study of theory in sociology, as was Anthony Giddens' *Capitalism and modern social theory* of 1971. Indeed, there is often no difference of meaning apparent. However, Marx, for example, would have seen his theoretical approach as broader then 'sociological', involving in an intimate way economics and history as well; this recognition applies certainly to the case of Giddens. Of theorists covered in the present book, Spencer deserves to be counted as a pioneer in sociological theory, but referring to him as a social theorist captures his wider normative theoretical concerns relating to social life, taking him and us into moral and political waters. Idealist thinkers, on the other hand, were clearly theorising about society (and morality and politics), but would not describe themselves as doing sociology (it can be argued that on occasion they could have done so, given their interests, but Spencer's name was associated with sociology; as we have seen, idealists wished to differentiate themselves sharply from Spencer). For den Otter (1996, pp 127-8), sociology, at least in the 1880s and 1890s, 'tended to refer to those theories which sought to apply biological evolutionary principles to the investigation of human societies. Attacks on the new discipline, therefore, were most often levelled at the kind of sociology advanced by Herbert Spencer... a figure who perhaps more than any other single contemporary shaped debate about the discipline of sociology'. On the whole then, it has seemed that 'social thought' and 'social theory' best indicate the nature of the ideas under consideration. This field itself is not confined to the output of academics: theory becomes embedded in policy documents and everyday reflections on ordinary life. I have tried to reflect that breadth, particularly in discussing non-idealist thought in the later years of the poor law.

It should be stated clearly from the beginning that the book is concerned with a fundamental contrast in the kind of social theory influencing social policy. Sometimes, indeed, an entire policy or service area can be interpreted as non-idealist, or idealist, in nature: the poor law, for instance is presented as non-idealist. Quite common, though, are cases where an area of policy or service provision displays elements of both idealism and non-idealism. These tend to be instances featuring cash benefits where the thrust of the policy is idealist but choices about how the benefit is spent are left to claimants, an element of non-idealism. The compulsory health insurance scheme introduced by the Liberal government in 1911, for instance, had idealist objectives. A greater sense of security in the workforce would pay dividends in terms of social cohesion and economic performance. Indeed, this kind of objective was underlined by the structure of contributions to the scheme: each insured person contributed, but so too did that person's employer, and the state also added to the total contribution in respect of each insured person. Moreover, the state did not run the scheme itself directly but in partnership with 'approved societies' drawn from the business and voluntary sectors, hence the scheme crossed boundaries and promoted organic unity in society in an authentic idealist manner. How the benefit was spent when claimed, however, was left to the claimant. Some idealist theorists in fact argued against the payments, preferring instead more direct health service provision (this example is discussed further in Chapter Five). This study, then, is primarily about a key divergence in the *social theories influencing* policy, rather than between policies themselves.

The analysis of the ideas about what form social policy *should* take in Britain since the 1830s, rather than simply the ideas present in the form that social policies as a matter of fact assumed, is thus my ultimate concern. This approach, it is hoped, will serve to complement other accounts of the history of social policy which focus on it as in fact implemented (of which Fraser's *Evolution of the British welfare state,* 1973, 3rd edition, 2003, remains the best known). In placing 'intellectual history' in the title I do not mean to refer to the history of ideas held by individual public-figure 'intellectuals', as they might have been termed in recent times, though that might well be a worthwhile topic of study, but instead to the history of those ideas that might reasonably be argued to have contoured the nature of the conception of problems and policy over the long run in the past two centuries or so in Britain.

The book begins with an examination of social theory about the poor law in Britain and Ireland in the 1830s. Much theoretical analysis afterwards rested on assumptions about what had been intended and for what reasons in the innovations of that decade. Unless we are unwisely prepared to take those representations at face value it is vital to get the thinking at the time as clear as possible. The introduction of a poor law to Ireland is considered in tandem with the case advanced for reform in England: the almost habitual neglect of the Irish innovation has been regrettable since it is revealing in itself in theoretical terms and contains ingredients which clarify the reasoning of players in the English reforms. Peter Mandler's (1990) emphasis on the centrality of evangelical and liberal Tory thought in the 1830s was of great assistance in the excavation. For some time the specific theological dimensions of policy in the nineteenth century have suffered neglect compared with its economic and political origins and consequences, in history in general as well as in the special area of the history of social policy, and it is good to be able to draw on Mandler and others to give a less 'materialist' appreciation of poor law thought.

The second chapter shifts the action to my paradigm non-idealist, Herbert Spencer. It considers both his arguments against welfare provisions emanating from the state and his support for 'private beneficence', for charities, and for the expanded administration of civil justice which he felt could make an enduring contribution to the enhancement of welfare. In effect, Spencer was laying out a sophisticated version of welfare pluralism in the last decade or so of Victoria's reign. The following chapter examines Spencer's complex interpretation of individuals and social life. Difficulties in this interpretation, chiefly over his account of human agency which worried his contemporary critics, including idealists, are discussed. This chapter is intended to show the range of targets that idealists were to believe they had found in Spencer: not his political analysis alone but his 'natural history' approach to moral sentiments and his conception of psychology and sociology. It also discusses more recent attempts to find in Spencer a champion of a liberal idea of community and rights-based utilitarianism for our own times. In doing so the chapter is neither encouraging nor discouraging the discovery of enduring 'life' in Spencer's ideas. The point is to show up the multi-layered nature of his thought, which revisionist interpretations need to address.

A 'case study' of theoretically grounded approaches to the care of older people is the subject of the next chapter. The familial tensions and financial difficulties in the absence of state pensions associated with the onset of old age were topical as the twentieth century began. Idealist preferences for supervision and surveillance in the care of older people are displayed in a close examination of the majority and minority reports which the Royal Commission on the Poor Law issued in 1909. Attention is also drawn to the notably different priorities which non-idealist thought brought to the fore, especially the obligations of sons and daughters towards their parents as they become advanced in years and increasingly dependent on others for coping with the demands of everyday life.

The fifth chapter treats in much greater depth theoretical themes that arose in connection with the discussion of the treatment of older people, and in previous chapters, drawing together and discussing the pivotal substantive differences between idealist and non-idealist social thought. Idealist conceptions of society as a moral organism and of freedom are introduced and a range of collectivist theoretical positions is identified, all of which, it is argued, are indebted to idealist social thought. Also examined are the divergent images held in idealist and non-idealist thought of ordinary people as agents in everyday life and of freedom, tutelary direction and moral progress.

Chapter Six is concerned with the deep-seated differences between the two traditions over the status accorded to informal care. Significant theoretical strands are seen to join together the 'classic idealists' such as Green, Jones and Bosanquet, and Richard Titmuss. In a consideration of the influence of Titmuss on the nascent academic discipline of social administration, an account of the idealist nature of its intellectual orientation in the 1950s and 1960s is advanced. Alongside the strikingly rapid sprouting of interest in the 'new' topic of informal care in the 1970s, however, the subject was slipping its anchorage in idealist assumptions.

The following chapter develops a framework in which to analyse the contrasting ways in which idealist and non-idealist social thought have interpreted the place of voluntary organisations in social life and the manner in which they can have a positive impact on welfare. It covers the divergence apparent *within* idealist thought over the most appropriate spheres of activity for the state and voluntary organisations, and also Auberon Herbert's non-idealist advocacy of 'voluntaryism' in late Victorian times. The contributions of William Beveridge and also the idealist philosopher, A.D. Lindsay, writing on and engaging with adult education in the first half of the twentieth century, are introduced to probe precisely how, at a time when pro-state rather than pro-voluntary idealist thought held sway in social policy thought, a case for voluntary action could be constructed. The shift away from pro-state idealism in particular in the 1970s, already noted in the previous chapter, is related to the theoretical features of a revival of interest in voluntary action. The chapter highlights that idealist and non-idealist interpretations of the role of voluntary action are held within voluntary organisations *themselves* and shape their missions accordingly. It discusses too the recent work of Etzioni on voluntary organisations and communitarianism, and a renewed idealist-inspired disposition towards voluntary action associated with 'New Labour', in connection with which voluntary organisations that understand their own aims in non-idealist terms may encounter pitfalls.

The final chapter applies the master contrast developed in previous chapters between idealist and non-idealist social thought to shed light on why there was significant popular support for the poor law in the early twentieth century during a time of high unemployment. By this time poor law relief had kept at bay idealist attempts to annex it to a programme of moral reform (as in the majority report) or to compulsory curative treatment of 'problems' (as in the minority report). Assistance now might well be awarded where there was need without being related to what might or might not hasten the 'good society' – in other words the poor law was in effect perceived as a quintessentially non-idealist source of social security, and thus acceptable because it left people to make their own choices freely, albeit limited of course by the low levels of financial support available. This chapter also discusses the recent and continuing emphasis in social policy, especially in connection with health care and education, on developing administrative mechanisms to facilitate consumer choice. Julian Le Grand's view that in policy circles users have come to be seen as decision-making 'queens' rather than passive 'pawns', and professionals and other service providers seen as potentially self-interested 'knaves' rather than altruistically inspired 'knights', is related to the distinction between idealist and non-idealist thought, in particular to a shift away from idealist assumptions in the construction of social policy. This chapter also applies the master distinction to a discussion of 'social capital', and considers the influence of the idealist John Macmurray on New Labour.

I should like to add that this study was prepared alongside of the heavy teaching, administrative and postgraduate supervision responsibilities now characteristic of university life in the United Kingdom. Time has not permitted the application of the master distinction to as many instances of theoretical input to the world of social policy as I would have liked, in particular in the field of economic thought. Nevertheless, I think that the argument, the core of the project, is presented in as complete a form as I can at present picture it. The neck is stuck out; critics can hack.

ONE

'Virtue' and the poor law in Britain and Ireland in the 1830s

Rethinking the poor law

It is nearly 60 years since the demise of poor law legislation in 1948, though workhouse buildings (already then designated public assistance institutions) survived longer, sometimes to this day, with new functions within health and social service provision. At least one is a 'heritage' icon (Southwell in Nottinghamshire, owned by the National Trust). Within historical studies the poor law still receives reassessment (Brundage, 1978; Digby, 1978; Dunkley, 1982; Neuman, 1982; Crowther, 1983; Mandler, 1990; and Harris, 1992). Within social policy studies, however, the 'moral defects' of poor law practice and theory tend to be emphasised, in contrast to the enlightenment embodied in the new legislation enacted in the 1940s on health provision, social security, education and the care of children, though there are exceptions such as Deacon (1981, 1982) and Pinker (1964). Histories of a discipline from 'within' tend to be conceptualised as stepping stones towards the present-day key achievements and concerns (Lewis, 1995). This chapter sets out to avoid this tendency and draws into the picture some wider interpretative concerns relating to the poor law, particularly its theoretical sources. As Edward Norman observed:

> After a long bleak interlude, historians are once more beginning to take the religious issues in nineteenth-century England seriously. For decades 'secular' historians have tended to regard the incidence of Christian belief, where they have come across it either in the lives of particular statesmen or in social groups, as a fringe cultural phenomenon, perhaps useful as a matter of social control. What they have not perceived as of importance in the modern world has not seemed to them, as noticed in the immediate past, as much more than the lingering evidence of a discarded order. When Morley, for example, wrote his

famous biography of Gladstone he could not, as an atheist, bring himself to regard Gladstone's religious priorities as real priorities. The result, with an enduring legacy, was a depiction of Gladstone as a moralist (for atheists can understand moral priorities) rather than a man motivated by a religious view of the world. (1987, p 56)

However, as explained in the Introduction, this chapter is also designed to contribute to an intellectual framework that, it will be contended, assists us in making new sense of conceptions of the individual user of services in social policy and social policy studies in the twentieth century and beyond. One way this is approached here is by examining and developing recent work of Le Grand (2003). Le Grand pinpointed how assumptions about agency and motivation held by policy makers affect policy. He divides the way agency is imputed to service users, with 'pawns' as mute and powerless recipients of what is prescribed contrasted with 'queens' exercising choice. Service providers are categorised as 'knights' (motivated by altruistic sentiments) and 'knaves' (motivated by self-interest). Le Grand found movement in the 1970s and 1980s towards users as 'queens' and providers as 'knaves'. The distinction between 'pawns' and 'queens' in particular, with adjustment to introduce 'lapsed queens', helps interpret the 1830s.

The chapter begins by considering the prominence Mandler (1990) has accorded to the ideas of the 'Noetics' in shaping poor law reform in England in the 1830s and the conflict in events heralding the introduction of a poor law to Ireland in 1838, conflict often overlooked but revealing about the foundations of reform in England.

Intellectuals and poor law reform in England in the 1830s

Revolution in France, the Napoleonic wars, the Act of Union with Ireland, and economists' alarms over the costs and consequences of outdoor relief (including Malthus' concern that population growth would outstrip the resources to support it) formed the backcloth to poor law thought in the 1830s. Governments stalled on reform in this hothouse climate: the 'old' poor law perhaps kept the peace at home. However, in 1830 the rural insurrection of the Swing disturbances erupted in the southern counties of England. If the poor law no longer guaranteed social stability, the case for reform triumphed (Dunkley, 1982). As is well known, a royal commission to inquire into the poor law was established in 1832. However, the pivotal role of liberal Tories of the day in the process of making appointments to the commission and as appointees, the production of its report in 1834 and the Act of the same year, and in the appointment of a separate commission on the suitability of a poor law for Ireland (there was no 'old' poor law), has often been eclipsed. By contrast, prominence has been accorded to the writings of Bentham and their transmission via Edwin Chadwick.[1]

This situation Mandler (1990) has tried to redress. Nassau Senior, he reminds us, was co-author of the report in 1834 with Chadwick. But Chadwick was 'an outsider and effectively an isolate' – most commissioners 'were neither Benthamites nor liberals nor even Whigs, but liberal tories' (Mandler, 1990, p 82). By the 1820s a liberal Tory position was emerging that fused economic liberalism fuelled by the Scottish enlightenment with political authoritarianism. In intellectual form this was a combination of natural theology, which sought to demonstrate evidence of God's existence, with political economy, pioneered particularly at Oriel College, Oxford by the so-called Noetics (the word is from Greek, meaning 'reasoners'). Mandler applies the term Noetic to those in and around Oriel College in the 1820s, such as Edward Coplestone, John Davison, Richard Whately, and Senior, and also to others who shared their fundamental views on political economy. The natural progress of human improvement came through the striving by individuals for higher levels of virtue, not in the pursuit of happiness or material goods. Providence reinforces duty through the presence of scarcity, and its potentially catastrophic consequences: key virtues are prudence and industry, with the accumulation of wealth as a sign of virtue, enabling further moral achievement through benevolence. Conservatism followed, with the Noetics 'unabashed believers in rule by the virtuous – that is, the wealthy – who were best able to monitor and foster the progress of morality' (Mandler, 1990, p 88). Governance was their province, but governments were unable to create virtue or prevent sin, though through impious measures they could hinder virtue and encourage vice.

Liberal Tories infused with Noetic beliefs derived from Oxford days were a powerful grouping in the 1820s and 1830s. They assumed important positions in the Church of England, the law and as Tory MPs. There was scope for sympathy with Benthamite reform, and sufficient tensions within the Tory Party over reform for them to give conditional support to the new Whig government. Nassau Senior's connections before 1830 had been liberal Tory, but he 'had been assiduously worming his way into high ministerial circles since the day the Whigs took office' (Mandler, 1990, p 97). Senior must have been in at the birth of the idea of a royal commission in January 1832, and subsequently headed the list of the eight members appointed. Alongside Senior, Mandler identifies William Sturges Bourne, Bishop Sumner of Chester, Bishop Blomfield of London, and the Revd Henry Bishop as the core of the commission 'all connected with the Noetics' (1990, p 98). Of the others, Henry Gawler was a lawyer with views on the poor law that 'perfectly accorded with those of the Noetics' (Mandler, 1990, p 99), James Traill made no apparent contribution, and the Benthamite Walter Coulson was an old pupil of Senior. Chadwick, known to the Noetics as a contributor to their *London Review*, was initially an assistant commissioner. At least ten of the 25 assistant commissioners had Noetic links. For the Webbs to describe the majority of the royal commissioners as Benthamite was a distortion: 'although this tory dog had a Benthamite tail, it was the dog which wagged the tail and not vice versa' (Mandler, 1990, p 83). For the Noetics, unlike the Benthamites, their end

> was not utility but the propagation of virtue. Whereas utility
> could be judged by human government, virtue could not.
> Like the Benthamites, they understood the limits of self-
> interest in achieving desirable ends, but, unlike them, they
> were reluctant to direct or override it. If the exercise of
> self-interest had deleterious consequences, often it was
> because God intended it to be so. Ignorance and misery
> could only be surmounted by the learning of duty and
> virtue ... (Mandler, 1990, p 95)

The Noetics had reached the 'Principle of Less Eligibility' independent of the Benthamites. This principle deserves to be given in full here to display the distinctive Noetic concern with virtue and vice. It declared that the situation of a person receiving poor relief should not

> be made really or apparently so eligible as the situation of
> the independent labourer of the lowest class. Throughout
> the evidence it is shown that in proportion as the condition
> of any pauper class is elevated above the condition of
> independent labourers, the condition of the independent
> class is depressed; their industry is impaired, their
> employment becomes unsteady, and its remuneration in
> wages is diminished. Such persons, therefore, are under the
> strongest inducements to quit the less eligible class of
> labourers and enter the more eligible class of paupers. The

converse is the effect when the pauper class is placed in its proper position, below the condition of the independent labourer. Every penny bestowed that tends to render the condition of the pauper more eligible than that of the independent labourer, is a bounty on indolence and vice. (Poor Law Report, 1974, p 335)

Outdoor relief to the able-bodied was, therefore, the 'master evil of the present system' (Poor Law Report, 1974, p 395)[2].

The Noetics also controlled the process of advising on the contents of the Poor Law Amendment Bill of 1834 and the appointment of the parliamentary draughtsmen. On the permanent Poor Law Commission to implement the Act the Noetics were again in the driving seat. Chadwick was secretary but the commissioners and assistant commissioners tended to be Noetics; after 1841, when George Cornewall Lewis and Edmund Head became commissioners, differences with Chadwick over the direction of poor law policy became rancorous. Chadwick repeatedly worked against his superiors' desire to interfere again in the labour market by hiring out paupers for less than ordinary wages and to extend outdoor relief (see Finer, 1952, pp 120-1 and 181-92). At a fundamental level the issues involved differences in principle between Noetics and Benthamites about ends rather than means:

while they agreed on the starting-point established by the 1834 report, their differences were bound to surface thereafter. Basically, the Benthamites were true believers in the power of scientific government. They defended poor laws in principle, and considered them to be powerful engines of improvement in practice. The permanent Poor Law Commission could be the nucleus of a 'preventive police' whose aim was to scour out evil influences whenever they reared their head. The Union workhouse would be but the first of an array of institutions – schoolhouses, hospitals, asylums, sanitary boards – all aiming to make people happy and secure. For the Noetics much of this was utopian and impious. Happiness and security could only be earned through the performance of virtue. The permanent Poor Law Commission's task was to wean landlords and labourers from this deadly dependence, not to devise new means of interference. The workhouse was to deter, not to improve; it would work best if it remained empty. Improvement was to be left to individual character. (Mandler, 1990, p 101)

The overarching objective of repositioning the poor law so that it ceased to hinder virtue and encourage vice (no such agency could create virtue) was to be secured, so the 1834 report proclaimed, by abolishing outdoor relief to the able-bodied, furnishing relief only on the condition that the recipient entered a workhouse. At a stroke, to receive relief would place individuals in a 'less eligible' position than individual labourers. This method of implementing the poor law was already in place in some parishes and it impressed the commissioners deeply, as putting back in place the intentions of the original Elizabethan legislation, and hence displaying how best to proceed across the whole country. These model dispauperised parishes had been fortunate in possessing (Poor Law Report, 1974, p 399) 'an individual of remarkable firmness and ability, often joined with a strong interest in good administration, great influence to overcome opposition, and leisure to establish good management. In the majority of instances the change originated with the clergyman or some of the largest holders of land within the parish.' The report frequently cites evidence to this effect from Southwell in Nottinghamshire, and from Faringdon, Swallowfield and, in particular, Cookham, all in Berkshire. However, in the absence of such individuals, the abuses continued. Thus in Cookham (Poor Law Report, 1974, p 399) 'the benefits of the improved administration have been manifested since the year 1822, but manifested without imitation' in neighbouring parishes.

It is important to be clear that the report was setting its face against apportioning relief according to a person's merit, that is, whether or not they were seen as 'deserving' or 'undeserving'. Harmful consequences of this practice are deemed unavoidable and prevalent. In the county of Cambridge, it appeared (Poor Law Report, 1974, p 120) 'that such endeavours to constitute the distribution of relief into a tribunal for the reward of merit, out of the property of others, have not only failed in effecting the benevolent intentions of their promoters, but have become sources of fraud on the part of the distributors, and of discontent and violence on the part of the claimants'.

On realising that he lacked adequate knowledge of his parishioners' circumstances, the rector of Ufton altered his practice (Poor Law Report, 1974, p 121): 'When first I came to this parish, I instituted rewards for virtuous conduct ... but I soon found that I did more mischief than good by the proceeding, and I was compelled to abandon it'. The practice had indeed been sanctioned (Dunkley, 1982, p 67):

'After 1815 it became well-nigh official policy to discriminate between the "deserving" and "undeserving" poor when distributing the rates, select committees of the House of Commons in 1817, 1819, and 1824 urging local authorities to consider the character of the applicant before granting an appeal'.

In practice, this approach to relief had led to higher expenditure. The 1834 report (Poor Law Report, 1974, p 141), and indeed Whately's third report on Ireland (Third Report, 1836), drew attention to the experience of the parish of Cholesbury in Buckinghamshire. By 1832 this parish had virtually ceased to function. Landowners, farmers and even the clergyman faced a financial collapse: the rates charged to finance poor relief now simply outstripped their revenues, and surrounding parishes were obliged to step in to support Cholesbury's poor. Cholesbury in fact appeared to be a unique 'black hole', but other parishes were approaching its fate. Here, outdoor relief to able-bodied persons in the previous three decades had cumulatively increased poor rates and the number of births, and reduced labour and depressed wages, with the parish economy finally spiralling down to a crash. Not only were virtuous individuals being punished by the old poor law's impact; so too was the virtuous community. If this fate could befall parishes in relatively prosperous England, to introduce any system of relief for the able-bodied poor of Ireland might well be deemed a high-risk venture. The report applauds one magistrate's statement of defiance:

> I do not think that the character of a pauper, even if he is in distress, can be taken into consideration; for the Poor Laws were not established as a reward for good conduct, but as a provision for the person in immediate distress, and a person just discharged from the house of correction, or a prostitute, is as much entitled to relief as the most respectable pauper in the parish, because the principle of the English Poor Law is that no one shall starve; therefore the magistrates are obliged to order relief to bad characters as well as good if they are incapable of supporting themselves. (Poor Law Report, 1974, p 235)

In tune with this opinion, and recognising the practical difficulties of judging character in a manner 'to obtain sufficient popular confidence to remove the impression of the possible rejection of some deserving cases' (Poor Law Report, 1974, p 387), the report roundly declares that 'destitution, not merit, is the only safe ground of relief' (Poor Law

Report, 1974, p 392). Once the workhouse was instituted as the sole source of relief, it brought into being 'a self-acting test of the status of the applicant' (Poor Law Report, 1974, p 378). By such means, 'the line between those who do and those who do not need relief is drawn, and drawn perfectly. If the claimant does not comply with the terms on which relief is given to the destitute, he gets nothing; and if he does comply, the compliance proves the truth of the claim – namely his destitution.'

By definition, the workhouse ensures that no person 'in need' – understood as destitution – is refused relief, and that no person not destitute receives it. The inherent symmetry and simplicity is toasted with enthusiasm.[3]

> If, then, regulations were established and enforced with the degree of strictness that has been obtained in the dispauperised parishes, the workhouse doors might be thrown open to all who would enter them and conform to the regulations. Not only would no agency for contending against fraudulent rapacity and perjury, no stages of appeals (vexatious to the appellants and painful to the magistrates), be requisite to keep the able-bodied from the parish; but the intentions of the Statute of Elizabeth, in setting the idle to work, might be accomplished, and vagrants and mendicants actually forced on the parish; that is, forced into a condition of salutary restriction and labour. (Poor Law Report, 1974, p 378)

The report concluded by looking to the future, convinced that their recommendations should remove or diminish the evils of the present system, and in the same degree remove the obstacles 'which now impede the progress of instruction, and intercept its results, and will afford a freer scope to the operation of every instrument which may be employed, for elevating the intellectual and moral condition of the poorer classes' (Poor Law Report, 1974, p 378). Nevertheless, subsequent poor law practice often continued to evade the neat logic: the 'master evil' of outdoor relief to able-bodied persons persisted (it was cheaper than indoor relief), local areas dragged their feet over workhouse construction (Lees, 1998) and scope for substituting merit for destitution survived.

Chadwick, although he was secretary to the permanent commission, soon found the field of sanitary reform more congenial, and issued his *Report on the sanitary conditions of the labouring population of Great Britain* in 1842. His fellow utilitarian, John Stuart Mill, read it 'slowly and carefully', and found 'the strength and largeness of practical views which are characteristic of all you do' (letter to Chadwick, in Finer, 1952, p 210). Later in the decade, Mill clearly aligned himself with the deductive core of the poor law report. For Mill, destitution creates a strong claim for assistance: there is 'the amplest reason for making the relief of so extreme an exigency as certain to those who require it, as by any arrangements of society it can be made' (Mill, 1970, p 333). A reliance upon charity would exhibit two shortcomings: charity would 'almost certainly' be geographically uneven in its provision, and, since the state 'must necessarily provide subsistence for the criminal poor while undergoing punishment, not to do the same for the poor who have not offended is to give a premium on crime' (Mill, 1970, p 335). However, relief is injurious if people come to rely upon it. If assistance is given in a manner which 'leaves to everyone a strong motive to do without it if he can, it is then for the most part beneficial. This principle, applied to a system of public charity, is that of the Poor Law of 1834' (Mill, 1970, p 334). Seeking to yoke together individual liberty and utility, Mill adds, however, that the state

> cannot undertake to discriminate between the deserving and the undeserving indigent. It owes no more than subsistence to the first, and can give no less to the last. What is said about the injustice of a law which has no better treatment for the merely unfortunate poor than for the ill-conducted, is founded on a misconception of the province of law and public authority. The dispensers of public relief have no business to be inquisitors. Guardians and overseers are not fit to be trusted to give or withhold other people's money according to their verdict on the morality of the person soliciting it, and it would show much ignorance of the ways of mankind to suppose that such persons, even in the almost impossible case of their being qualified, will take the trouble of ascertaining and sifting the past conduct of a person in distress, so as to form a rational judgement on it. (Mill, 1970, pp 335-6)

'A manifest hiatus': towards a poor law in Ireland

Accompanying the English question of poor law reform a debate had been running over whether or not a poor law should be introduced in Ireland, and, if it was, of what sort: 'one of the most important questions which at present affects the interests of England', according to J.E. Bicheno in 1830 (1830, p 231)[4]. Here another well-connected Noetic, Richard Whately, played a large role. His brother Thomas, rector of Cookham, Berkshire, had reformed parish relief along Noetic lines, and was, as we have seen, commended in the 1834 report. An Oriel Fellow, Whately tutored Senior (they remained in close contact); his publications on logic, theology and economics were widely read. In the 1820s, after initiating poor law reform in Halesworth, Suffolk, he became Professor of Political Economy at Oxford, departing in 1831 for Dublin to become archbishop there. Unavailable in England, Whately, with Senior's recommendation,[5] chaired the Irish inquiry established in 1833.

With reference to his published letter of 1831 to Lord Howick on Irish poor laws, Senior wrote in 1836 to Lord John Russell, the home secretary, to give broad endorsement to Whately's third and final report on recommendations of the same year:

> In that letter I protested against any compulsory provision for the able-bodied or their families. The only change that subsequent experience has produced in my opinion is, that I now believe that in England, or in any other country in which the standard of subsistence is high, a provision for the able-bodied in strictly managed workhouses, in which their condition shall be inferior to that of the independent labourer, may be safely, and even advantageously made. But, as this is not the state of Ireland, as the standard of subsistence in that country is so low, that any provision which the State could offer must be superior, so far as physical comfort is concerned, to that obtained by the independent labourer, this change of opinion does not apply to Ireland, and I am forced, therefore, as far as Ireland is concerned, to adhere to that letter. (Senior, 1837, p 4)

Whately knew Senior's position. He was also familiar with the most recent report of 1830 from the select committee on the state of the poor in Ireland, which had declined to recommend a poor law (Report of Select Committee, 1830, p 55). Bicheno, who had already written in Noetic vein on the English poor law and, fresh from a visit to Ireland, had given evidence that the country was characterised by charitable activity among the poor themselves as well as from the gentry: a poor law would destroy the active charity that already existed and would 'break up what is of vital importance to a good state of society, the virtuous exercise of the social feelings' (Report of Select Committee, Minutes of Evidence, 1830, p 380). Bicheno was himself now a member of Whately's commission. Whately's third report argued that Irish provision must differ from English: with no established right to support there was no duty to provide even deterrent workhouses. Moreover, in Ireland 'we see that the labouring class are eager for work, that work there is not for them, and that they are therefore, and not from any fault of their own, in permanent want. This is just the state of circumstances to which the Poor Law Commissioners of England say the workhouse system is not applicable' (Third Report, 1836, p 5). The land could not support the charge of a rate to support the able-bodied poor: 'As the parish of Cholesbury became to other parishes in England, so … the whole of Ireland would soon have to lean on Great Britain for support' (Third Report, 1836, p 6). Legislation to help improve the country, increasing the demand for free and profitable labour, was essential 'for ameliorating the condition of the poor' (Third Report, 1836, p 8). The impotent should be relieved, but able-bodied persons unable to find worthwhile employment 'should be secured support only through emigration, or as a preliminary to it' (Third Report, 1836, p 8). Emigration was no permanent panacea: but for now it was 'an auxiliary essential to a commencing course of amelioration' (Third Report, 1836, p 17). A board of improvement would bring land into cultivation, provide road, and drainage, improve land under cultivation, and establish an 'agricultural model school' (Third Report, 1836, p 22).

The report categorises the impotent poor, indicating the legal provision necessary. Public institutions are required (Third Report, 1836, p 25): 'for the relief and support of incurable as well as curable lunatics, of idiots, epileptic persons, cripples, deaf and dumb, and blind poor, and all who labour under permanent bodily infirmities …', and also for 'the relief of the sick poor in hospitals, infirmaries, and convalescent establishments'. External attendance and 'a supply of food as well as medicine' should be provided 'where the persons to be relieved are not in a state to be removed from home'. Further institutional provision is required for 'the purpose of emigration, for the support of penitentiaries to which vagrants may be sent, and for the maintenance of deserted children; also towards the relief of aged and infirm persons, of orphans, of helpless widows with young children, of the families of sick persons, and of casual destitution'. Implementation requires a permanent poor law commission, elected boards of guardians, and powers to award grants to voluntary associations for the building of alms-houses and other purposes.

Nevertheless, the report observes that the effectiveness of remedies 'under Providence' mainly depends:

> upon those who possess power and influence in the country. It is only through these that the poor can be put into proper courses of industry, taught the value of comforts, or animated to exertions to procure them. In proportion as such persons are raised high, they have high duties to perform; they are endowed with wealth and intelligence, not as means of self-indulgence, or for effecting any sordid object of ambition, but as trusts for the good of their fellow-creatures. (Third Report, 1836, p 31)

G.C. Lewis (1837) provided an important critical response to the report, the title page describing it as 'drawn up by the desire of the Chancellor of the Exchequer for the purpose of being submitted to His Majesty's Government'. Lewis points to the absence of a test that the impotent poor to be relieved are indigent, and to the cross-cutting class of 'casual destitute' and its indistinctness from able-bodied indigence that the report vows to exclude from relief. 'On what ground,' Lewis asks, 'is a man in real want to be denied relief, because he is able-bodied, while a man whose want is no greater, receives relief because he is not able-bodied' (1837, p 7). Lewis then criticises the claim that less eligibility would be inapplicable to Irish workhouses because 'the standard of existence among the labouring population is already the lowest upon which life can be sustained' (1837, p 9). Lewis does not charge Whately with this argument (though clearly Senior was committed to it), but believes it to be widely accepted. It is not the quantity or quality of food that enforces less eligibility, but compulsory labour and confinement. Workhouses are practicable in Ireland. Moreover, the workhouse test ascertains destitution: as a consequence 'there is no apparent ground for not relieving the able-bodied as well as the widow and the man infirm through age' (Lewis, 1837, p 16). Lewis raises questions of practicability in respect of the no fewer than eight classes of public institutions to come under the control of the commissioners, excluding, of course, the workhouse, 'the most important of all' (1837, p 19). There is 'a manifest hiatus in their system' (Lewis, 1837, p 27) without workhouse provision for able-bodied persons; for the commissioners dismiss emigration as a policy to be pursued permanently and extensively for able-bodied persons. Refusing workhouse-based relief would be 'a powerful and perpetual incentive to imposture and immorality, and would create a new class of evils peculiar to this kind of poor law' (Lewis, 1837, p 22). Lewis also complains that the report asserts 'the duty of the state to find employment for the people' (1837, p 27). This principle is, however, absent from the English poor law; contrary to the report's belief, setting to work is a *condition* of relief only. Finally, Lewis is critical of proposals to improve the land:

> A Government can only, as it seems to me, attempt to accelerate the improvement of the soil by *indirect* means. In this, as in most other cases connected with the *material* part of civilization, its functions are simply negative; it can do no more than remove obstacles to amelioration, and suffer a society to proceed unchecked in its natural career of enhancement. All attempts to give a positive onward impulse to the creation of wealth may be expected to turn out like the efforts of a paralytic man, whose limb moves in a contrary direction to his will. (1837, p 30)

Government might indeed undertake to build roads in the public interest in the absence of private proprietorial efforts but this scheme 'of the Government managing everything for individuals ... very captivating and plausible at first sight ... invariably ends by producing lethargy and helplessness in the people, and by counterworking the very end which it is intended to promote' (Lewis, 1837, p 29).

Lewis, then, advocated an English-style poor law for Ireland, workhouse-based and affording relief to the destitute. He had reached this conclusion by at least August, 1834: 'From what I can learn of the run ... of the evidence ... the evils of the present system of maintaining the destitute poor in Ireland ... appear so great that a well organised workhouse system would be far preferable' (Lewis, 1870, p 35). Lewis was in Ireland at this time, as an assistant commissioner to Whately's inquiry, investigating the poor Irish resident in England and Scotland, and also serving as a commissioner on the state of the established Church in Ireland.[6] Lewis' father, Thomas Frankland Lewis, was of Noetic sympathies and interested in English poor law concerns (he became one of the first members of the permanent English poor law commission) and no doubt discussed matters with his son. When Whately's third report first appeared in April 1836, G.C. Lewis had characterised it as containing 'all kinds of absurd projects no sane Government will ever think of introducing' (Lewis, 1870, p 48). By July the same year he was submitting to the government the *Remarks*.

There was, indeed, 'a difference of opinion on Ireland within the

Noetic camp' (Mandler, 1990, p 101), particularly over whether or not to allow a *right* to relief to able-bodied persons, though, as G.C. Lewis wrote to Head in April 1837 regarding the Irish Poor Law Bill, the refusal 'of the *express* right to relief will be quite illusory: practice will establish what the legislature will not grant' (Lewis, 1870, p 76). However, Whately had also described the labouring population as 'not from any fault of their own, in permanent want' (Third Report, 1836, p 5). Even his friend Senior found this statement unpalatable:

> I cannot admit that they are in want *not from any fault of their own*. If the Irish labourers allow their numbers to increase without any reference to the means of subsistence, a portion of them must every year, or at every unfavourable season, perish from want, and all of them be in a state of permanent distress, or apprehension of distress. And as this state of things would be the necessary result of their own previous conduct, I cannot admit that it would occur *without* any fault of their own. (Senior, 1837, p 2)

Orthodox Noetic belief was that Providence reinforced the duty to be virtuous and industrious through the Malthusian pressure on population: to deny to labouring people in Ireland any responsibility in this circumstance would threaten in substantial measure that belief. Here, perhaps, lay the origin of the dispute.

The Whig government turned to George Nicholls, a Birmingham banker and friend of Peel, to find a way forward. Nicholls was one of the three permanent English poor law commissioners, known for strict enforcement of the conditions on which relief was granted at Southwell, Nottinghamshire in the 1820s. On 22 August 1836, Russell, the home secretary, wrote requesting that Nicholls go to Ireland to examine the soundness of Whately's views on poor relief, workhouses and emigration. The list of topics to examine reflects the matters that concerned Lewis. Nicholls reported on 15 November. He favoured a workhouse-based system of relief covering *all* destitution, with no outdoor relief (Nicholls, 1837, p 21). He cautioned that a general famine is 'a contingency altogether above the powers of a Poor Law to provide for' (Nicholls, 1837, p 21), and that a general policy of emigration would lower the quality of the population remaining, with the strongest persons most likely to leave (Nicholls, 1837, p 31). An excess of population was 'an evil', with prevention possible through 'improved moral and prudential habits', which in Ireland 'prevail in a very imperfect degree', with marriages contracted with 'the most reckless improvidence' (1837, p 31). In this manner, the 'sphere of wretchedness and want' was extended (Nicholls, 1837, p 32). Nicholls may not have been an Oriel man, but this was music to conventional Noetic ears.

Nicholls' proposals, striking a chord with those of Lewis, formed the basis of the Irish poor law legislation of 1838.[7] To Lewis, Nicholls' report seemed 'generally right in its opinions and recommendations' (Lewis, 1870, p 76). Whately's commission thus had no effect on legislation. Whately possessed a markedly independent turn of mind; a Protestant archbishop, he espoused Catholic emancipation, disestablishment, and non-sectarian education, and was thus a controversial figure. The English report of 1834 had pointed to generous outdoor relief to able-bodied people, regardless of their innate character, as the taproot of imprudence and dependency. The important thing was to remove this incentive. In Ireland, there was no 'old' poor law at which to point the finger, though there was over-population. Senior and Lewis in these circumstances blamed the destitute themselves, at least in part, as the cause of their own suffering, but Whately did not (nor did Bicheno, 1836, p 13: 'their vices have sprung from their situation, not their situation from their vices'). Key factors in this dissent were the social and economic organisation in Ireland, including land ownership. This analysis, chiming with Whately's general commitment to reform, was in the van of ideas at the time: little wonder that a more orthodox reformed poor law of the sort now embedding itself in England was the preferred option of the dominant members of the Whig government.

Whately's position on the question of a poor law for Ireland had not been reached in a casual manner: it seems to reflect his critical reading of Malthus. In his *An essay on the principle of population* of 1798, Malthus had criticised the poor law for allowing the population to increase more than it would without the poor law and, through poor rates, for reducing the living standard of labourers: he called for the abolition of parish laws relating to relief, and, in cases of extreme distress, for county workhouses funded by 'rates upon the whole kingdom' (1970, p 102). In 1832 in his *Introductory lectures on political economy*, Whately had identified a crucial ambiguity in Malthus' argument (Whately, 1832, ch IX, paras 43-4). For Whately, the doctrine that

> since there is a tendency in population to increase faster
> than the means of subsistence, hence, the pressure of
> population against subsistence may be expected to become

greater and greater in each successive generation (unless
new and extraordinary remedies are resorted to), and thus
to produce a progressive diminution of human welfare...
may be traced chiefly to an undetected ambiguity in the
word 'tendency' which forms a part of ... the argument.

By a 'tendency' towards a particular result can be meant 'the existence
of a cause which, if *operating unimpeded*, would produce that result'.
But, instead, it may be taken to mean 'the existence of such a state of
things that that result *may be expected to take place*'. In this second sense,
as society progresses, and contrary to Malthus' imputation, the evidence
suggests in fact that 'subsistence has a tendency to increase at a greater
rate than population'.

For Whately, Malthus is mistaken in claiming a tendency in the
(second) sense, that the result may be expected to take place. When
Whately disagrees with Senior over personal responsibility for the
population circumstances of Ireland it is not, it must be underlined,
because Whately has adopted some providentialist or fatalistic belief
that the tendency, in the first sense, ought not to be, or even cannot be,
impeded. This would indeed be unwarranted since it would be to
misread it as a law-like statement about actualities rather than a (very
wide) range of potentialities. Whately instead agrees with Senior that
the alleged 'tendency' (in the second sense) towards an expected
particular and historical result – an actual crisis of excess population –
is, in fact, not a 'tendency' (it is emphatically preventable), but disagrees
with him over the responsibility for avoiding such an event: for Whately
this is a matter beyond the control of poor people, but within the
control of people with proven virtue who thus possess power and
influence in the country, and of government.

Whately's commission was prepared to look 'for the causes of poverty
in the social structure of the country rather than perceive poverty as a
sign of personal failure', according to Burke (1987, p 32). Given the
Noetic context it may be less appropriate to view Whately's position
as displaying a 'deeper understanding' of poverty (Burke, 1987, p 37)
than as a genuine difference with intellectual sympathisers over the
'space' for virtue. Moreover, it must also be remembered that the reports
of Lewis and Nicholls, and the Act itself, provided for relief to non-
disabled destitute people. Whately's scheme of reforms did not (except
accidentally through the ambiguities of the concept of the 'casually
destitute'): a manifest hiatus indeed.[8]

Conclusion: virtue, agency and the poor law

The discussion to this point has helped to refocus attention on the neglected social theory that actually motivated the investigation and method of reform of the English poor laws and the intimately linked process of introducing a poor law to Ireland. For, through Noetic thought forged out of theology and political economics, the liberal Tories possessed a theory of how social life could be conducted, with implications for a poor law in the scheme of things. The ideological points of dispute over Ireland among the Noetics help to display the English poor law reform in the full context of Noetic concerns of the day. Moreover, the fractious relationship between Chadwick and the Lewises, father and son, on the permanent poor law commission emerges as a clash of social theories rather than merely of personalities (Finer, 1952).[9]

The review of the decisive Noetic and liberal Tory emphasis on virtue, not utility, has also clarified Victorian poor law thought on agency. Approaching the poor law aware of the fundamental and contrasted conceptions of agency as described by Le Grand illuminates many topics. Whately, as has been shown, differed from Senior, Lewis and Nicholls on when poor people were responsible for circumstances: living virtuously was unlikely to triumph over the destitution accompanying an excess of population. But they agreed it was impious for government to seek directly the 'good society'. Individuals could be 'freed up' to learn the values of virtue, but not made virtuous. In most circumstances, to need poor relief when able-bodied signalled a lapse: less eligibility would rekindle in the 'lapsed queen' the desire to strive again for prudence and industry as a 'restored queen' (the adoption of Whately's Irish scheme would have made this, according to critics, a protracted process not least because it lacked a test of destitution).

Thomas Spencer was one clergyman who quickly responded to the poor law report and Act of 1834. He reorganised poor relief on the new lines in his parish of Hinton Charterhouse, to the south of Bath, and became the first chairman of the Bath Poor Law Union Board of Guardians.[10] He wrote several influential pamphlets on poor law reform at this time, including *The successful application of the new poor law to the parish of Hinton Charterhouse* of 1836. The combination of sound theology and political economics had delivered an upswing in employment: political economy, indeed, 'is inferior only to religion itself in importance' (T. Spencer, 1836, p 5). In these years too he was personally responsible for the education of his nephew, Herbert. The next two chapters discuss Herbert Spencer's social theory and its bearing on thinking about welfare: his thought, as well as the Noetic and liberal Tory thought explored in this chapter, will there be described, in a way, still to be explained, as 'non-idealist'.

TWO

Spencer and a liberal road to welfare: the eclipse of a vision

Introduction

This book deals at some length with Herbert Spencer as an example of non-idealist social thought. Since today Spencer's thought is not generally familiar (his name certainly remains known from his phrase 'survival of the fittest') the present chapter begins with a brief outline of his ideas and their context.

Over a century ago, Spencer was an acknowledged leading light in Victorian intellectual life with a reputation that permeated popular thought. His books were rapidly translated into the major languages, including Japanese. T.H. Green, Henry Sidgwick, A.J. Balfour and G.E. Moore gave his work careful philosophical criticism. As sociology grew as a discipline Spencer's pioneering contributions were explicitly engaged with as Tönnies (Offer, 1991) and Durkheim (Perrin, 1995) fashioned their own distinctive analyses of fundamental forms of social relationships, social change and social cohesion. Beatrice Webb, committed to social research and social reform, listed at length her indebtedness to Spencer in her autobiographical *My apprenticeship* (1926) and in her letters and diaries. In economics Alfred Marshall read Spencer closely on the course and direction of social and industrial change and wrote in 1904,

> There is probably no one who gave as strong a stimulus to the thoughts of the younger Cambridge graduates thirty years or forty years ago as he (H. Spencer). He opened out a new world of promise, he set men on high enterprise in many different directions, and though he may have regulated English intellectual work less than Mill did, I believe he did much more towards increasing its vitality. (in Marshall, 1925, p 507)

From the 1850s onwards Spencer was part of a circle of science-minded movers and shakers, which included Professor T.H. Huxley, Professor Alexander Bain, Professor David Masson, Professor John Tyndall and Sir Joseph Dalton Hooker, who combined shared conviviality with constructive criticism of each other's works (one forum with these purposes was the 'X club', on which see Jensen, 1970 and Barton, 1990). His letters record numerous further exchanges with Darwin, J.E. Cairnes, John Stuart Mill, the industrialist and philanthropist Andrew Carnegie, and a great many others. Among creative writers of his time Grant Allen (1904), W.H. Hudson (1904) and Lynn Linton (1894) held him in high regard and he was personally close to Marian Evans (George Eliot) up to her death, despite a lop-sided emotional entanglement between them in the 1850s, Spencer being the less enthusiastic (Hughes, 1998). Three writers in whose work Spencer figures were Jack London, Arnold Bennett and H.G. Wells. In London's semi-autobiographical *Martin Eden* the eponymous hero read Spencer and marvelled:'here was the man Spencer, organising all knowledge...reducing everything to unity' (1910, p 109). To give up Spencer would be like 'a navigator throwing the compass and chronometer overboard' (1910, p 113). Armed with Spencer he could wrong-foot complacent bourgeois figures; he alone comprehended life. In Arnold Bennett's *Sacred and profane love* the young heroine Carlotta read *The study of sociology* all night: 'I had not guessed that anything so honest, and so courageous, and so simple, and so convincing had ever been written'. Spencer taught her intellectual courage: 'nothing is sacred that will not bear inspection, and I adore his memory' (1906, pp 22-3). In his own *Journals*, Bennett hailed *First principles* as one of the greatest books ever written. It had filled him up 'with the sense of causation everywhere', and could be seen 'in nearly every line I write' (1971, p 335).

It was the unification of knowledge rather than the challenges to conventional wisdom that won over the composer and principal of the Royal College of Music, Sir Hubert Parry, who met Spencer in 1874 and felt 'quite overwhelmed by the honour so that I could hardly speak without trembling' (Graves, 1926, vol I, p 146). Spencer's theory of evolution in large measure structured Parry's *The art of music* of 1893, issued in a revised form three years later as *The evolution of the art of music* in E.L. Youmans' influential *International scientific series*. Youmans himself was a friend and ally of Spencer in America (Fiske, 1894). Spencer assisted in developing the series; his *The study of sociology* appeared in it.

There were also contacts with the world of politics. Spencer breakfasted with Gladstone (Duncan, 1911, p 215). At Spencer's request John Morley brought A.J. Balfour (who became prime minister in 1902) to see him in 1896. Next day Balfour reflected that the request could not be taken as 'otherwise than a high compliment, so off we set together in a hansom to call on the old philosopher (he is 76 and has just finished the endless volumes of his so-called Synthetic Philosophy) in St John's Wood' (in Dugdale, 1939, pp 150-1). In 1874, coming to the end of a brief period as Liberal MP for Nottingham, Auberon Herbert met with Spencer, and then read his work. For Herbert the great law-making machine of the House of Commons at once lost its charm: 'a new window was opened in my mind ... I saw that thinking and acting for others had always hindered not helped the real progress, that all forms of compulsion deadened the living forces in a nation' (Hutchinson Harris, 1943, p 156; and Greenleaf, 1983).

Herbert Spencer was born in 1820 in Derby. His father was a teacher and passed on a passion for unearthing the causes of things, religious scepticism and the scientific developments of the day. In June 1833 his education became the responsibility of his Cambridge-educated uncle Thomas at Hinton Charterhouse. Thomas was at the evangelical end of the established church and a political radical. His commitment to principle rather than expediency in politics found favour with his nephew. Besides acquiring a fair amount of mathematics, but no history and little in the way of languages, Spencer assisted with his uncle's proof-reading and aspired to write on his own account. Lessons ended in 1837 and, intelligent but prone to being didactic and disrespectful of authority, the son evaded university studies, being eased into employment in civil engineering and allied work by one of his father's contacts in the burgeoning world of railway construction, introducing him in the process to London life. Thomas, however, helped ensure that his nephew's desire to write on political matters was not extinguished. Early essays appeared in the *Nonconformist*: Thomas knew Edward Miall, the editor. Then, in 1849, a letter from Thomas expedited Herbert's appointment as sub-editor with the *Economist* in London. Cultural life enriched and friendships blossoming, he now completed his first substantial publication, *Social statics*, which appeared in December 1850, according to Spencer, although it is dated 1851. Spencer here wedded himself to Lamarck's mechanism of biological change, the inheritance of characteristics acquired by parents by their offspring. Adaptation to circumstances would thus lead to improved adjustment to surroundings in the organic world at large, including the human world, by which 'perfect individuation, both of man and of society is achieved' (Spencer, 1851, p 462). In the circumstances of social life it is requisite that all people have the chance to adapt and progress towards perfection (Spencer, 1851, p 103): 'Every man has freedom to do all that he wills, provided he infringes not the equal freedom of any other man'. This was Spencer's key principle in *Social statics* and later publications – the equal freedom principle, or principle of justice. If the state did more than enforce this principle it interfered with the process of adaptation and acted unjustly. Hence Spencer's opposition to a poor law, public health legislation and an established Church, and also his insistence on the same rights for men and women: he criticised compulsory sanitary reforms in the 1848 Public Health Act and other measures demanded by Chadwick, seeing public bureaucracies as inefficient and the measures as contrary to justice. The desired reforms would come about without such intervention through advances already occurring and reflecting the preferences of purchasers.

Social statics began the process of public recognition. It is primarily a book with a particular social and moral philosophy, though in the process it establishes a framework for sociological study. In the following years Spencer encountered and accepted the idea of the division of labour (from Milne-Edwards) and the claim made by the embryologist Von Baer of a movement from homogeneity to heterogeneity in embryological growth. These ideas led Spencer to write essays on the cause and direction of development more generally. In 1855 he also published his *Principles of psychology*. Mental adaptation had been assumed rather than explained in *Social statics*. Now Spencer placed associationism in a developmental or 'evolutionary' context in a concerted attempt to treat 'mind' as part of nature, though avoiding, he hoped, the charge of materialism. In brief, he was arguing for a sophisticated kind of psycho-neural parallelism in which the evolution of consciousness can be traced in the animal and human worlds, accounted for by the accumulated effects of adaptation in psychic and physical structures (on Spencer's psychology see Chapter Three, and Mivart, 1873; Smith, 1982; and Taylor, 1992).

Intensive work on the *Psychology* led to a breakdown in health; anxiety about his health and insomnia were recurrent concerns for the rest of his life. Nevertheless, by 1857 Spencer felt he had the ingredients for a theory of evolution, which encompassed the forces and direction of change, with adaptation as the mechanism of change, and applied to all phenomena, inorganic as well as organic. Between 1862 and 1896 this theory and its exemplification appeared as the ten volumes of his 'System of synthetic philosophy'. *First principles* came out in 1862, followed by the *Principles of biology* (two volumes, 1864 and 1867), a two-volume revised version of the *Principles of psychology* (1870 and 1872), then the *Principles of ethics* in two volumes (1892a and 1893a), and the *Principles of sociology* in three volumes (1877, 1882 and 1896). Although logically the *Ethics* was the culmination of the 'System', Spencer completed it ahead of the third volume of the *Sociology*.[1]

The 'System' for a while brought Spencer the reputation of the synthesiser and organiser of all the knowledge available to the Victorians, and, with ordered and inter-related change, social and otherwise, as its leitmotif, it attracted the acclaim of many who were no longer able to accept the certainties of religious faith or simply felt adrift in a rapidly changing world. More particularly the *Ethics* and *The man versus the state* (1884) championed political individualism, and the *Sociology* and *The study of sociology* (1873) helped to found the new discipline and encourage an interest in regularities lying beneath surface events, calling into question orthodox beliefs and thus giving a sense of liberation to those who felt trapped by them.

With the 'System' safely completed, Spencer died in Brighton on 8 December 1903. His ashes were placed in Highgate Cemetery, not far from Marx's resting place. His reputation was already on the wane. *The Times*' obituary, although noting that he had been compared with Aristotle, cast doubt on Spencer's durability in posterity. It did however, single out as significant his 'application of scientific conceptions to the study of the conditions of social welfare'. The *Manchester Guardian* affirmed that 'when socialism begins to produce reaction Spencer's political writings will be a mine of arguments for the critics of paternal government'.

Spencer's sustained opposition to statutory welfare provisions, based on his theory of social and general evolution, was twinned with less noted aspects: his arguments in favour of what he calls 'positive private beneficence' (which today would be called 'informal welfare' or 'informal care'), his analysis of the role of charitable organisations and his backing of an expansion of the administration of civil justice to enhance welfare. In fact, Spencer was laying out a form of welfare pluralism at the close of the last century. The remainder of this chapter argues that Spencer's work is not only significant in the history of social theory and welfare but is intrinsic to the process of interpreting present-day debates and research priorities in welfare studies.

Although there is encouraging evidence of a renewal of interest in Spencer's social and political thought (Gray, 1981 and 1996; Taylor, 1992; Offer, 1994), his views about how social and political life might develop in a state such as the United Kingdom after his death, and about the prospects for individual welfare in particular, are not well known. In studies of social policy his unyielding hostility towards forms of welfare provided by the state, whether services such as health and education or cash benefits, has often been noted (Pinker, 1971; and Titmuss, 1974, for example). However, as soon as one begins to think about the achievement of welfare in more pluralistic and participatory terms, as is of course now the case, Spencer can become very interesting.

Spencer's ideas about the future of welfare and the social and political life that will support them are presented in a range of his writings, not one text. One key element is his discussion of 'private beneficence'. In today's lexicon 'private beneficence' would be referred to as 'informal care', and has, usually without reference to Spencer, become the subject of much recent research (Parker, 1990, provides a review)[2] and a central plank indeed in community care policy. Spencer did tend to hide his light under a bushel: he emphasised at the expense of his positive views his despair at the 'socialistic' way he thought matters were actually developing, a recrudescence of barbarism arising from a return to compulsory forms of cooperation fostered by Gladstonian liberalism and abetted by writers such as H.M. Hyndman, and Canon Blackley on national insurance. Indeed, he did not believe that the active publicising of his views in general could have more than a marginal effect upon political and social life. To his American ally, J.A. Skilton, he wrote in February 1895:

> *You* believe that the course of things in society is to be changed by teaching. *I* do not believe any such thing. Every-where I have contended, and I contend still, that feelings, not ideas, determine social results, – that everything depends, not upon intellect, but upon character; and character is not to be changed in a day or in a generation. (Spencer, 1904a, p 1004)

A true theory of social progress is not, he wrote in the same letter, 'a *cause* of movement but is simply oil to the movement – serves simply to remove friction. The force producing the movement is the aggregate of men's instincts and sentiments, and these are not to be changed by a theory.' Nevertheless, his work was very widely discussed: it was Spencer's theory of evolutionary progress (and the possibility of regression) that led the *Manchester Guardian*'s obituarist to claim that he was 'among the two or three most influential writers of the last half-century', a by no means extreme claim at the time. It was also this theory and its impact which led Hilton (1988, p 311) to describe

Spencer as 'a key figure in the mid-Victorian slide into unbelief'. The early neglect of his positive views about welfare is thus in fact itself historically and sociologically interesting, as I hope to show, and appears to be in no simple way the result of criticisms of his theory of the mechanism and direction of evolution. Darwin crucially argued for the natural selection of variations produced spontaneously as the major mechanism of change against the inheritance of acquired characteristics, and took much less interest in any *direction* to change (Offer, 1994).

This chapter explores exactly what Spencer's liberal vision of the future for the well-being of individuals amounted to, and the nature of the social and individual life and the political structures and functions that he believed to be the necessary pre-conditions for it. Spencer's ideas relating to welfare are mostly to be found in his *Principles of ethics* and *Principles of sociology*. Perhaps the best place to begin is with his relatively systematic discussion of the nature of and prospects for that part of 'positive beneficence' that is 'private beneficence', and the associated critical comments on the 'positive beneficence' provided *both* by the state *and* by philanthropic organisations (the field of 'negative beneficence' covers such matters as not inflicting a penalty even when its enforcement would be just, but pedantic).

The context of Spencer's comments on private beneficence

Spencer's most extended discussion of 'private beneficence' comes in part VI of the *Principles of ethics*. The two volumes of the *Principles of ethics*, completed in 1892 and 1893, were the culmination of his statement of the theory of the evolution of all things, organic and inorganic.

For Spencer, in social life as in natural life, progressive evolution shows through in general as individuals adapt to their circumstances and in particular in the products of specialisation associated with an increasing division of labour. When it comes to ethical matters it is crucial that the proper sphere of government is identified. Failure by government to do its duties in this sphere, and transgressing this sphere of duties, will lead, says Spencer, to social advance being thrown into reverse. The fundamental character of individuals cannot be changed 'artificially', it must adapt naturally to circumstances; and the aggregate of individual characters makes up society. As Taylor has noted, the objective of Spencerian social theory, unlike the theory of Comte or Mill, 'was not to serve as a basis for social engineering, but rather to show that all such engineering was an impossibility' (1992, p 132).

Government action outside its 'proper sphere' will protect people artificially from consequences of non-adaptation; this is doubly counter to evolutionary advance in Spencer's sense because it both retards their ability to adapt and punishes and discourages those who have adapted, through the raising of taxes and so forth to finance the intervention of government.

The *Ethics* has itself in Spencer's sense an evolutionary relationship with his earlier *Social statics* (1851). That book predated his theory of evolution by some years. The task of the *Ethics* was to relate logically what Spencer still regarded as the correct positions of the earlier book to his evolutionary theory, though Spencer also issued an abridged and revised version of *Social statics* in 1892 (1892b). (On the logical problems of 'evolutionary ethics' see Flew, 1967.)

Spencer's definition of justice in the *Ethics* is not changed significantly from its form in *Social statics*. It is 'every man is free to do that which he wills, provided he infringes not the equal freedom of any other man' (Spencer, 1910, vol II, p 46). The proper task of government is to enforce justice, no more and no less (Gray, 1981, provides a useful exposition of Spencer's idea of justice as referring to entitlements rather than deserts). For Spencer, justice is one form of altruism. There is another form – beneficence. In Spencer's evolutionary account of social life, justice, and governments to provide it, become necessary for social equilibrium. Justice is a matter of public concern; it needs, however, to be supplemented by 'the prompting of kindness' (Spencer, 1910, vol II, p 270). Beneficence, or kindness, is needful 'before life, individual and social, can reach their highest forms' (Spencer, 1910, vol II, p 270. This aspect of Spencer's thought is emphasised in Hiskes, 1983). However, it is of private not public concern. If beneficence was exercised by society in its corporate capacity the principle of justice would be violated with the disaster ensuing for social evolution of rewarding the unadapted and punishing the adapted. Beneficence responsibly endowed increases social coherence and stability through its reciprocal benefits to benefactors and beneficiaries. Irresponsible beneficence, beneficence that ignores conduct and character in the beneficiary, is another matter.

The dimensions of beneficence

A review of Spencer's treatment of positive beneficence in general has logically to begin with his comments on cash transfers, since with them he pioneers a categorisation of welfare activities which is itself of considerable significance yet often omitted in accounts of the development of policy analysis. 'We have,' writes Spencer:

> the law-established relief for the poor by distribution of
> money compulsorily exacted; with which may fitly be
> joined the alms derived from endowments. We have relief
> of the poor carried on by spontaneously organised societies,
> to which funds are voluntarily contributed. And then, lastly,
> we have the help privately given – now to those who stand
> in some relation of dependence, now to those concerning
> whose claims partial knowledge has been obtained, and
> now haphazard to beggars. (1910, vol II, p 376)

Spencer is here distinguishing between the state, the voluntary sector
and 'private beneficence' as sources of cash aid. He inveighs against
state beneficence for the poor; it makes dependent the recipient and
hinders natural adaptation to surrounding circumstances, it penalises
those who have adapted and are able through paying rates to fund
relief, and it is of course contrary to his view of justice. Moreover, it is
extravagant in that much of the total fund raised goes to maintain the
machinery, to pay the salaries of poor law staff, staff who may indeed
have self-interest at heart.

Less familiar is the fact that Spencer finds aspects of the voluntary
sector wanting too. On occasion he has been described as a source of
the Charity Organisation Society's (COS) ideas (for example, Heraud,
1970, p 4. On the nature and significance of the COS see Lewis,
1995). The main influences in fact appear to be independent of and
indeed different to Spencer. As Harris observes (1993, p 231): 'Within
the Charity Organisation Society – a body often typecast as the last
bastion of laissez-faire individualism – there was in fact a striking
contrast between the atomistic philosophy of older members like
Thomas Mackay and a younger generation who supported the organic
"social collectivism" preached by Bernard and Helen Bosanquet and
Thomas Hancock Nunn.'

The poor law historian and Individualist Mackay ('a permanent
fixture on the council of the Charity Organisation Society' (Taylor,
1992, p 24)) appears to be the only significant COS figure for whom
Spencer was a mentor: 'It only remains for the author to avow his
obligation to the teaching of Mr Herbert Spencer,' wrote Mackay in
the Preface to his *The English poor* (1889) (Mackay is discussed further
in Offer, 1983 and Taylor, 1992). Doubtless, had Spencer thought that
the COS in general was following his ideas, he would have exempted
it from his criticisms of voluntary relief (he does, though, substantiate

his criticisms by reference to the COS's own accounts of lax practice by charities). Evils akin to those found in state beneficence abound: 'They force on us the truth that, be it compulsory or non-compulsory, social *machinery* wastes power, and works other effects than those intended. In proportion as beneficence operates indirectly instead of directly, it fails in its end' (Spencer, 1910, vol II, p 386. Aspects of voluntary action approved by Spencer are discussed later, in Chapter Seven). These reservations, stated with force, appear to be overlooked in Pinker's (1971) account of Spencer's 'positive' disposition towards charity.

Even private beneficence regarding pecuniary matters, although preferable, is not free of criticism. There is still the risk of inadequate inquiry and supervision regarding the worthiness of the beneficiary. However, the risks of Spencer's incubus becoming reality – evolutionary advance thrown into reverse – are least when beneficiary and benefactor are known to each other. 'Within the intricate plexus of social relations surrounding each citizen,' Spencer says, 'there is a special plexus more familiar to him than any other and which has established greater claims on him than any other' (1910, vol II, p 390).

Spencer surmises that the substitution of the system of contract for the system of status has meant that the emergent universal principle of so much service for so much money has weakened the impulse to acts of kindness. Yet the impulse could and should be strengthened; it would be so strengthened 'by the gradual disappearance of artificial agencies for distributing aid' (Spencer, 1910, vol II, p 391), which, of course, he urges.

Private beneficence as identified by Spencer embraces more than pecuniary assistance. Spencer's discussion of other kinds of beneficence is much more focused on the familial dimension, with a discussion first of beneficence in general within marriage and from children towards parents. On both of these related themes his position can be indicated briefly. If, as Spencer says, marital beneficence must be reciprocal, the chapter nonetheless begins by underlining discrepancies: 'In the history of humanity as written, the saddest part concerns the treatment of women' (1910, vol II, p 336). On filial beneficence towards older parents the reciprocity required is such as to avoid mental starvation, not simply physical starvation, which is usually forthcoming. When Spencer turns his attention separately and explicitly to aid for the ill and injured, the topics are still addressed from a familial perspective. Illness or accident requires beneficence from within the family, whether a spouse or children are involved: 'In the natural order of things the house becomes at need a hospital and its inmates nurses' (Spencer, 1910, vol II, p 355).

Some irreverent characterisation follows, which must do much to counter any suspicion that Spencer will now fall victim to bias in terms of gender:

> Husbands in the decline of life who have married young wives, and presently make them little else than nurses – objecting even to have other nurses share the burden with them – require awakening to a due sense not of others' duties to them but of their own duties to others. A man is not absolved from the obligations of beneficence because he is ill; and if he rightly feels these obligations he will insist that others shall not injure themselves for his benefit. (Spencer, 1910, vol II, p 357)

In general, though, Spencer makes his innovative points about the 'costs' and 'burdens' of caring – topics that he is here raising – in a less picaresque but equally effective manner:

> Here is a wife whose sole occupation for a decennium has been that of nursing a gouty husband; and who, as a result, dies of a worn-out physique before he does. Here is a daughter who, after many years' attendance on an invalid mother, is shortly after required to give similar attendance to an invalid aunt; and who, now that she had lived through these long periods of daily abnegations and wearisome duties, is becoming mentally unhinged. And here is a husband whose latter days are made miserable by the task of safeguarding, in his own house, an insane wife. (Spencer 1910, vol II, pp 356-7)

If Spencer was lacking a solution to the dilemma of self-sacrifice or self-preservation in the face of such demands on beneficence – and he was – he deserves acknowledgement for expressing the dilemma early and pat.

Spencer's treatment of 'positive beneficence' and the location of 'private beneficence' within it thus emerges as analytically sharp, and, even if it is somewhat anecdotal in empirical content, its existence is noteworthy. There is sociological shrewdness about who gives care and to whom, not least in respect of gender.

For Spencer, private beneficence, whether it takes the form of cash or care, must reflect the moral conduct and character of the beneficiary, the more direct the contact, the less the risk of a demoralising effect upon the beneficiary, with practical ethics suggesting that there are legitimate limits to what it is reasonable to supply or to demand as to beneficence, according to the circumstances of the beneficiary and benefactor. Most importantly, the existence and expansion of informal care is welcomed by Spencer; it combines the merits of advancing altruistic sentiments in the benefactor and enhancing the welfare of beneficiaries. Private beneficence benefits both benefactor and beneficiary, is needful for individual and social life to reach their highest forms, and increases social coherence and stability. In short, it allows, according to Spencer, social evolution to progress, unlike beneficence provided by the state or even often by voluntary organisations.

History, private beneficence and informal care

In the *Ethics* Spencer was, in an original way, asking some important questions about private beneficence, or informal care, and advocating it from within his own specific theoretical framework. But moral and political concern with informal care was, however, already an established feature of debate about poor law policy and practice. The *Report on the poor laws* of 1834 (Poor Law Report, 1974) had as a theme the need for virtue to be rewarded and vice punished. As a consequence policy and provision whereby relatives were in effect rewarded for neglecting their responsibilities for dependants were to be reversed.[3] Mackay's *The English poor* (1889) is but one example of continued concern with relationships between the poor law and family life. Shortly after Spencer's death came a further commission of inquiry into the poor laws, resulting in a report of 1909, of which the first two volumes form the views of the majority of the commissioners, with volume III forming the views of the minority (on the report see Vincent, 1984; and McBriar, 1987).[4] As Harris has said:

> The Royal Commission antipodized public opinion on
> social issues, between supporters of the majority report –
> largely embodying the views of the COS Council – and
> supporters of the minority report – drafted by Sidney and
> Beatrice Webb. To this day, the historiography of the Poor
> Law Commission is still heavily influenced by the
> manichean struggle between collectivism and individualism,
> progress and reaction so dramatically portrayed in the diaries
> of Mrs Webb. (Harris, 1989, pp 37-8)

The majority report regarded it a duty on both the state and voluntary organisations to arrange nursing to assist informal care where it was deemed necessary, with powers to remove compulsorily to the infirmary cases where the recipient failed to maintain 'a healthy domicile and good habits', or cases such as 'aged sick persons living alone, who have no friends or relatives to look after them' (Poor Law Report, 1909, vol I, p 360). A more sceptical, inquisitorial stance emerges from the Webbs' minority report, with such assistance withheld 'where the patient persistently malingers or refuses to conform to the prescribed regimen' (Poor Law Report, 1909, vol III, p 231). This report also criticises boards of guardians who press relatives to care for dependants rather than provide relief themselves.[5]

Oversimplifying matters a little, the majority report was willing, provided certain moral conditions were met, to assist informal care through the state or voluntary organisations, as well as to specify them as having caring responsibilities of the last resort; the minority report, however, looked to the state to take a strong tutelary role, and to displace informal care whenever 'expert' opinion so decreed. Neither report, it is important to note (see Chapter Six), was specifying as a primary role for social policy the promotion or support of informal care per se, though clearly the majority report took a less negative view of it than the minority. Spencer could not have approved of either position: both violated his view of justice and the role of the state. The possible ameliorations of suffering through the righting of 'injustices', however, occupied Spencer considerably. But before addressing these matters in the next section, the fact that it matters that all the material on informal care just discussed has been neglected needs some amplification.

Political and social debate about social policy in the 1980s and 1990s has focused on, among other matters, an (allegedly) de-moralising effect of 'the welfare state' (for example, Green, 1993; Himmelfarb, 1995; and Marsland, 1996); on voluntary organisations as an alternative source of provision to the state (Finlayson, 1994; Lewis, 1995; and Whelan, 1996); on the existence or not of an underclass (Macnicol, 1987; Murray, 1990; and Marsland, 1996); and, of course, on the nature and extent of informal care and its relationship to statutory responsibilities for 'community care' (Griffiths Report, 1988; Bamford, 1990; and Green, 1996). In many cases parallels with the situation a century ago have been explored.

The main exception, though, has been informal care; without consideration of Spencer's work and poor law literature, especially the 1909 reports, the impression has arisen that informal care was the one corresponding topic not being debated about a century ago. To the extent that it is possible to improve our critical understanding of the present by considering the cognate debates of the past, the case for looking carefully at late Victorian and Edwardian social theory and policy is further fortified by the rediscovery of these comments.

Spencer's own interest in informal care did not suffer from any pejorative judgement about it; he judged it positively, since it chimed in with, indeed was essential to bringing about, the higher evolution of social life as he saw it. To his credit, he was aware of the costs, problems and gender imbalances of caring, in spite of his theoretical commitment to it. He viewed it sympathetically, and not as an unproblematic, reflex function, but as an intriguing social phenomenon with a sociologically interesting domestic politics and logic. An awareness of Spencer's approach to informal care may serve as an antidote to the risk of judging it and interpreting it through a framework assuming the superior quality of provision by the state and the subordinate status of other provision, rather than understanding it in its own terms (a risk addressed in, for example, Bulmer, 1986; Cecil, Offer and St Leger, 1987; Lewis and Meredith, 1988; Finch and Mason, 1993; and Twigg and Atkin, 1994).[6]

One of Spencer's main tasks was to map, rather in the manner of a Victorian explorer, what he saw as the fundamental differences between forms of social life, particularly between the nature of routinised bureaucratised social life, in which the state displays a coercive 'militant' type of activity, and private, personalised life – a classic illustration of which was, for Spencer, private beneficence. Control by the state of welfare matters epitomised for Spencer what he called the 'militant' type of society, whereas autonomy in these matters characterised the 'industrial' type. Private beneficence was a sign of evolutionary progress because of the altruism it displayed; it was also a sign of progress because 'industrial' social life was itself an advance on 'militant' life – Webbian surveillance represented a personal nightmare.

Spencer's types of society or social life are discussed further later. Spencer's younger contemporary, Tönnies, explicitly criticising and extending Spencer's work, substituted for the distinction the well-known contrast between formal, impersonal gesellschaft life and informal and 'natural' gemeinschaft life.[7] Better known, but less faithful in representing Spencer's emphasis on altruism in 'industrial' life, are Durkheim's criticisms (on which see Corning, 1982).

Private beneficence, justice and the Spencerian future of welfare

Although of great importance for Spencer, private beneficence or informal care was not the only welfare-promoting element that he found congruent with the development of social evolution as he conceived it. Justice, if defined and administered by the state in ways prescribed by Spencer, would prove no less important.

As we have already seen, the sole domestic task of government, according to Spencer, is to enforce 'justice'. Stock criticisms of government from Spencer, for example in *The man versus the state*, are that it does things justice does not demand and therefore interferes with social evolutionary progress, and that it fails to administer justice where there is injustice. Looking to the future in the section of *The principles of sociology* entitled 'Political institutions', Spencer writes that the state's responsibility for enforcing justice is at an end (1891a, pp 660-1), 'only when the State undertakes to administer civil justice to the citizen free of cost, as it now undertakes, free of cost, to protect his person and punish criminal aggression on him'.

As it happens, Spencer had first taken this position in his twenties; in *The proper sphere of government* the fact that taxes have been duly paid to government by its subjects is taken to imply that 'after men had thus prepaid the government, it would be a most unjust proceeding for that government to put them to additional expense whenever it was called upon to perform its duty towards them' (Spencer, 1843, p 50). Accessible and expeditious courts of justice, free of charge, would do much to correct the state of affairs where the defence of the poor man 'against the aggressions of his rich neighbour' (Spencer, 1843, p 51) is only possible through the ruination of his own pocket.[8]

Again, in February 1884, he broached the same topic, this time in the somewhat surprising context of declining a request to allow his name to be put forward as a candidate to represent Leicester in Parliament:

> My views on political matters are widely divergent from those of all political parties at present existing. That which I hold to be the chief business of legislation – an administration of justice such as shall secure to each person, with certainty and without cost, the maintenance of his equitable claims – is a business to which little attention is paid; while attention is absorbed in doing things which I hold should not be done at all. (Duncan, 1911, pp 240-1)

In response, *The Times* of 14 March was concerned that the costless administration of justice would immensely increase litigation. To Youmans, Spencer wrote expressing the converse view: 'were justice prompt, certain and costless, the result would be not increase but decrease; since the larger amount of civil aggression results from the belief that it will not bring any penalty' (Duncan, 1911, p 242).

Some indication of how far into social life this enforcement of justice might reach is indicated in a letter to the Earl of Wemyss of 1892:

> For a generation past the stupid English public have tamely submitted to the enormous evil inflicted upon them by railway companies at every large town in the kingdom – the evil of peace disturbed day and night by the shrieks of railway whistles. With their dull, bovine unintelligence, they have let it be tacitly assumed that railway companies, and even private manufacturers, have a right to make noises of any degree of loudness, with any degree of frequency, at whatever times they please ... These daily aggressions on hundreds of thousands of people – to some serious and to all annoying – ought to be peremptorily forbidden, even had railway companies to suffer in consequence considerable inconvenience and cost. (Duncan, 1911, p 314)

From these passages it seems clear that, according to Spencer, the proper administration of justice will in due course emerge as a remedy for that poverty, disadvantage and illness that results from injustice. It will also be the means whereby unjust discrimination in employment on, for example, grounds of race, and also unjust environmental pollution, can be rectified. Logically, compensation should be payable to those who can make a successful claim that their freedom, according to Spencer's definition of justice, has been infringed. Once opened, this door swings very wide indeed (as was noted by Sidgwick, for example. On Sidgwick and on the large question of the justification of the private ownership of land for Spencer, see Taylor, 1992, ch 7).

Matters are further amplified when a secondary injunction regarding justice is noted:

> Living and working within the restraints imposed by one another's presence, justice requires that individuals shall severally take the consequences of their conduct, neither increased nor decreased. The superior shall have the good of his superiority; and the inferior the evil of his inferiority.

> A veto is therefore put on all public action which abstracts
> from some men part of the advantages they have earned,
> and awards to other men advantages they have not earned.
> (Spencer, 1891a, p 610)

A reasonable inference from this passage must be that, provided equal work of equal quality can be demonstrated as having been furnished, the normal connections between acts and results must make it an injustice – a violation of entitlement – to discriminate in rates of remuneration between men and women or on grounds of race or ethnicity. On the other hand, the person whose work is, on economic grounds, 'superior' is entitled to the advantages earned over one whose work is 'inferior'.

Spencer acknowledged that these considerations could lead to changed and perhaps expanded law-making (see Duncan, 1911, p 351), though he pointed out elsewhere that it would be considerably mitigated by the sentiments of justice rather than injustice becoming ever more spontaneously followed by those individuals living the advanced civilised life, and hence coming to predominate in social life viewed in general:

> To one who is ruled by a predominant sentiment of justice,
> the thought of profiting in any way, direct or indirect, at
> the expense of another, is repugnant; and in a community
> of such, none will desire to achieve by public agency at the
> cost of all, benefits which a part do not participate in, or do
> not wish for. (Spencer, 1891a, p 658)

With these concerns in mind, Spencer anticipated that a greater emphasis on local rather than central government would characterise the future. Thus, as he viewed the situation, 'the inhabitants of each locality will object to be controlled by the inhabitants of other localities, in matters of purely local concern' (Spencer, 1891a, p 655). How far he intended such devolution of powers to go is a most vexing topic. He opposed Home Rule for Ireland, but did so on inconsistent grounds. In 1890 he wrote to Auberon Herbert in the following trenchant manner:

> From Home Rule, for example, I utterly dissent. All nations
> have been welded together not by peaceful and equitable
> means, but by violent and inequitable means, and I do not
> believe that nations could ever have been formed in any

other way. To dissolve unions because they were inequitably formed I hold, now that they have been formed, to be a mistake – a retrograde step. Were it possible to go back upon the past and undo all the bad things that have been done, society would forthwith dissolve. (Duncan, 1911, pp 300-1)

Two years later the reason for his opposition to Home Rule had changed. His view was now that Ireland was not ready for it. His opposition now had weaker justification, it was simply conditional on his judgement that the 'goodness of ... institutions is purely relative to the natures of the men living under them' (Duncan, 1911, p 315).

On the other hand, Spencer was willing to sketch out in 1894 a relatively detailed scheme for the devolution of the administration of justice. To the Individualist Wordsworth Donisthorpe, a fellow contributor to the 1891 libertarian volume supported by the Liberty and Property Defence League, *A plea for liberty*, he wrote saying that if the state became responsible for the administration of civil justice – a doctrine he had explicitly enunciated – then:

> The State would now not stand in the position of umpire, but would become an active investigator. On complaint being made to the local authority that some aggression had been committed or some non-fulfilment of an agreement, the first step might be that of sending an appointed functionary – an officer of first instance – to interview jointly the two disputants, and hear from them their respective statements, and explain to them the law affecting the matter. In nine cases out of ten the presence or absence of a wrong is clear enough, and the opinion of this official on the matter would suffice to effect a settlement. (Duncan 1911, p 360)

In addition, Spencer described two further legs to the process: there might be, if requested, a reference to a higher authority, and if that failed to produce an acceptable result to all parties an appeal might be made, with no cost to the appellant, 'where the interpretation of the law in the particular case might fairly be considered a matter of doubt' (Duncan, 1911, p 360).

On the further dissemination of these bold and radical ideas, Spencer got cold feet. No reason is given. It was constitutionally unlike Spencer to abandon a long-held belief, however iconoclastic its implications. Perhaps his pessimism about the readiness of character to change resurfaced, or perhaps he feared a tiring public controversy. Two days after the letter just cited to Donisthorpe, he again wrote to him this time with the curt and cryptic command: 'Please say nothing about my views on the administration of civil justice' (Duncan, 1911, p 360).

Once again, the critics of Spencer's liberalism were at his heels, finding *injustice* in the fact that some individuals through various privileges had better chances in life than others (see Wiltshire, 1978, ch 7). The pursuit of welfare was to involve 'social justice', and the meeting of 'needs', not compensation for aggressions suffered and the devolution of the administration of justice. Henry Sidgwick (1892, p 116), one of the more sympathetic critics, commented on a worrying lacuna in Spencer's schema: 'When we are inquiring what compensation is justly due to persons whose rights have admittedly been encroached upon, supposing the encroachments have been sanctioned by law and custom and complicated by subsequent exchange, it is evident that the Law of Equal Freedom cannot help us; we want some quite different principle of Distributive or Reparative Justice'.

Spencer's support for private beneficence and increased attention by the state to matters of civil justice are the main positive aspects of his picture of the development of welfare. One further aspect, though, deserves a brief mention. Spencer does not say much on the topic but in reviewing the likely future of religion he remarks (1891a, pp 825-6): 'All matters concerning individual and social welfare will come to be dealt with; and a chief function of one who stands in the place of a minister, will be not so much that of emphasising precepts already accepted, as that of developing men's judgements and sentiments'.

In predicting the secularisation of priestly functions and an associated heightened individual concern for self-knowledge, Spencer proved a good prophet: the private purchase of a bewildering variety of counselling, therapy and guidance services seems to have been an area of great expansion as individual concern and responsibility for enhanced well-being have become landmarks of personal probity.

Militancy, industrialism and the prospects for welfare

As has already been shown, Spencer's picture of the future of individual and societal welfare was not to be achieved through education, and to a very limited extent through the broadcasting of his own theory of how social evolution occurred and the direction it might take. Instead the changes could arise almost entirely only through the necessarily slow process of individual character or human natures adapting to social circumstances. Nor was there any guarantee about the direction of this process: on the contrary, such change was a delicate growth and highly vulnerable to being undermined by other developments in social life over which Spencer repeatedly fretted. A letter of 1892 finds him writing: 'In efforts towards ethical culture there is constantly overlooked the one effort more important than all the others – the effort to suppress militancy. Abundant proof exists that with war come all the vices, and with peace come all the virtues' (Spencer, 1904a, p 1003).

In the *Principles of sociology* he observed that 'the possibility of a high social state, political as well as general, fundamentally depends on the cessation of war' (Spencer, 1891a, p 663). Little cause for comfort to him came from his own theoretical inference that 'from war has been gained all that it had to give' (Spencer, 1891a, p 664). Either in world affairs or in domestic politics he found fuel to stoke up his apocalyptic vision of reborn militancy: at home Liberals 'vied with the opposite party in multiplying State-administrations which diminish individual liberty' (Spencer, 1893b, p 573).

At this point more must be said on Spencer's well-known categorisation of mostly modern societies into predominantly 'militant' or predominantly 'industrial' types (on which see also Peel, 1971, ch 8). In a nutshell, as has been indicated, 'militant' social relations predominate when a society is geared to war, with strong internal regulation of affairs by the state, and 'compulsory co-operation'; 'industrial' social relations predominate when a society is geared to peace, with individual freedom, industrial enterprise and contract governing internal affairs, and voluntary cooperation. For Spencer, militant social relations make realisation of his picture of the future impossible. But a question now presents itself, is it 'industrial' social relations that are necessary for his picture to be realisable, or a 'third type' of society, lying in the future, that he introduced into his sociological analysis?

The first thing to be done is to describe Spencer's 'third type'. In the *Principles of sociology* he introduces the idea of a possible future social type that differs as much from the industrial as this does from the militant. It is a type:

> which, having a sustaining system more fully developed than any we know at present, will use the products of industry neither for maintaining a militant organization nor exclusively for material aggrandizement; but will devote them to the carrying on of higher activities. As the contrast between the militant and the industrial types, is indicated

by inversion of the belief that individuals exist for the benefit of the State into the belief that the State exists for the benefit of individuals; so the contrast between the industrial type and the type likely to be evolved from it, is indicated by inversion of the belief that life is for work into the belief that work is for life. (Spencer, 1893b, p 563)

This passage first appeared in 1876. It is alluded to, consciously or unconsciously, in Spencer's *Autobiography* when narrating the events of his visit to America in 1882. He recalled that the theme on which he enlarged in an address – specifically directed at his audience – was that (Spencer, 1904b, vol II, pp 406-7): 'life is not for learning nor is life for working, but learning and working are for life. And a corollary was that the future has in store a new ideal, differing as much from the present ideal of industrialism as that ideal differs from [the] past ideal of militancy.'

Apart from this one reappearance of the 'third' social type, the idea of a post-capitalist utopia was, in fact, left in limbo immediately after its first very brief outing of 1876. Spencer's picture of the future of welfare does not *depend*, then, on the infrastructure of this new type of society being realised, but rather on the existence of the social relations that characterise his industrial type of society: it represents, indeed, part of his view of the evolutionary development of modern 'industrial' societies, the United Kingdom in particular. In 1881, Spencer had become sufficiently anguished over an apparent reawakening of militancy to participate actively in anti-aggression propaganda, describing himself as at the time 'profoundly impressed with the belief that the possibility of a higher civilization depends wholly on the cessation of militancy and the growth of industrialism' (Spencer, 1904b, vol II, pp 375-6).

Conclusion: coming within an ace?

This chapter has argued that Spencer had a positive and, in his own opinion, liberal view of the future of welfare centred around what he called 'private beneficence' and the expanded administration of 'justice' as he had defined it. It has also explored the precise specification of the political, social and individual circumstances that he believed, constrained as he was by his understanding of 'social evolution', to be necessary for such a picture of the future to become reality. However, as has already been indicated, the impact of these ideas on practical politics at the time was subdued; I want to conclude by exploring how this came about.

As we have seen, Spencer himself was reluctant to promote his ideas – he was both pessimistic about the future and sceptical of the power of theory to engender change. In political terms his closest adherents were to be found in the Liberty and Property Defence League (on which see Taylor, 1992). However, the league's members were almost uniformly committed to blocking 'socialistic' measures rather than advocating any innovative alternative. Benjamin Kidd[9] and T. H. Huxley, and L. T. Hobhouse too, steered evolutionary thought towards idealist tolerance of state intervention by variations on the argument that the mechanisms and direction of social evolution could be influenced by social control. A key task of Chapters Four and Five of this book is to identify Spencer's thoughts as profoundly at odds with the ideas of many of his critics, who were idealist, defined broadly. Hobhouse, in his *Social evolution and political theory* of 1911, for instance, having praised such developments as state-funded pensions for older people (in 1908), which would have horrified Spencer, though he sensed their imminence, argued:

> The turning-point in the evolution of thought ... is reached when the conception of the development of humanity enters into explicit consciousness as the directing principle of human endeavour, and, in proportion as the phrase is adequately understood, is seen to include within it the sum of human purpose in all its manifold variety. In particular, it can be seen to be the conception necessary to give consistency and unity of aim to the vastly increased power of controlling the conditions, external and internal, of life, which the advance of knowledge is constantly yielding to mankind. (Hobhouse, 1911a, pp 155-6)

Beatrice Potter, to whom Spencer had been a mentor, also broke ranks on similar grounds, embracing both Sidney Webb and Fabian socialism, and with her husband drafting the minority report of 1909.

Spencer's ideas on welfare, in fact, lacked powerful friends, a situation not helped by his own diffidence towards the application of his ideas. The most promising prospects would have appeared to be with the intellectual leadership of the COS. But this society, dating back to 1869, and with its strong impact on the majority report of 1909 had, as we have seen, failed to receive Spencer's imprimatur.

Some kind of alliance with the society ought to have been possible.

It was, after all, committed to administering charitable funds in ways designed to re-moralise rather than de-moralise character. In 1891 it had been reported in the *Pall Mall Gazette* of 15 May that Spencer had become a member of the Society for the Prevention of Cruelty to Children. On 28 May the *Gazette* published Spencer's views on the work of the society: 'though, by protecting the children of bad parents (who are on the average of cases themselves bad), there is some interference with the survival of the fittest, yet it is a defensible conclusion that in the social state, philanthropic feelings may, to this extent, mitigate the rigour of natural law' (quoted in Offer, 1983, p 737).

In a sense, then, the reasons for withholding support to the work of the COS seem to have been thin indeed. Here, after all is non-compulsory social machinery, which wastes power, nonetheless winning Spencer's approval. However, as Spencer well knew, there was an unbridgeable chasm between his philosophical position and that of Bernard Bosanquet, the COS's leading apologist. Bosanquet may indeed have signed the letter of congratulation to Spencer in 1896 to mark the completion of his 'System': only a year before he had dipped his pen in vitriol (Bosanquet, 1895, see also McBriar, 1987, p 126). As Vincent remarks, 'Bosanquet contrasted what he called the ethical individual against the Spencerian atomic individual' (1984, p 353). Bosanquet, his teacher T.H. Green and other idealist philosophers, with debts to Hegel, and Rousseau's 'general will', were in a different camp, well brought out by Harris:

> Green, like Herbert Spencer, viewed society as an 'organism',
> and like Spencer he believed that the true arena of social
> progress lay in voluntaristic cooperation among human
> beings rather than in direction by the state. Unlike Spencer,
> though, he saw the 'organic character of society' as rational
> and purposive rather than natural and predetermined, and
> the true sphere of rights and laws as being not nature but
> human consciousness and will. A fully organic 'society' was
> a group of interdependent rational beings with a common
> moral purpose, embodied in a 'general will'. Only in 'society'
> could human beings find true freedom or 'moral liberation';
> and morality did not consist merely in private acts of virtue,
> but in the bringing of the individual will into conformity
> with the rules and well-being of the wider organic whole.
> (Harris, 1993, p 228)

Spencer was diametrically opposed to this philosophy in general, and the philosophy of social action and the view of positive freedom and justice that it supported in particular. Late in life to his old friend the psychologist Alexander Bain, he wrote:

> I not infrequently think of the disgust you must feel at the fate which has overtaken *Mind*. That you, after establishing the thing and maintaining it for so many years at your own cost, should now find it turned into an organ for German idealism must be extremely exasperating ... Oxford and Cambridge have been captured by this old-world nonsense. What about Scotland? I suppose Hegelianism is rife there also. (Duncan, 1911, p 457)

Mind, it may be noted, promised an obituary of Spencer, but in fact never published one. Spencer, in thus baulking at giving his support to the COS, and in the process omitting to state his support for non-idealist voluntary organisations, failed to develop to the full a picture of welfare pluralism that he could, logically, have supported.

However, whether or not a picture of the future of welfare made up of strong espousal of voluntary action (on non-idealist grounds), 'private beneficence' and the expanded administration of justice that Spencer envisaged could have changed the course of events in social policy legislation in a more pluralistic direction before the First World War is impossible to tell. Certainly Spencer, who came within a whisker of committing himself to the first element, and was beyond doubt committed to the other two, could have argued for this strong 'package' in a powerful way and made it a part of social thought. It is interesting that, for better or worse, some such package, without acknowledging Spencer's pioneering steps, has appeared in post-idealist times in Green's *Reinventing civil society* (1993) and Himmelfarb's *The de-moralization of society* (1995), and, with a debt to Spencer made clear, in Marsland (1996). Perhaps, indeed, as Hutton says, '[t]he England of Adam Smith, John Stuart Mill and Herbert Spencer had been submerged ... by the welfare state and the attempt at government direction of the economy, but it had not been extinguished' (1996, pp 53-4).

THREE

Free agent or 'conscious automaton'? The individual in Spencer's social theory

Introduction

This chapter is concerned primarily with how Spencer understood 'social individuals' and 'social life', and to comment in this light on some recent interpretations of Spencer on moral and political ideas. The present book does not seek to *advocate* a particular position but to clarify patterns of social thought relating to social policy matters. Nevertheless, to guard against possible confusion, it is necessary to identify problematic facets presented by some of the new interpretations of Spencer, and to make clear my own interpretative stance. Accordingly, the chapter looks in some detail at Spencer's work on psychology and sociology as well as on ethics, seeking to establish how Spencer understood people as social individuals. In particular the neglect of Spencer's denial of freedom of the will is identified as a problem in some recent interpretations. One of his contemporary critics, the Millite economist, John Elliott Cairnes (1875, p 143), charged that Spencer's own theory of social evolution left even Spencer himself the status of only a 'conscious automaton'. This chapter, drawing on a range of past and present interpretative discussions of Spencer, seeks to show that Spencerian individuals are psychically and socially so constituted as to be only indirectly responsive to moral suasion, even to that of his own *Principles of ethics* as he himself acknowledged. While overtly reconstructionist projects to develop a liberal utilitarianism out of Spencer to enliven political and philosophical debate for today are worthwhile – dead theorists have uses – care needs to be taken that the original context and its concerns with the processes associated with innovation (and decay) in social life are not thereby eclipsed, the more so since in some important respects they have recently received little systematic attention, even though the issues have contemporary relevance in understanding social life. While for the analytical purpose of this book no harm arises from adopting the procedure of putting

Spencer's denial of freedom of the will 'on ice' in considering, for instance, informal care (as is done), it is important that the underlying structure of Spencer's social thought is made clear to avoid as far as possible the risk of misleading anyone who may wish to use his work to some other end.

Spencer wrote a great deal through a long life and on a very wide range of topics. From the 1850s onwards he wrote as a synthesiser, developing a directional theory of evolution encompassing all phenomena. The mechanism of change was the inheritance of acquired characteristics, although after the publication of Darwin's *Origin of species* in 1859, which advocated the occurrence of spontaneous variations subject to selective survival as the principal mechanism of change, named natural selection, Spencer also found a place for this new mechanism in his theory as 'indirect equilibration' (see Spencer, 1864). Even before he embarked on the 'System of synthetic philosophy' the exploration of linkages between biology, psychology, sociology and moral and political ideas were of paramount interest in his pursuit of a principle to determine the role of the state – 'justice'. Nevertheless, the 'System' in its ten volumes was the definitive account of his evolutionary science.

Modern critical commentary on Spencer thus faces a serious challenge. Specialism has usurped genericism in scholarship in very large measure. Sociologists will tend to focus on Spencer's sociology, and moral philosophers on the *Ethics*. In practice it is a struggle for both groups, who tend nowadays to be those most interested in Spencer, to master, for example, his *Psychology*. Yet Spencer meant there to be strong logical linkages from the beginning to the end of his 'System'. Of course one may wish to explore one part in particular, but if justice is to be done to Spencer's meaning it is a perilous activity to bracket off other parts for long: usually wider excavation is required even if only one part is the main focus.

In a wider sense too, consideration of Spencer's work in a generic kind of way is timely. There are live questions today about the nature of the interfaces between sociology on the one hand and psychological and biological explanations of social life on the other, and in this context reflection on Spencer's characteristic focus on the processes of innovation and oblivion in social life (but much less so his concern with the *direction* of change which is pre-Darwinian) chimes well with the contemporary theoretical orientation of, for example, Runciman (1998) towards a selectionist paradigm.[1]

In this chapter, then, I want to offer an evaluation of some recent interpretations of aspects of Spencer's oeuvre. My comments will keep in mind the potential legitimacy of the view that mining a dead theorist to develop contemporary ideas is a profitable activity – the orientation to past theorists dubbed 'presentism' by Turner (1985, p 8). Nevertheless the probable conflict between contemporary utility and fidelity to the original author's intentions and products will be a matter for critical review.

Liberty and utility

Recently, David Weinstein provided an overdue re-examination of the nature of Spencer's social and moral thought, drawing attention to his commitment to utilitarianism. Liberal utilitarians, says Weinstein,

> Permit the principle of utility to serve as a standard for assessing classes of actions and institutions while denying it service as a source of direct obligation. For them, strong moral rights serve as sources of direct obligation, making their version of indirect utilitarianism *liberal* utilitarianism … general utility is best maximized over the long run when individuals assiduously fulfil their fundamental juridical obligations and thereby indirectly promote the flourishing of individuality. Maximizing happiness consists in fostering individuality which, in turn, requires that we channel out actions along broad avenues permitted by stringent moral rights. (1998, pp 1-2)

The strong right provided by Spencer as a source of direct obligation is his principle of equal freedom, stated in the *Ethics* thus: 'Every man is free to do that which he wills provided he infringes not the equal freedom of any other man' (Spencer, 1910, vol II, p 46).[2]

There is much to praise in Weinstein's attempt to give the basic structure of Spencer's moral thinking, and indeed in the detailed revisionist discussions of its relationship to the ideas of Bentham, Mill, Sidgwick and G. E. Moore, and of Spencer's position on 'natural rights', 'rational utilitarianism' and his arguments to the equal freedom principle. And Weinstein at least attempts to locate his discussion in the synthetic evolutionary perspective, particularly regarding the analyses of the *Psychology* and *Sociology*, from which the 'mature' moral philosophy contained in the *Ethics* sprang. Significantly, though, Weinstein says in a footnote (1998, p 7): 'Spencer never used the expression "liberal utilitarianism" when referring to his own moral and political theory … The fact that neither Mill nor Spencer explicitly identified themselves as liberal utilitarians naturally opens liberal utilitarian interpretations of them to the charge of being rational reconstructions.' He also adds, wisely, that interpreting Spencer is 'an exegetical labyrinth even for the initiated' (Weinstein, 1998, p 9).

I am not concerned to tackle either the claim that a plausible 'reconstruction' of Spencer along these lines is of value in developing moral philosophy in our own times or the claim, at least not head on, that he is actually best described, as a moral philosopher, as a liberal utilitarian. On the other hand I think my concerns are over more than matters of nuance or finesse. The peculiar nature of Spencer's moral philosophy, it seems to me, is not in Weinstein's hands brought to the surface – odd features, some profound, traceable to the evolutionary envelope in which it comes, are, to put it lightly, muffled.

In addition to Weinstein's comments, contributions by John Gray (1982 and 1995) and Richard Hiskes (1983) will also be discussed. Gray identifies Spencer as a liberal utilitarian in ways comparable to Weinstein. However, Gray says next to nothing about the psychological and sociological setting of Spencer's moral philosophy, or rather merely dismisses it as misguided (1982, p 246): 'the evolutionary theory … specified no plausible *mechanism* for the evolution of societies'. Spencer's Lamarckian inheritance of acquired characteristics may indeed be implausible. Nevertheless, as I will try to show, it imbued the moral thinking with peculiar constraints on its role in personal and social life. There may be potential to develop out of Spencer a 'rational' liberal utilitarianism, but as Gray himself observes the theory that emerges may 'have little in common with Spencer's' (Gray, 1982, p 248). Hiskes (1983) is not concerned with the moral philosophy but with a liberal idea of community that he finds in Spencer's *Ethics* accompanied by an elevated status for voluntaryism. Again there may be special constraints to be noticed, eclipsed by too little regard for man and agency as conceptualised in the *Psychology* and the *Sociology*, in Hiskes' case the *Psychology* in particular.

In my attempt to flag some of the underlying difficulties and complications involved in assessing Spencer's thought on social life and ethics in the context of his overall scheme of things, I have tried to avoid two tempting but I think unprofitable lines of approach, and it may be best to say what they are. The first line is to argue that, because Spencer said so-and-so in one place or another, he cannot really hold its converse at some other point. Inconsistency of course ought not to occur, but it can. Apparent contradictions can be real. The second line of approach I try to avoid is saying that, because one position logically implies another, this second position may also be inferred as held. Again, it must not be assumed that Spencer actually held a position to which he was in fact logically committed. My aim here is to indicate some of the distinctive wider theoretical positions held by Spencer that need to be kept in mind in future accounts of his social and moral thought that are excavated from his work, in connection with wider reconstructionist projects in liberal thought, and to emphasise some important but often overlooked exegetical points more generally in the field of Spencer's sociological and psychological thought.

'Character', 'circumstances' and freedom of the will

Let us begin by considering Spencer's minimalist attitude to the relevance and impact of his writings, in particular but not only his sociological and ethical writings, on everyday life. In the *Sociology* we find:

> A general congruity has to be maintained between the social state at any time necessitated by circumstances, and the accepted theories of conduct, political and individual. Such acceptance as there may be of doctrines at variance with the temporary needs, can never be more than nominal in degree, or limited in range, or both. The acceptance which guides conduct will always be of such theories, no matter how logically indefensible, as are consistent with the average modes of action, public and private. All that can be done by diffusing a doctrine much in advance of the time, is to facilitate the action of forces tending to cause advance. The forces themselves can be but in small degrees increased; but something may be done by preventing misdirection of them. (Spencer, 1891, p 666)

The study of sociology concludes that the man of 'higher type' should understand how little can be done to advance reform: 'philanthropic energy' must be united with 'philosophic calm'. In support, Spencer observes (1873, pp 402-3): 'before there arise in human nature and human institutions, changes having that permanence which makes them an acquired inheritance for the human race, there must go immeasurable recurrences of the thoughts, and feelings, and actions, conducive to such changes. The process cannot be abridged; and must be gone through with due patience.'

A letter of 1895 to J.A. Skilton, the American author of *The evolution of society* of 1889, reinforces the message (in Duncan, 1911, p 367): 'No adequate change of character can be produced in a year, or in a generation, or in a century. All which teaching can do – all which may, perhaps, be done by a wider diffusion of the principles of sociology, is the checking of retrograde action …' The specific concerns of these passages reflect Spencer's distinctive but problematic conceptualisation of flesh-and-blood human beings at large in social life, and of 'society'. For Spencer, in social life human beings are locked into a process whereby 'character' or 'human nature' is (slowly) adjusting to the acknowledged existence of others and of social institutions. Over generations, through the inheritance of acquired characteristics achieved by adaptation, humans become more fitted to social life, and, at the same time, social life and its institutions also undergo social evolution. This mechanism of social change is in essence based on the method of change for individual members of species developed in the *Psychology*, as will shortly be shown.

In his own time, and subsequently, Spencer has often been interpreted as viewing a person's capacity to believe or feel certain things as determined by their levels of psychological and social adaptation (as examples see Mivart, 1873; Cairnes, 1875; and Wiltshire, 1978). This interpretation squares with the albeit limited space for 'teachings' that Spencer concedes only if the contents of books and lectures and so forth have a simply unconscious, part-of-the-environment, kind of impact on the process of adaptation. And, even so, the further question would need to be raised – how can a new thought to be taught arise, except, of course, as a result of the author having superior psychic and social adaptation? In this interpretation conscious human agency can never be what it seems.

A different interpretation, however, is available. Spencer does from time-to-time refer to 'average modes of action, public and private' (1891a, p 666) and 'average human nature' (1873, p 395). Perhaps Spencer is attempting to identify 'structural', 'underlying', or 'relatively permanent' levels of personal and social reality in contrast to 'surface' levels of relatively unimportant and transitory ideas, feelings and happenings. Sociologists today would, I think, tend to see such distinctions as leading to the exclusion from view of much that is of central importance in making sense of social and individual life. Nevertheless such an interpretation would yield up in principle the logical space for Spencer for a non-reductionist idea of conscious agency. With some people capable of actions above 'average' human nature, there would be scope here for the conscious production of new ideas and for teaching to have some point, a conscious reaction on the part of some individuals. In practice, though, there would be a negligible effect on social life precisely because such individuals are in advance of average modes of action and average human nature. We are brought back to the first interpretation, and thus (most) people are again conceptualised very differently to how they are ordinarily understood to be.

It might be hoped that a further probing of Spencer's writings on, say, rapid political transformations would resolve the question of his acceptance of conscious human agency. However, his discussions of major events in France, America and Britain refer both to changes produced by 'accident' and as consequences of a lack of 'duly adapted character', and to changes that might indicate a role for innovative human agency. Nevertheless, political institutions cannot be effectually modified faster than the characters of citizens are modified. It follows, therefore, according to Spencer:

> that if greater modifications are by any accident produced, the excess of change is sure to be undone by some counter-change. When, as in France, people undisciplined in freedom are suddenly made politically free, they show by some *plebiscite* that they willingly deliver over their power to an autocrat, or they work their parliamentary system in such way as to make a popular statesman into a dictator. When, as in the United States, republican institutions, instead of being slowly evolved, are all at once created, there grows up within them an agency of wire-pulling politicians, exercising a real rule which overrides the nominal rule of the people at large. When, as at home, the extended franchise, very soon re-extended, vastly augments the mass of those who, having before been controlled are made controllers, they presently fall under the rule of an organized body that chooses their candidates and arranges for them a political programme, which they must either accept or be powerless. So that in the absence of a duly adapted character, liberty given in one direction is lost in another. (1891a, pp 661-2)

Perhaps at this stage one may make four observations. First, that it is highly doubtful that Spencer subscribed to a commonsense idea of conscious human agency. Second, as far as he did concur with this idea, it was clouded by concerns with psychical and social causal factors.

Third, that the power of human agency, deliberate or otherwise, to influence social life was much more severely limited than would ordinarily be supposed. And, fourth, it is possible either that Spencer was vulnerable to the charge of inconsistency in this area, or that his position can be clarified, as I now propose, by looking elsewhere in his work.

With these points in mind it may be helpful to shift the focus to some aspects of Spencer's *Principles of psychology*. The *Psychology* is now one of Spencer's least-read titles; certainly it is dense in style and organisation. It is, though, arguably the key to his work on human evolution in general. In 1854 he confided to his father his opinion that 'it will ultimately stand beside Newton's *Principia*' (in Duncan, 1911, p 75). (On Spencer's psychology in general see Young, 1970 and Smith, 1982.)

In the *Psychology*, which first appeared in 1855, Spencer asks if we possess free-will. An extensively revised and reorganised second edition in two volumes came out in 1870 and 1872, and a third edition in 1880. Common to all editions is a denial of freedom of the will. Thus in the 1880 edition Spencer states that, while everyone is at liberty to do what he desires to do (supposing there are no external hindrances) no one is at liberty 'to desire or not to desire' (1880, vol I, p 500). The reason is that 'all actions whatever must be determined by those psychical connexions which experience has generated – either in the life of the individual, or in that general antecedent life of which the accumulated results are organized in his constitution'.

The point is emphasised with explicit linkage to evolution in the 1855 and 1870 editions, though not the 1880 edition, in the following manner:

> To reduce the general question to its simplest form:-
> Psychical changes either conform to law or they do not. If they do not conform to law, this work, in common with all works on the subject, is sheer nonsense: no science of Psychology is possible. If they do conform to law, there cannot be any such thing as free-will.
>
> Respecting this matter I will only further say, that free-will, did it exist, would be entirely at variance with that beneficent necessity displayed in the progressive evolution of the correspondence between the organism and its environment. (Spencer, 1855, pp 207-8)

St George Jackson Mivart was one who homed in on the denial of free-will. Mivart, seven years younger than Spencer, became a Catholic in 1844 but pursued a distinguished career as a zoologist. With Huxley's recommendation he became lecturer in comparative anatomy at St Mary's Hospital, Paddington, in 1862. His Catholicism and interest in metaphysics led him to publish articles that criticised Darwin and Spencer over what he regarded as the special status of man as a knowing and moral being. Darwin took Mivart seriously as a critic, but what was perceived as a personal criticism of himself and his family led to Mivart's exclusion from a circle of evolution-minded scientists with whom he was previously on good terms. Mivart published ten articles that painstakingly dissected the *Psychology* (the second edition). He viewed Spencer as denying to human will 'any more power of choice than a fragment of paper thrown into a furnace has a choice concerning its ignition' (Mivart, 1873, p 220). The *Psychology* undermined a sense of moral responsibility and possessed a form of expression that 'would lend itself to confusion between the sorting faculty of the apertures of a sieve and the sorting faculty of the man who employed it for sorting' (Mivart, 1873, p 222). We have, he says, of the *Psychology*:

> the most ingenious and interesting construction of sensible perceptions of increasing degrees of complexity wrought out with an abundance of illustration and a facility of research truly admirable. But what is the outcome? We feel indeed we have an insight into the power of mere sensation and the consequent faculties of brutes, such as we never had before, as also into the *materials* of our own thoughts; but we have no increased knowledge of our own *intelligence* itself. Our cat's mind is indeed made clear to us, but not our own. (Mivart, 1873, p 221)

Another of Spencer's early critics linked Spencer's denial of free-will to logical shortcomings in *The study of sociology*. J.E. Cairnes successively held chairs in political economy at Dublin, Galway and University College London. In his 'Mr. Spencer on social evolution', while noting Spencer's commitment to causal antecedents operating everywhere, he observed that Spencer:

> if I correctly understand him, refuses to admit that an individual has the power, by an effort of will, to make his character other than it must inevitably be. He thus, no doubt, escapes a difficulty; but only, as it seems to me, to encounter

another still more formidable. For, on the supposition that self-improvement is impossible, and that consequently the whole course of human affairs is predetermined, to what purpose devote ourselves to the study of sociology? To what purpose warn mankind against the dangers of over-legislation? Or to preach the duty of letting social evolution go on unhindered? Is Mr Spencer prepared to accept the conclusion that these too – his own words and actions – are but links in the chain of destiny, and that he himself is but a 'conscious automaton'? (Cairnes, 1875, p 143)

Spencer had two responses to concerns of this sort. The first was that it was absurd to think of social evolution going on apart from the activities of component individuals. Towards the close of *The study of sociology*, Spencer commented:

> If, as seems likely, some should propose to draw the seemingly awkward corollary, that it matters not what we believe, or what we teach, since the process of social evolution will take its own course in spite of us; I reply that, while this corollary is in one sense true, it is in another sense untrue. Doubtless, from all that has been said, it follows that, supposing surrounding conditions continue the same, the evolution of a society cannot be in any essential way diverted from its general course; though it also follows (and here the corollary is at fault) that the thoughts and actions of individuals, being natural factors that arise in the course of the evolution itself and aid in further advancing it, cannot be dispensed with, but must be severally valued as increments of the aggregate force producing change. (1836, pp 400-1)

Much later Spencer returned to this point in an essay 'Social evolution and social duty', published in *Various fragments* (1897a). But now the emphasis had shifted to account for the misconception. By critics, he notes first (1897, p 120):

> It is supposed that societies, too, passively evolve apart from any conscious agency; and the inference is that, according to the evolutionary doctrine, it is needless for individuals to have any care about progress, since progress will take care of itself. Hence, the assertion that 'evolution erected

into the paramount law of man's moral and social life becomes a paralyzing and immoral fatalism'.

But again this assertion, adds Spencer, is an error. It is absurd to expect that social evolution 'will go on apart from the normal activities, bodily and mental, of the component individuals'. Now, however, the error is presented as the result of

> failing to see that the citizen has to regard himself at once subjectively and objectively – subjectively as possessing sympathetic sentiments (which are themselves the products of evolution); objectively as one among many social units having like sentiments, by the combined operation of which certain social effects are produced. He has to look on himself individually as being moved by emotions which promote philanthropic actions, while, as a member of society, he has to look on himself as an agent through which these emotions work out improvements in social life. (1897, p 122)

Yet Spencer has not retracted his denial of free-will for individuals nor met Cairnes' 'conscious automaton' challenge. Spencer also made an explicit but still opaque reply to Cairnes, declaring that (Spencer, 1897a, pp 17-18): 'the difficulty lies in recognizing human actions as, under one aspect, voluntary, and under another pre-determined. I have said elsewhere all I have to say on this point. Here I wish only to point out that the conclusion he draws from my premises is utterly different from the conclusion I draw'.

The second response was prompted by T.H. Huxley's Romanes Lecture of 1893, 'Evolution and ethics', and its concerns about the place of humankind in an evolutionary context. Later in the year Spencer wrote to J.A. Skilton:

> The position he takes, that we have to struggle against or correct the cosmic process, involves the assumption that there exists something in us which is not a product of the cosmic process and is practically a going back to the old theological notions, which put Man and Nature in antithesis. Any rational, comprehensive view of evolution involves that, in the course of social evolution, the human mind is disciplined into that form which itself puts a check

upon that part of the cosmic process which consists in the unqualified struggle for existence. (in Duncan, 1911, p 336)

Unexceptionable in itself, the view of evolution given here sits uneasily with the apparent contrast between Nature and government legislation and action to which Spencer appealed in *The man versus the state* and elsewhere (see later). Again the question of the freedom of the will is not raised.

To get matters clearer as to why Spencer denied freedom of the will we need to probe deeper into the *Psychology*. In essence, the *Psychology* had developed a dualist 'inner-outer' psychoneural theory of mind (see Smith, 1982). The evolutionary process of compounding and recompounding of sensations was paralleled by a process whereby the central nervous system grew in complexity, definiteness and heterogeneity. For Spencer, according to Taylor:

> for each occurrence of a sensation there was a corresponding disturbance of the nervous system, and that these were to be regarded as the mental and physical instantiations of the same event. This was not a materialist theory of mind, a charge Spencer repeatedly denied, but was a species of what modern philosophers would describe as 'psychophysical parallelism', the theory that for every mental phenomenon there must be a neural counterpart. Spencer argued that what was subjectively a mental event was objectively a molecular motion ... (Taylor, 1992, p 109)

To the extent that Spencer is committed to 'psychosocial parallelism' he need claim no more than that what we call examples of the exercise of free-will, or, I think we might add, original thought, always have some parallel neural story. Spencer tends not to relate his psychology to events in personal everyday life. There seem to be no answers to such questions as: what disturbances in my central neural system parallel my efforts to master and criticise the *Principles of psychology*, or my choice to visit someone today or tomorrow? But I assume the parallels are to be in some way so closely textured as to apply to all the experience of individuals (as suggested by Spencer's discussion of 'original' ideas in this context, 1880, vol II, p 534). In which case no negative indication in relation to ideas of or acts of free-will might seem called for, the matter might seem untouched. However, once it is noted that these co-evolving parallel tracks are the 'inner' and 'outer' manifestations of a unified evolutionary process – neural activity on the one hand, consciousness on the other, both evolving together – it becomes clear that the evolutionary process of the adaptation of an individual to the environment (including the social environment) together with the inheritance of acquired mental characteristics (physical and psychic) is determining and locking together the form and content of both consciousness and parallel neural structures and processes.

Cairnes' charge that Spencer construes individuals as 'conscious automata' needs revision only to the extent that their programmes are slowly updated during their lives. The *Psychology* shows that the humans whose activities are so indispensable to the continuation of social evolution only have the appearance of exercising free-will; we may believe in the voluntary nature of actions, but the belief is unfounded. Contrary to the Cartesian tradition and immensely to the chagrin of his idealist contemporaries, Spencer accords human consciousness no special status.

There is no reason to think that the fact that Spencer shortened his remarks on free-will in the third edition of the *Psychology* is of particular significance: the denial of it remains clear and intact. Armed with the *Psychology* and the general evolutionary theory showing only slow psychic and social change as possible, Spencer could point to the hopelessness of schemes for rapid legal, political and social change on the one hand and the lack of 'higher' social and psychical sentiments among primitive man (1880, vol II, p 530), those of 'undeveloped' intelligence or 'lower' races, and women (1880, vol I, pp 582-3) on the other. All chimed well with individualist and conservative thinking in the late nineteenth century, and offered an alternative to a range of reformist and interventionist proposals associated with the idealist social thought as broadly defined by Harris (1992, see also den Otter, 1996) of T.H. Green, Bernard Bosanquet, D.G. Ritchie, J.A. Hobson, and Sidney and Beatrice Webb, among others.

Two examples may serve to illustrate Spencer's style of psychological thought on these matters. On the development of 'imagination' Spencer observes that at the 'highest' level:

> we pass in the most civilized to constructive imagination –
> *or rather, in a scattered few of the most civilized* [emphasis added].
> This, which is the highest intellectual faculty, underlies every
> high order of intellectual achievement ... Instead of
> constructive imagination being, as commonly supposed,
> an endowment peculiar to the poet and the writer of fiction,
> it is questionable whether the man of science, truly so called,

> does not possess even more of it. (Spencer, 1880, vol II, pp 534-5)

On the distance of the 'average mind' from complete fitness for the social state, in the discussion of 'corollaries' in the *Psychology* (Spencer's nascent social psychology) he writes:

> And here we see how far men at present are from that highest moral state, in which the supreme and most powerful sentiments are those called forth by contemplation of conduct itself, and not by contemplation of other persons' opinions of conduct. In the average mind the pain constituted by consciousness of having done something intrinsically wrong, bears but a small ratio to the pain constituted by the consciousness of others' reprobation: even though this reprobation is excited by something not intrinsically wrong. Consider how difficult it would be to get a lady to wheel a costermonger's barrow down Regent-street, and how easily she may be led to say a malicious thing about some lady she is jealous of – contrast the intense repugnance to the one act, which is not in itself reprehensible; and then infer how great is the evolution of the moral sentiments yet required to bring human nature into complete fitness for the social state. (Spencer, 1880, vol II, pp 605-6)

Spencer's social beings, certainly the most intellectually developed, are in many ways indistinguishable from people as we would ordinarily understand them. They have consciousness and moral sentiments. However, they do not choose what to say or do, even if it appears so; instead what is said or done is the result of complex and subtle causes that determine how incoming 'sensations' are received and structured in consciousness, and which are paralleled by slowly evolving complex neural structures and processes, all of which are actively interacting, and in due course yielding up more advanced minds through use-inheritance over time. Ultimately it is as if a locomotive rather than its driver is described as being in charge of its train.

So far as I can ascertain, Spencer never disowns his condemnation of the idea of free-will. People may commit 'spontaneous' acts of, for example, generosity (see Weinstein, 1998, p 49), but these are not voluntary or 'free' actions, even though they may seem so to the doer. Late in the day came a reply to the Revd J. Llewelyn Davies, a prominent

Christian socialist, reprinted as an appendix in the second volume of the *Ethics,* in which Spencer declares that 'the consciousness of "ought" as existing among men of superior types is simply the voice of certain governing sentiments developed by the higher forms of social life, which are in each individual endorsed by transmitted beliefs and current opinion' (1910, vol II, pp 449-50). This is consolidation, not recantation.

Seeing beyond the shackles

Weinstein's treatment of Spencer's moral thought confronts neither his denial of free-will nor the fact that the denial is embedded in his psychology and sociology. Instead he observes that for Spencer 'evolution simply makes us better strategists because it makes us better social scientists' (1998, p 168). However, 'strategists' here demands strong inverted commas: our knowledge of our evolutionary past, knowledge even of Spencer's particular theory, *explains* our desires, however 'enlightened'. We are not free 'to desire or not'; if we show 'self-restraint' such behaviour is no less conditioned. Spencer, as we have seen, goes to great lengths to emphasise how little practical impact a theory or teachings can have. They may be understood by men of 'higher intelligence' but they can impact more widely only as 'average' character adapts to them initially as environmental factors, in which form they may remove the 'friction' that impedes progress. Ideas that are held ahead of the competence of component individuals and their level of adaptation to the social state, problematic as it is how this might come about, are doomed to have negative consequences for the social fabric.

As has already been suggested and is well known, Spencer was hostile to 'socialistic' ideas and practices in general and to government intervention that 'transgressed' rather than upheld the equal freedom principle in particular, epitomised perhaps by the arguments of *The man versus the state*. Yet it is hard to see how, given Spencer's own psychological and sociological evolutionary premises, such 'deviancy' can come about in the first place. One could sketch the answer that it is the product of 'regressive' forces, harking back to a more primitive (or to a 'militant') social form, but this risks charges of tautology as the theory becomes compromised by ambiguity, robbing his hostility of logical power. Spencer inveighs against the consequences of proposals that 'interfere' with Nature (yet, if 'Nature' or 'laws of nature' can be so 'interfered' with this suggests rather that they have been identified arbitrarily – damaging for Spencer's whole edifice), but, with no concession to free-will, can give us no reason for the ability of the proposals to arise at all. There is a telling passage in the *Pall Mall*

Gazette of 28 May 1891, in which Spencer recorded his objections to the founding of the Society for the Prevention of Cruelty to Children:

> It is surprising with what light hearts people are led to abrogate the order of Nature and to substitute an order of their own devising. All life on the Earth has risen to its present height under the system of parental obligation. Throughout, the process has so worked that the best nurtured offspring of the best parents have survived and maintained the race, while offspring inadequately nurtured have failed to leave self-sufficing posterity. And now it has come to be thought that these strong parental feelings … may with advantage be replaced by public sentiment working through State-machinery! I hold, contrariwise, that the replacing of parental responsibilities will inevitably cause degradation and eventual extinction. (in Offer, 1983, p 352)

In the same vein, in the *Ethics* he puts the question 'What can be a more extreme absurdity than that of proposing to improve social life by breaking the fundamental law of social life?' (1910, vol II, p 260). Here Spencer means the link in all life between conduct and consequences. However, the objection remains that to point to 'exceptions' to a law of nature is to show the law is not what it claims to be, and to describe some elements of social life as 'non-natural' is arbitrary.[3]

Weinstein is, of course, concerned to liberate a theory of 'liberal utilitarianism' from Spencer. As said earlier the intention here is not to make direct comments on the merits or otherwise of such a self-avowed exercise in reconstruction. Rather, I am concerned to understand Spencer, and the place of his moral thought in the context of his wider thought. So far, at some length, the concentration has been on the special, complex and contradictory conception (given his political criticisms) that Spencer has of social beings, with its explicit disavowal of free-will, which fails to figure in Weinstein's re-working. Weinstein is also possibly unhelpful for the purpose here in his treatment of Spencer's distinction between empirical utilitarianism and rational utilitarianism. Rational utilitarianism was taken by Spencer to be his own innovation, but for Weinstein (1998, p 213): 'Spencer's claim to have derived stringent moral rights from the principle of equal freedom by logical deduction is not persuasive. Contrary to what he maintains, moral rights are not logical derivations from the principle of equal freedom. Thus his endeavour to replace "empirical" Benthamite utilitarianism with a more methodologically severe "rational" utilitarianism falls short. When all is said and done, Spencer's "rational" utilitarianism is just another variety of "empirical" utilitarianism, albeit a variety that tries to be more scientific.'

Now for Spencer – although Weinstein does not appear to say so – the principle of equal freedom is, among other things:

> a belief deducible from the conditions to be fulfilled, firstly for the maintenance of life at large, and secondly for the maintenance of social life.
>
> Examination of the facts has shown it to be a fundamental law, by conformity to which life has evolved from its lowest up to its highest forms, that each adult individual shall take the consequences of its own nature and actions: survival of the fittest being the result. And the necessary implication is an assertion of that full liberty to act which forms the positive element in the formula of justice; since, without full liberty to act, the relation between conduct and consequences cannot be maintained … among gregarious creatures this freedom of each to act, has to be restricted; since if it is unrestricted there must arise such clashing of actions as prevents the gregariousness. And the fact that, relatively unintelligent though they are, inferior gregarious creatures inflict penalties for breaches of the needful restrictions, shows how regard for them has come to be unconsciously established as a condition to persistent social life. (Spencer, 1910, vol II, pp 60-1)

We are enabled to 'affiliate' this belief, continues Spencer, 'on the experiences of living creatures at large, and to perceive that it is but a conscious response to certain necessary relations in the order of nature. No higher warrant can be imagined …'

When Weinstein in his reworking interprets Spencer's references to the basis of moral rights as causally necessary conditions for maximising utility, complementing the principle of equal freedom, he is entitled to find them ultimately empirical in nature, rather than deductive. But *for Spencer himself*, they, like the 'parent' principle of equal freedom itself, are very much grounded in the laws of his theory of evolution; he intended them to be seen as deductively tethered to evolutionary dynamics. It is also relevant to note that Weinstein finds Spencer's substantial and unambiguous references to 'animal ethics' something of a naturalistic oddity (Weinstein, 1998, p 143). Yet for Spencer the idea of an 'ethical' continuum through at least the later stages of biological, psychical and social evolution is centre-stage.

I would like now to move the focus to two aspects of Weinstein's interpretation of Spencer's social and moral thought that seem particularly helpful from the point of view of understanding Spencer's ideas as such. The first aspect is a discussion of the relationship of the equal freedom principle to what Tim Gray (1981, p 391), for example, has referred to as a 'subordinate' injunction regarding 'justice' in Spencer: 'Living and working within the restraints imposed by one another's presence, justice requires that individuals shall severally take the consequences of their conduct, neither increased nor decreased' (Spencer, 1891, p 610).

Weinstein, however, points to passages in Spencer where he is 'suggesting that the principle of desert and the principle of equal freedom are identical principles with equal freedom being the form which desert takes in sociality' (Weinstein, 1998, p 60; compare also the passage quoted from Spencer earlier (1910, vol II, pp 60-1)). However, there is also a useful passage not introduced by Weinstein. Following a discussion in the *Ethics* that points in the past to the dominance of at one time inequality and at another equality, Spencer remarks:

> For if each of these opposite conceptions of justice is accepted as true in part, and then supplemented by the other, there results that conception of justice which arises on contemplating the laws of life as carried on in the social state. The equality concerns the mutually-limited spheres of action which must be maintained if associated men are to co-operate harmoniously. The inequality concerns the results which each may achieve by carrying on his actions within the implied limits. No incongruity exists when the ideas of equality and inequality are applied the one to the bounds and the other to the benefits. Contrariwise, the two may be, and must be simultaneously asserted. (1910, vol II, pp 42-3)

If the 'formula' of justice as subsequently given by Spencer – to repeat 'every man is free to do that which he wills, provided he infringes not the equal freedom of any other man' (1910, vol II, p 46) – has shortcomings in terms of attention to benefits or desert (or entitlement in Tim Gray's analysis), it is beyond doubt that it was intended to cover these matters as indicated.

With the meaning of 'equal freedom' so understood it is possible to comment critically on some recent ideas about what are or are not breaches of the principle. It may well be, provided equal work of equal quality can be demonstrated as having been furnished, that for Spencer the normal connections between acts and results must make it an injustice to discriminate in rates of remuneration between men and women or on grounds of race or ethnicity. In this respect Paul Rowlandson may himself be in error in stating that a mistake arises 'in suggesting that Spencer might have approved legislation specifically opposing race and gender discrimination' (2000, p 473). Weinstein cites a passage in the 'Industrial institutions' section of the *Sociology* (Spencer, 1897b, pp 515-16) in which Spencer alights upon the privations suffered by contemporary factory workmen, comparing mill-work to slavery. Weinstein declares that 'if wage labor violates exchange, then it partially robs laborers of what they deserve. Hence it contravenes the principle of equal freedom' (1998, p 202).

The second aspect of Weinstein's interpretation of Spencer that is helpful in understanding Spencer's ideas is that Weinstein notices, albeit briefly, that for Spencer justice is only one part of the category of 'altruism', also important are 'positive' and 'negative' private 'beneficence' (discussed in Chapter Two). In advanced societies individuals have acquired 'sympathy'. It improves the life of each individual to be 'sympathetic' to the freedom and interests of others. 'Self-restraint' in actions is of great importance in advanced social life, as is action of a 'positively beneficent' nature, the rendering of services not dictated by 'justice' as such: 'The requirements of equity must be supplemented by the promptings of kindness' (Spencer, 1910, vol II, p 270). Acting with self-restraint and with kindness in line with 'sympathy' for the lives of others – beneficence – is necessary but it is different from and not to be confused with the realm of 'justice'. 'Justice' is 'needful for social equilibrium, and therefore of public concern', whereas 'beneficence' is 'not needful for social equilibrium, and therefore only of private concern' (Spencer, 1910, vol II, p 270). The public acknowledgement and maintenance of justice as defined by Spencer facilitates the further development of this area of negative and positive beneficence – 'virtuous' behaviour – as a feature of social evolution. Eventually a perfect society would be reached in which sympathetic behaviour would be fully evolved alongside respect for justice. Indeed, Spencer made a distinction between 'absolute' and 'relative' ethics, where 'absolute' ethics – the ethics actually espoused by the *Principles of ethics* (and *Social statics*) – were the ethics suited to life in the promised perfect social state. A degree of compromise was acknowledged by Spencer in relating the *Ethics* to the circumstances of everyday contemporary social life (the idea and relevance of 'absolute' ethics was the subject of trenchant criticism from Henry Sidgwick, 1880).

The point has already been made earlier that Spencer had a vision of a 'welfare society' from a liberal and non-idealist point of view that stood against fashionable idealist recipes for social reform aimed at directly securing the 'good society' at the turn of the century. Support for charitable 'sympathetic' action by like-minded individuals, though not large voluntary organisations, ready access to the means whereby 'justice' could be enforced and disputes settled, and private beneficence exercised by families, friends and neighbours provided a vision of how the welfare of individuals could be directly bolstered and communal solidarity indirectly advanced. In particular this was a non-idealist view of welfare promotion that was critical of the coercion and encouraging of dependency it detected in idealist schemes of reform encompassing both organised charity and the state already being canvassed by the 1880s.

Indeed, Hiskes (1983) has argued that Spencer's thought embraces a non-collectivist liberal idea of the growth of community through the emphasis on altruistic actions and associations as a feature of advanced social evolution. Interestingly though, Hiskes finds in Spencer's discussion of social evolution 'a pervasive determinism in the description of that process which challenges the liberal faith in human freedom'. Spencer, he says, 'handcuffs' individuals: 'The laws of evolution shackle individuals in their search for community by informing them that though community is inevitable as the end stage of evolution, it is not to be consciously sought. To do so would be to interfere with the natural process that will bring community about in exactly the same way that governmental interference will hinder its development' (Hiskes, 1983, p 48).

However, note that Hiskes is here calling into play Spencer's *social* determinism, the belief in a law of social progress (on the unilinearity of which Spencer expressed reservations). The *psychological* determinism, discussed above, goes unacknowledged. While the direction of social change in Spencer, for Hiskes, is determined, he does not confront the point that 'voluntary', 'altruistic' action *on a day-to-day basis* is not, for Spencer, what it seems: our physical constitutions, shaped by the inheritance of acquired characteristics, permit but a simulacrum of autonomy.

Spencer may write in places as if he subscribes to freedom of the will. Yet the evidence is plain from the *Psychology* and his sociology: in the structure of his theory we are conceived of as, to recall Cairnes' apt phrase, 'conscious automata'. Moreover, Spencer *was* capable of inconsistency. At one point he himself found an exception to the ubiquity of evolution, denying that harmony could be considered as having 'evolved' from an identical melody being sung alongside another in fugal fashion. He wrote in 1891: 'the new kind of effect suddenly achieved cannot be considered as *evolved*, without stretching somewhat unduly the meaning of the word' (1891b, p 537). Spencer's problem here was not merely the lack of a convincing evolutionary explanation to hand, it was that 'harmony' meant something more than the accidental simultaneous sounding of two or more notes – it was, then, invented rather than evolved. Even further inconsistency ensued, he was here overlooking a passage in *First principles* that claimed that harmony *had* 'evolved' in such a fashion (Spencer, 1870, p 357. See Offer, 1983).

In this chapter I have tried to consider sympathetically recent attempts by Weinstein and others to disinter from Spencer a version of liberal utilitarianism and cognate social principles. I have not quarrelled head-on with these efforts at 'reconstruction', for dead theorists can certainly be the source of contemporary inspiration, and in the process valuable new light can be thrown on 'classic' issues involved in interpreting an author. Indeed, Weinstein's valuable interpretation of Spencer's equal freedom principle and its relationship to the principles of conduct and consequences has been recognised, and his own and Hiskes' comments on beneficence have also been welcomed critically.

'Conscious automaton', 'handcuffed', 'shackled': descriptions of this nature nevertheless epitomise Spencer's conception, psychically and socially, of the social individual in advanced social circumstances. The reconstructionist projects to which I have drawn attention would have served ill the development of our understanding of Spencer's social and moral thought if these 'awkward' facets of Spencer's oeuvre were closeted as a consequence. To the extent that, in order to analyse fundamental contrasts in the social theory embodied in social policy, this book also puts 'on hold' Spencer's denial of freedom of the will, the same caveat must apply.

FOUR

The case of older people: social thought and divergent prescriptions for care

Introduction

In Britain the years between 1880 and 1910 were something of a cauldron for the production and discussion of ideas about social life, the aims of social policy, and the roles of charity and government (a recent review is Haggard, 2001). While considerable attention has been paid to proposals for old-age pensions, little has been said on other forms of support and care for older people and the social theory that nourished them. This chapter discusses this topic as addressed by Spencer, and by the two reports of the royal commission on the poor laws of 1909. These two reports, known usually as the 'majority' and 'minority' reports, were chiefly associated with Helen Bosanquet and other members of the Charity Organisation Society (COS) on the one hand, and Beatrice Webb and the thought of Fabian socialism on the other.[1] Spencer's concern with 'filial obligation' is examined, and the differing emphases on institutional care and compulsion between the Bosanquets and the Webbs are discussed.

The discussion of older people thus serves as a case study of divergent ways of approaching social problems, with Spencer identified as non-idealist in contrast to *both* of the reports, which share idealist characteristics in spite of differences of substance; they agree over social ends, but not over the means to their realisation. This case study is intended to pave the way for the more detailed analysis of the theoretical and conceptual roots of these positions, the subject of the following chapter. Key divergences in social and political principles in thinking about support and care for older people are clarified, with some aspects of their relevance to present-day dilemmas surrounding 'social care' indicated.

The selection of these three sources for review is deliberate. In each case there is a distinctive interplay between sociological analysis, a philosophy of 'the good' and a political agenda. Moreover, the three cases represent the main intellectual approaches to the 'social questions' of the time. Spencer was, as we have already seen, a leading 'Individualist'. Helen Bosanquet and her husband Bernard championed charity as a means to enhance reciprocity, citizenship and the good society. They wrote in sympathy with the COS and within a tradition of social philosophy of considerable strength in the universities, which was profoundly tied in with moral and political reform, sometimes of a specifically Christian character. Beatrice Webb and her husband Sidney, as Fabian socialists, espoused state action allied with administrative reform and the exercise of professional expertise as the means to social and economic reform in the shape of a 'national minimum of civilised life' (McBriar, 1987). It may be noted too that each viewed as a protagonist tended to take the kind of positions adopted by the others as a cause for direct critical comment.

Two related objectives drive this chapter. The first is to try to chart the range of thinking about the care of older people in the period from 1880 to the 1910s since a specific focus on thinking about older people is indeed seldom adopted (though see Thane, 2000). The second is to illustrate the differing theoretical and/or conceptual assumptions underpinning the range of thought on older people that is identified, in the process explicitly preparing the ground for the ensuing more detailed examination. Acknowledging Harris' (1992) contribution, the chapter gives a sneak preview of the idea of 'idealist social thought' (defined as broader than Idealist philosophy, though encompassing it) as coming to provide the dominant intellectual framework for envisioning social policy and social problems of the time, and as assisting in showing up family relationships between ideas – such as Idealism and Fabian socialism – often viewed as unconnected. However, Harris does not explore the clearly implied contrast with what I call 'non-idealist social thought'. This contrast deserves attention and has received a preliminary exploration with the earlier identification of Spencer as a 'non-idealist'. Within the specific context of theoretically charged comments on the care of older people the present chapter takes the opportunity to test the variations around the theme of idealist social thought as conceptualised by Harris and the value of the implied contrast with non-idealist thought.

The rest of the chapter falls into five sections. The first outlines the nature of Spencer's concern, generally neglected, with the treatment of parents late in their lives by their offspring. The second explores the comments on older people of the majority report of 1909, and the third does the same for the minority report: both reports, it will be noted, reflect what Harris calls idealist styles of social thought. The fourth section highlights key features of Harris' claims about the nature and importance of 'idealist social thought' and explores the 'power' of this concept and the implied contrasting concept of 'non-idealist social thought' in the identification of divergences and commonalities in the three sources. The concluding section comments briefly in this light on some recent developments in policy and research.

Spencer, 'filial beneficence' and the care of older people

One seldom-noticed facet of the later writings of Spencer is his interest in older people, particularly the treatment of older parents by their offspring.[2] His comments come in the *Principles of ethics*, especially the second volume, and in the third volume of the *Principles of sociology*.

The comments in the *Ethics* arise out of the baleful consequences, as Spencer sees them, of 'intrusions' by the state into the education and upbringing of children in the contemporary scene. For the parents, the sense of fulfilment and the rewards associated with devoted parental care have been diminished. Diminished too are the feelings of care for parents that may be evoked in children reared under the discharge of 'high parental functions'. However, the discharge of such functions would bring 'the reward in old age consisting of an affectionate care by children, much greater than is now known' (Spencer, 1910, vol I, pp 549-50). At the time, public provision through the poor law was 'undertaking, in a measure, the charge of parents not supported by their children' (1893b, p 705).

As suggested, Spencer makes his remarks in the context of the need for moral and material reciprocity, so that 'endeavours to make the old age of parents happy' shall 'correspond with the endeavours they made to render happy the early days of their children'. Developing his position, he comments:

> In few directions is existing human nature so deficient as in this. Though, among the civilized, the aged are not left, as among various rude savages, to die of bodily starvation, yet they are often left to pine away in a condition that may be figuratively called mental starvation. Left by one child after another as these marry, they often come at length to lead lives which are almost or quite solitary. No longer energetic enough for the pleasures of activity, and not furnished with the passive pleasures which the social circle yields, they suffer the weariness of monotonous days. From

time to time there comes, now from one child and now from another, a visit which serves nominally to discharge filial obligation, and to still the qualms of conscience in natures which are sympathetic enough to feel any qualms; but there is rarely such an amount of affectionate attention as make their latter days enjoyable, as they should be. For in a rightly-constituted order, these latter days should bring the reward for a life well passed and duties well discharged. (Spencer, 1910, vol II, p 353)

Spencer can find no procedure for the effective encouragement of filial sentiments towards parents in their old age. 'Filial beneficence' is, he declares, 'a crying need', yet it cannot be demanded by the already old, since this would in the circumstances be coercion, and to demand it of the young 'implies their deficiency in the sentiment which makes it needful'. By the 'official expounders of rectitude the subject is but rarely dealt with'. According to Spencer, the outcome is that the young themselves will suffer pain or unhappiness as they in turn grow old:

If those who are appointed to instruct men in the conduct of life, fail properly to emphasize filial beneficence in the interests of parents, still more do they fail to emphasize it in the interests of the children themselves. Neglecting to enforce the claims of fathers and mothers on their offspring, they leave those offspring to suffer, in declining life, from the consciousness of duties unperformed, when there is no longer a possibility of performing them – leave them a prey to painful thoughts about the dreary latter days of those they should have tenderly cared for – dreary days which they begin to realize when their own latter days have become dreary. (Spencer, 1910, vol II, p 354)

In the *Sociology* Spencer's main comments on the treatment of older people are found in the final chapter of the division, entitled 'Domestic institutions'. Here Spencer's concern is with the future of the family unit in the context of his theory of social evolution. The care of parents by offspring, which, in terms of social evolution, is the most recent of the bonds that hold the family unit together to manifest itself, is the bond that has most room to increase.

Absent among brutes, small among primitive men, considerable among the partially civilized, and tolerably strong among the best of those around us, filial affection is a feeling that admits of much further growth; and this is needed to make the cycle of domestic life complete. At present the latter days of the old whose married children live away from home, are made dreary by the lack of those pleasures yielded by the constant society of descendants; but a time may be expected when this evil will be met by an attachment of adults to their aged parents, which, if not as strong as that of parents to children, approaches it in strength. (Spencer, 1893b, p 760)

Filial affection will develop, according to Spencer, through the enlightened education of their children being undertaken as the direct responsibility of parents. Spencer had written extensively on education earlier (in the 1860s), developing a scorn for orthodox teaching techniques:

When the minds of children are no longer stunted and deformed by the mechanical lessons of stupid teachers – when instruction, instead of giving mutual pain gives mutual pleasure, by ministering in proper order to faculties which are eager to appropriate fit conceptions presented in fit forms – when among adults wide-spread knowledge is joined with rational ideas of teaching, at the same time that in the young there is an easy unfolding of the mind such as is even now shown by exceptional facility of acquisition – when the earlier stages of education passed through in the domestic circle have come to yield, as they will in ways scarcely dreamed of at present, daily occasions for the strengthening of sympathy, intellectual and moral, then will the latter days of life be smoothed by a greater filial care, reciprocating the greater parental care bestowed in earlier life. (Spencer, 1893b, p 761)

By the early 1890s, working on the *Ethics*, Spencer was in his early 70s. It is possible that his own age, his single and childless status, anxieties about his health, and the loss of close personal ties through illness and death prompted his reflections on old age in particular. However, they are firmly rooted in a wider set of theoretical concerns. Within social and moral life Spencer had identified altruism as a vital sentiment. Altruistic actions could be categorised as matters of 'justice' or matters of 'beneficence'. For Spencer, as discussed in Chapter Three, the formula of justice must unite positive and negative elements in respect of each and every person.

> It must be positive in so far as it asserts for each that, since he is to receive and suffer the good and evil results of his actions, he must be allowed to act. And it must be negative, in so far as, by asserting this of everyone, it implies that each can be allowed to act only under the restraint imposed by the presence of others having like claims to act. (Spencer, 1910, vol II, p 45)

Living by this rule of justice maximises happiness for each individual as a consequence. For Spencer the sole function of government is to enforce 'justice'. 'Justice' is a matter of public concern; social equilibrium depends upon it. Spencer bewails the tendency of governments to trespass in their actions beyond enforcing 'justice' while neglecting its proper administration. Much pain could be avoided if complainants had free access to conscientiously administered mechanisms for the speedy resolution of disputes over injustices.

By contrast, 'beneficence' is a private matter that covers acts arising from 'sympathy' for others in respect of acts of restraint (negative beneficence) and acts of generosity (positive beneficence), they are acts not, however, required by considerations of justice strictly interpreted. Spencer's emphasis on 'voluntaryism' has led him to be considered a champion of a distinctively liberal idea of community (see Herbert, 1908; Hiskes, 1983; and Offer, 2003b. On Herbert see Hutchinson Harris, 1943). Spencer certainly opposed action by government to promote beneficence directly. The proper sphere of government action was 'justice', and going beyond this entailed the coercion of individuals and a destabilising interference in a process by which Spencer set huge store, individuals adapting naturally to their circumstances, passing on adaptations through generations via the inheritance of acquired characteristics. By this means 'social evolution' occurred. Organised charities, however, such as the Society for the Prevention of Cruelty to Children, while they could do good, could also be remote, bureaucratic and damaging in their actions since these risked disrupting the relationship between conduct and consequences, preventing adaptation or perverting the course of it (see Offer, 1983, and also the previous chapter). However, private and voluntary action with beneficent aims towards individuals in mind, aims that chime with and reinforce the mechanism and direction of social evolution, win Spencer's *imprimatur*.

If the gradual disappearance of what Spencer terms 'artificial agencies for distributing aid' (such as the poor law) and the levying of associated rates could be secured, the performance of acts of private beneficence would be vitalised afresh in scale and scope. Sympathy evoked, the resources available would give it expression. Defining at least in part the field of what today is called informal welfare, he observes:

> Within the intricate plexus of social relations surrounding each citizen, there is a special plexus more familiar to him than any other, and which has established greater claim on him than any other. Everyone who can afford to give assistance, is brought by his daily activities into immediate contact with a cluster of those who by illness, by loss of work, by a death, or by other calamity, are severally liable to fall into a state calling for aid; and there should be recognized a claim possessed by each member of this particular cluster. (Spencer, 1910, vol II, p 390)

Similarly, beneficent and cooperative voluntary organisations can come to flourish in support: 'a provident beneficence suggests the acquirement of such surgical and medical knowledge as may be of avail to sufferers before professional aid can be obtained. Unqualified applause, then, must be given to those Ambulance Societies and kindred bodies, which seek to diffuse the requisite information and give by discipline the requisite skill' (Spencer, 1910, vol II, p 361).

For Spencer, then, 'filial beneficence' is part of a wider field in which individuals voluntarily practise beneficence, in the process giving expression to their social sentiments and strengthening them through repetition, hence advancing psychological and social evolution. Moreover, when coupled with the activities of enlightened voluntary organisations and with the state enforcing justice and policing injustice, we have on view in Spencer an intriguing vision of how individual welfare and strong community ties might be achieved, and how in particular the quality of the lives of older people could be enriched and honoured.[3]

Older people, the majority report and maintaining morale

Spencer's comments on the care of older people can be contrasted with a pair of other sources: the majority and minority reports issued by the royal commission on the poor laws of 1909. The majority report was in large measure written by Helen Bosanquet, prominent in the COS, and indeed COS luminaries and sympathisers formed the bulk of the royal commission's membership. The minority report (the subject of the next section) was largely the work of Beatrice Webb, with strong Fabian socialist associations. Spencer had been a mentor to Beatrice as a family friend but by now there were fissures on theoretical and political matters.

Bernard Bosanquet, his wife Helen, and Charles Loch shared a view of charity as the engine of social progress, delivering 'tutored' democratic citizens, understanding that to be fully free was to act *in certain ways*. All three were prominent in the COS, seeking to fulfil the vision through the casework method and by a division of labour between charity and the poor law, attending to the 'helpable' but shunning the intractable 'unhelpable'. By the early twentieth century it was natural that many of the commissioners of 1909 had first-hand knowledge of COS work (Loch and Helen Bosanquet were members of the commission, but not Bernard Bosanquet).

The majority emphasised that a strong voluntary sector acting in a coordinated manner with publicly provided services was required. The poor law was to be remodelled as public assistance, with the geographically larger unit of local councils replacing boards of guardians. The first line of defence for the older poor of good character should be voluntary aid, coupled with an assurance of adequate public assistance to support them at home. Only if relatives and friends were unable to provide support should indoor relief be provided, of a kind recognising their characters, and on a separate site to that for able-bodied persons. The majority explicitly rejected medical testimony that indoor relief rather than outdoor relief was always preferable, arguing instead for 'a better supervision of the people on out-relief'.

The details of the majority's comments on older people are of considerable interest. The majority noted divergences in respect of contemporary practice regarding both indoor and outdoor relief for the older poor between poor law unions. For policy for the future the role of powers to remove older persons from their homes to institutions was weighed with care. Such powers, it thought, were needed only on occasion: 'for the most part the old people who are too infirm to look after themselves, and have no friends to look after them, are glad to find a refuge in the infirmary or workhouse before their state becomes such as to call for active interference' (Poor Law Report, 1909, vol I, p 225).

As indicated, the report also recorded that medical evidence had been presented suggesting that *no* outdoor relief should be granted to the aged poor, quoting support for institutional care advanced by representatives of the Association of Poor Law Medical Officers (Poor Law Report, 1909, vol I, p 225): 'The opinion of Poor Law medical officers is overwhelmingly in favour of provision in institutions. The replies are all to the same effect, that the aged are kept cleaner and in better health in institutions than if you give them outdoor relief, and that they really suffer in health and in every other way if they are left to provide for themselves outdoors'. The report rejected this illiberal counsel, countering that the difficulties 'might be met by a better supervision of the people on out-relief, and that the number of cases becoming so neglected as to require compulsory removal might be diminished if they were properly looked after from the first'. Thus it recommends that outdoor relief should be adequate in amount and that older people 'should be periodically visited both by officers of the Local Authority (who might be women), and by voluntary visitors' (Poor Law Report, 1909, vol I, p 232).

Indeed voluntary aid, the report urged, should be organised in parallel with public assistance, and should be the initial point of contact (Poor Law Report, 1909, vol I, p 232). It is only when 'the inability of their friends or relatives to look after them in their own homes' (Poor Law Report, 1909, vol II, p 238) has become beyond doubt that older people should be subject to an order for continuous treatment. Such cases require 'very considerate treatment' (Poor Law Report, 1909, vol II, p 238), with an order granted on condition that a medical certificate is issued confirming that continuous care and treatment is necessary for the person's health or safety, and that there is sufficient proof that neither the person nor friends or relatives can provide the care and treatment (Poor Law Report, 1909, vol II, p 239).

Where indoor relief is in fact the route adopted for older people, they should have (Poor Law Report, 1909, vol I, p 232): 'accommodation and treatment apart from the able-bodied, and be housed on a separate site, and be further sub-divided into classes as far as practicable with reference to their physical condition and their moral character'. Cottage homes rather than large buildings are preferred, with residents tended by a matron. It is 'not ... at all desirable that old people who are given to drink, or are of dirty habits, should be enabled to remove themselves from control either by a pension, or by the granting of outdoor relief' (Poor Law Report, 1909, vol I, p 231).

'Depersonalising' risks associated with life in large institutions are highlighted (although the efforts made to maintain health and strength among the older poor therein are in fact recognised):

there is another human element which, under our present system, is not called into action – that is, the capacity and willingness of the old person to help himself. When the institution is on a large scale he may become a mere *numero*; the aged person is, day by day, fed, clothed, and accommodated mechanically as one unit amongst many. His everyday life is deprived of all opportunity for exertion, thought and independence, and this has its inevitable effect upon the *morale* of even the active and the willing. The physical comfort of such a life may be enhanced, but that again is purchased by the loss of much that makes existence pleasant and cheerful even to the aged. (Poor Law Report, 1909, vol II, p 220)

Also noted is an increase in old-age pauperism since 1900, attributed to the 'growing attractiveness of Poor Law institutions' and 'the tendency, consequent upon the old-age pensions movement, to regard outdoor relief as a pension' (Poor Law Report, 1909, vol I, p 232).[4] The authors add the comment, of some interest given Spencer's views:

It has also been suggested that a cause may be found in the weakness of a sense of filial responsibility in the present generation – but in our opinion, the increase of aged pauperism, and the decrease in filial duty, are both alike, effects of a common cause, viz., the general feeling that the State is able and willing to make provision, and even lavish provision for parents whose sons fail to support them. We believe that if the position is clearly defined and a consistent policy laid down both as to pensions and Poor Law relief, the natural feeling between parents and children will again assert itself. (Poor Law Report, 1909, vol I, p 232)

Key features of the majority report in respect of older people are thus a concern with 'character' and its protection from moral decline; some suspicion of the authority of medical knowledge; a view of family life as an important context for the lives of older people; a view of a quality of life that is important beyond mere health, including mental activity, exertion and independence; pronounced caution over institutional care as a panacea; an emphasis on provision by charity rather than the state; and a preference for sympathetic contact with rather than surveillance of individuals.

Older people, the minority report and the primacy of surveillance

We can now turn to the minority report. This report agreed with the majority on the abolition of boards of guardians but wanted a new structure of specialised committees, with expert staff to deal in terms of prevention as well as cure with specific categories of problem among the poor and more widely; the generic public assistance model was rejected as overlapping with provisions in, for example, public health that had grown up outside the poor law. This structure, though, risked another form of overlapping where several problems presented by one person or family would be dealt with by not one worker but by staff from several departments with different specialisms. Voluntary action was not to be an equal; it was to provide an 'extension ladder' of forms of aid beyond those required of the state to secure a guaranteed minimum of civilised life, perhaps in due course taken over by the state as that minimum rose.

This report also comments on the older poor. Greater prominence than in the majority report is given to those of bad conduct. They cannot be reformed, but they can be rendered 'unable to contaminate the rest of the community' (Poor Law Report, 1909, vol III, p 280). Persons of good conduct should be known to the public health authority, which should exercise 'guardianship over the citizen falling into second childhood' (Poor Law Report, 1909, vol III, p 278). On becoming 'a nuisance to the public' or endangering their own lives they should be found forms of accommodation according to need, characteristics and conduct. There is a general focus on the risks of 'elder abuse' from children and the financial probity of relationships between relatives and public agencies rather than on the support of relatives providing home-based care. Confidence in public health and medical personnel to frame the appropriate form of life for those at home, and in institutional care, eclipses concern for individual autonomy, independence and morale. Outdoor relief to the older poor tends to be 'insufficient to provide even the barest food, clothing and shelter' (Poor Law Report, 1909, vol III, p 256). Some unions in addition have a policy of refusing outdoor relief in particular cases 'as a means of inducing relations or friends to come forward and undertake the maintenance of the destitute aged person' (Poor Law Report, 1909, vol III, p 259). Although the same liability to contribute whether the relief is indoor or outdoor applies:

as there is usually a much greater repugnance in relations or friends to allowing a person in whom they are interested to enter the General Mixed Workhouse than to allowing him to receive Outdoor Relief, the Guardians, *without regard to the hardship to the destitute person himself*, play upon the repugnance, and refuse Outdoor Relief, with the object of exacting contributions from relations or friends who might otherwise refuse to make them. (Poor Law Report, 1909, vol III, p 259)

Inconsistency of administration is indeed one of the major themes on this and other topics of the minority report.

Again, some closer detail on the report's treatment of older people is revealing. Much space is devoted to the 'aged poor of bad conduct', the 'no inconsiderable class' of 'old men and women whose persistent addiction to drink makes it necessary to refuse them any but institutional provision' (Poor Law Report, 1909, vol III, p 279). The workhouse is insufficiently deterrent; they are able to pass in and out:

What seems essential in the institutional provision for this class is that it should be undertaken by an Authority having through its ordinary staff the means of becoming aware of the disreputable existence of such old persons, and providing suitable institutions for their reception, with powers, in cases in which they were leading grossly insanitary lives, of obtaining magisterial orders for compulsory removal and detention – not for the sake of punishing these old people, who cannot be reformed, and can hardly be made of any value to the community, but in order to place them where they will be as far as possible prevented from indulging their evil propensities, where they will be put to do such work as they may be capable of, and where they will, at any rate, be unable to contaminate the rest of the community. This need not be a prison. The aged person cannot usually be reformed, but experience shows that, within an institution, he is not, as a matter of fact, either recalcitrant or badly conducted. We cannot help thinking that the duty of looking after this class, to whom Outdoor Relief would be rigidly refused, seems, accordingly, to fall most appropriately to the Public Health Authority, with its constant 'searching out' of cases, and the compulsory powers of removal and detention which it already enjoys in cases of infectious disease. (Poor Law Report, 1909, vol III, p 280)

The report also treats at some length the older poor needing support in their own homes and the 'deserving' poor needing institutional accommodation. It advocates, on the lines of extant public health responsibilities towards infants, that the public health authority should exercise, as already noted, 'a similar guardianship over the citizen falling into second childhood', such that its staff are 'aware of cases in which the helpless deserving aged, notwithstanding their little pensions or the attentions of the charitable, are suffering from neglect or lack of care' (Poor Law Report, 1909, vol III, p 278). Such surveillance should be alert to tyranny and petty cruelty perpetrated even by their own children. Almshouses or 'homes for the aged' should be available as living alone becomes unsustainable, with care by 'nurses and doctors just as much as required' (Poor Law Report, 1909, vol III, p 279). Classification of accommodation, to be allocated according to physical need and present characteristics and conduct, is required. It would be of 'various grades of comfort' and 'permitting of various degrees of liberty' (Poor Law Report, 1909, vol III, pp 280-1): 'Into these the old people would be sorted, as far as may be in accordance with their present characteristics and conduct, with power to transfer inmates from grade to grade according to the occurrence of vacancies and to actual behaviour within the institution'. However, an underpinning of compulsory powers is needed 'with regard to all aged and infirm persons who are found to be endangering their own lives, or becoming, through mental or physical incapacity to take care of themselves, a nuisance to the public' (Poor Law Report, 1909, vol III, p 281).

Key features of the minority report on the treatment of older people are: a striking character-based emphasis on a sub-group with problems related to alcohol and draconian remedies to ensure their constraint, surveillance and inability to 'contaminate the community'; the wide-ranging empowerment of the state in the form of public health and medical personnel to both frame the regimen of living style for those at home and also to allocate, by 'sorting' the older people, the 'appropriate' accommodation in cases of 'second childhood' or 'helplessness', as well as to deal with problems of health as such; the concomitant absence of a concern with questions of individual autonomy, independence and morale; and a focus on the risks of 'elder abuse' from children and the financial rectitude of relationships between relatives and public agencies rather than on changes in the dynamics of 'filial obligations' in home-based care and support.

Idealism versus non-idealism: an introduction

Two further linked matters can now be introduced since they arise from the discussion of the care of older people; they will, though, be the subject of more thorough investigation in the following chapter. They are the nature of idealist social thought and its relationship with *non*-idealist social thought.

The crux of the matter is whether or not interventions associated with social policy (voluntary and statutory) should seek *directly* or at best *indirectly* in their interaction with individuals to promote an end state of social life such as the 'good' or 'healthy' society, as perhaps indicated by the 'general will'. There is ground here shared with the distinction made by Oakeshott between the state as, as Eccleshall (1990, p 16) expresses it, 'a civil association protecting individual liberties through the rule of law, and an enterprise promoting the common welfare'. Idealists are committed to using policy directly as a means to such an end; non-idealists may (or may not) hope for some such result indirectly, but leave it to be achieved by individuals as far as possible freely choosing and fulfilling *their own* projects in life, rather than having those projects imposed and executed in a manner designed to serve the 'good of all' (on general ideas of the state see Meadowcroft, 1995; on the implications of this non-idealist conception of society as catallaxy for ideas of distributive justice see Millar, 1989, ch 2). Non-idealists reject idealism on grounds philosophical as well as political: empowering individuals to pursue well-being as defined and pursued by themselves in their own lives is their objective. The reality of altruism means that solipsistic selfishness is not inevitable; social relations will result from uncoerced consent, not manipulation inspired by adherence to assumptions about social life. To use Le Grand's (2003) categories, for non-idealists, ordinary individuals are 'queens' not 'pawns'.

There are, as we have seen, differences in the schemes and sensitivities in the two reports. For the minority report where moral failings (what it calls the 'moral factor in destitution') are the root of dependency, whether for the older people of bad character or those unwilling to work (the 'born tired': S. and B. Webb, 1910, p 317), compulsory remedial or at least palliative measures are to be applied. But as is clear in the Scottish minority report of October 1909, most destitution is regarded as caused by other factors such as sickness, where no 'moral defect' is to be found. This is an explicit response to Bernard Bosanquet's argument (advanced in the *Sociological Review* for April, 1909) that where there is 'a failure of self-maintenance' there is 'a defect in the citizen character, or at least a grave danger to its integrity', and that cases of this kind raise problems that are 'moral' in the sense of 'affecting the whole capacity of self-management, to begin with in the person who has failed, and secondarily in the whole community so far as influenced by expectation and example' (quoted in Poor Law Report (Scotland), 1909, p 274). However, as Vincent (1984) has suggested, Bosanquet is not advocating the values of economic laissez faire, but making a more subtle and profound point about a 'failure' to be an ideal citizen, to have become unable to look to the common good in facing up to predicaments in which it is always possible to choose to act in one way rather than another, and display rational, independent will. Incapacities could be willed or unwilled, but the quality of the individual response was an ineliminable part of the picture. Voluntary action, practising casework guided by social therapeutics, could assist citizens to regain control of their circumstances rather than fall victim to them. Bosanquet, the COS and the majority report did not believe destitution was the product of moral inadequacy, except in circumstances where 'willed incapacity' to work for example arose, and here they agreed on a coercive role for the state with the minority. They were prepared to accept economic causes of temporary destitution and a wide range of 'environmental' ones (McBriar, 1987, p 300). Whatever the particular problem involved was, the majority were seeking preventive, curative and restorative treatment with the whole person in mind. For the majority, it was to the 'whole person' dimension that the minority report gave too little attention.

The idealist social thought with which the majority report is infused should now be apparent, as should some of the material differences with the minority report. However, it can also be argued that idealist social thought has an intimate connection with the minority report.

> Many social idealists, and others who were influenced by idealist modes of thought, dissented radically from the Bosanquets in their assessment of the desirable practical relationship between the citizen and the state. The Webbs, for example, wholly shared the Bosanquets' belief that private and public virtue were interdependent, that 'state-conscious idealism' was the goal of citizenship, and that social-welfare policies should be ethically as well as materially constructive: indeed Sidney once described himself as aiming to do in the social sphere what Rousseau had done in the political. But they claimed that the deviant or needy individual could far more easily be provoked into self-improvement from within the context of state social

services than if left to his own unaided efforts. (Harris, 1992, p 133)

The Webbs sought to realise 'social health' (S. and B. Webb, 1910, p 319) and believed that the opening of the twentieth century 'finds us all, to the dismay of the old-fashioned individualist, "thinking in communities"' (in Webb, 1948, pp 221-2). Moreover, towards the end of the Scottish minority report (written after the English and Irish[5] reports and hence informed by the public reaction to them) idealist aspirations are evident. The minority scheme of reform has a 'deeper significance' than economy or simplicity:

> The reform that we advocate, by emphas[is]ing everywhere the Principle of Prevention, and especially by systematically searching out neglected infancy and childhood, preventable sickness, uncontrolled feeble-mindedness and uncared-for epilepsy, unwanted vagrancy and that hopeless worklessness that is so demoralising to mind and body, brings with it the sure and certain hope that we may, at no distant date, by patient and persistent effort on these lines, remove from our midst the intolerable infamy to the Christian and civilised State of the persistence of a mass of chronic destitution, spreading like a cancerous growth from one generation to another of our fellow citizens. (Poor Law Report (Scotland), 1909, p 274)

To point to idealism in the Webbs and the minority reports should not be mistaken as a denial of their Fabian socialism. Rather, it is to draw attention to fundamental continuities of intellectual and theoretical disposition, which Harris' broad notion of idealist social thought pinpoints.[6]

Non-idealist social thought at the time was epitomised by Herbert Spencer. As we have seen, in his *Principles of ethics* (1892, vol I, and 1893a, vol II) he described and advocated 'private beneficence', now more familiar as informal care, supported unbureaucratic voluntary organisations, and demanded the comprehensive and accessible administration of justice, all of which would secure greater well-being. In his *Man versus the state* of 1884 he had heavily criticised the Liberals for 'unjust' interventions in social life and for failing to enforce 'justice'. For Spencer 'justice' maximises individual happiness. 'Justice' so understood sharply limits the duties of government to ensuring infringements of equal freedom, hence his critique of Gladstonian liberalism. Critics today of the state's 'swelling ambition to engineer the social sphere through energetic legislation and the adoption of a highly directive "audit culture"' (Peel, 2004, p 145) have a doughty friend in Spencer. Acts of justice along with acts of private beneficence (individually and socially desirable but not matters of 'justice') make up altruism, and for Spencer altruism is increasingly present in 'civilised' societies. The pursuit of 'justice' in social life leads to progressive social evolution, just as the desert element does in nature. In these matters Spencer's position is distinct from Darwin's, as indicated in Chapter Three (he is giving primacy to the now-discredited Lamarckian mechanism of inheritance of acquired characteristics as organisms adapt to circumstances rather than Darwin's 'natural selection' of variations as the cause of change, and adopting a pre-Darwinian concern with the *direction* of change).

Spencer thus articulated a non-idealist form of welfare pluralism. His individuals are social and altruistic. Spencer's thought, which had become well known by the 1870s was a prime target of idealist philosophers, including T.H. Green, and also of the Webbs, although Beatrice Webb was an admirer in her youth and close to Spencer. Writing shortly after Spencer's death one prominent idealist philosopher adopted a triumphalist tone (Pringle Pattison, 1904, p 256): 'the conception of man as essentially social, and of the state as the organ of the general will, has so firmly established itself that Spencer's pamphlets during the last twenty years sounded like a belated echo, and he had the air, even to himself, of one crying in the wilderness'. A similar parti pris opinion emanated from a later idealist, A.D. Lindsay, in 1919 when he derided the 'malignant theory' of 'scientific individualism' as swept into the dustbin of history (in Harris, 1992, p 135).[7]

Conclusion: echoes and memories

It would be easy to point to serious omissions in Spencer's concern with filial obligations (such as a consideration of other familial commitments and the constraints of poverty). It is really a larger non-idealist model of care for older people of which it is emblematic that matters, at least with present concerns in mind. Detailed discussion of idealist social thought, and the contrast with non-idealist social thought, comes in the next chapter, but it will be helpful to emphasise once more the basic distinction here. In idealist social thought, a concern with specific social problems was rendered subordinate to:

> a vision of reconstructing the whole of British society, together with reform of the rational understanding and moral character of individual British citizens. Social policy was not viewed as an end in itself, nor were the recipients of welfare ends in themselves; on the contrary, both policies and people were means to the end of attaining perfect justice and creating the ideal state. (Harris, 1992, p 126)

Idealist social thought involves thinking in terms of communities, of pursuing an end that is more than the aggregate of individual 'well-being' as in effect defined by the individuals, an end indicated by the 'general will' of the 'good society'. Contrary to the non-idealist position intervention in lives to pursue this end is seen as justified and desirable, with disagreements between idealists on the role of charity and the state in achieving the prescribed changes in individual lives and circumstances, and over the sanctions to be suffered by the non-compliant. The enlightened charity worker exercising supervision (for the majority report) and the well-trained professional vigilantly enacting surveillance (for the minority report) are better endowed with knowledge of the 'social good' than ordinary people, consequently their preferences and the preferences of those furnishing beneficence – or informal care – are accorded low priority.

Both reports shared an idealist style of thought, with differences over means rather than ends, whereas Spencer's comments are at odds with the chief tenets of idealist social thought. A vision of life for older people in which they are the experts about their well-being is at the heart of Spencer's thought. In a nutshell, Spencer's non-idealist social thought is that welfare is maximised if each individual lives according to the principle of justice. The growth in each individual of social sentiments such as positive beneficence, including a developed sense of filial obligations, are results of such a way of living, and will advance further. It is precisely this conception of sociability in Spencer that leads Hiskes (1983) to attribute to him a liberal idea of community.

A (non-Spencerian) contemporary non-idealist approach could indeed embrace supporting older people and their informal carers by directing voluntary action and health and social service provision to this end, and by insisting upon the adequacy of occupational pensions. Let me end, however, on a slightly different note. In part, a vision of the kind just identified finds echoes in the Griffiths Report *Community care: Agenda for action* (1988) and the White Paper *Modernising social services* (1998). The White Paper, though, is of particular interest since it includes an example of how a 'better' outcome for a service user can result from user involvement. It involves Mrs X a 72-year-old lady who is becoming frail, cared for by her son who lives with her and by other local family members. Having formerly coped well, the following events are recorded as her case is monitored.

> *June 1997*: Mrs X has a stroke and falls – accepts home help and subsequently admitted to hospital.

> *September 1997*: case conference: 'the medical and social work consensus was for residential care – all agreed except Mrs X' (Cases file). Weekly cost £335.
>   Mrs X accepts package of home help – 1 hour 3 times daily.

> *December 1997*: when visited by the review team Mrs X was delighted to still be in her home and her condition continues to improve. Weekly cost of care for the authority is less than half the cost of residential care. (*Modernising social services*, 1998, p 36)

This vignette encapsulates the continuing contrast between idealist and non-idealist social thinking. The extent to which professionals' own policies and the management of resources regularly permit the kind of optimum outcome recorded, especially at a time when it has become unexceptionable though to their disadvantage to refer to older people in hospital as 'bed-blockers', is a question beyond the scope of the present book.

It seems, then, that the idea of 'idealist social thought', and the further distinction between idealist and non-idealist modes of thinking, have a real potential to enhance the interpretation of the significant normative differences over the role of filial beneficence, domiciliary support from other sources, and institutions, which were earlier identified in past approaches to the care of older people. Understanding Spencer, the Bosanquets and the Webbs lays bare the traditions, and their associated echoes and memories, that should assist us in exploring, as Phillipson rightly desires, 'the roots of modern consciousness about ageing' (2001, p 520). More generally, the fact that dead sociologically minded theorists can bequeath enduring but unexcavated legacies to modern professional and everyday thought provides one of the compelling reasons why, contrary to Fuller (see Fuller, 1995, and Offer, 1996 for criticism), they merit continuing attention.

FIVE

Social policy and idealist versus non-idealist thought: the fundamental schism

Introduction: the late Victorian and Edwardian idealists

'British Idealism' had, as a philosophical movement, a fairly short preeminence at Oxford and universities in Scotland – broadly from about the 1880s to the First World War. Key figures include T.H. Green, F.H. Bradley, Bernard Bosanquet and D.G. Ritchie. Attacks on the meaning of its utterances came from G.E. Moore and Bertrand Russell, and later from A.J. Ayer (for a concise discussion see Passmore, 1968). However, if idealism was soon in retreat in philosophical circles, it maintained a cultural hegemony elsewhere, especially in the many areas of social thinking in which philosophers seldom participated.

In Boucher's view, exponents of idealist thought, in demonstrating the relevance of philosophy to ordinary life, 'exercised a considerable influence in providing a frame of reference for social policy, public administration and education reform well into the twentieth century' (1997, p xi). Harris argues that this influence is particularly marked in social policy (1989, and 1992, pp 135-7).[1] Social work's debt to idealist thought is also interesting in, for example, Canada. Moffatt and Irving (2002) have shown how John Watson and George Blewett, both students of Edward Caird at Oxford, influenced the development of social work in an idealist direction, particularly at the University of Toronto. This was reinforced with the arrival of the idealist E.J. Urwick from London in 1924: as first head of the department of social science and administration at the London School of Economics he had specified 'social philosophy' as the central discipline (Harris, 1992, p 125).

Harris' definition of idealist thought is usefully broader than the Idealist philosophical perspective at its core, and refers

> not just to philosophers who self-consciously adhered to the idealist school, but to anyone who thought that

> knowledge rested on certain a priori categories, who viewed
> society and/or the state as having a real corporate identity,
> and who saw the prime concerns of social science as being
> the interpretation of 'meaning' and 'purpose' rather than
> the discovery of causal laws. (Harris, 1992, p 123)

Only some idealist philosophical positions are of concern here, related
to its distinctive social, political and moral tenets. The organic view of
society and the obligations of individuals to others advanced by Plato
in the *Republic*, the idea that a people possessed a 'general will' – a
national character – that a government could embody, developed from
Rousseau, and the concern with 'mind' and 'history' in Hegel, all
contributed to a marked idealist turn in academic philosophy in British
universities, with T.H. Green at Oxford as the doyen. To an extent
logical relations became confounded with contingent relations: idealism
soon faded from respectability in philosophical analysis. As essentially
a social theory, however, idealism was well established in the departments
of social science introduced in the early twentieth century, usually
associated with idealists. Social reform and idealist social thought were
self-consciously entwined.

Thus these Hegelian views of historical development and of unity
between mind and nature and between society and individual, together
with Rousseau's idea of tutelary democracy expressing the 'general
will' and Plato's wisely-guiding 'guardians' of the *Republic* formed the
tap-root of idealism both narrowly and broadly defined. The concept
of absolute mind was used to defend something akin to immanentist
theology, thus providing at least in principle a reconciliation between
belief in God and evolutionary theory. Mind works through the world
to realise itself. Moreover, 'the presence of absolute mind within us
implies that we are vital, living beings whose behaviour can be
understood only in terms of our meanings, values and purposes' (Bevir
and O'Brien, 2003, p 307). For Harris, idealist patterns of thought
can be found in Rowntree (Harris, 1992, pp 123-4), Beatrice and
Sidney Webb (Harris, 1992, pp 124, 133), E.J. Urwick and R.H. Tawney
(see Harris, 1989, pp 50-5), as well as in J.A. Hobson and L.T.
Hobhouse,[2] overtly engaging in creative dialogue with the founders
of idealism. That it can be argued therefore 'that the mental outlook of
Titmuss was cast in a very similar mould' (Harris, 1989, p 54) is only
a matter for surprise in that it has come so late, given his enthusiasm
for Tawney (for example, Titmuss, 1958). Edward Caird, his ideas in
tune with Green's, and passionate about 'duty', was master of Balliol
College when both Tawney and Beveridge were students there at the

turn of the century. On graduation, both men gained practical experience, through work at Toynbee Hall, of the hardships faced by the unemployed. In 1908 Beveridge wrote in criticism of the Liberals' non-contributory old-age pension scheme, calling for a contributory scheme extending beyond old age:

> the state must get hold of its individual citizens, must know much more about them, must make them actually and consciously part of the social organisation. A non-contributory pension scheme sets up the State in the eyes of the individual as a source of free gifts. A contributory scheme sets up the State as a comprehensive organism to which the individual belongs and in which he, under compulsion if need be, plays his part. (in Beveridge, 1954, p 57)

It will be helpful very briefly to introduce some of the key idealists who are to figure in the discussion. Thomas Hill Green lived from 1836 to 1882, wielded influence through his teaching at Balliol College, and became professor of moral philosophy at Oxford: his *Prolegomena to ethics* came out in 1883. Benjamin Jowett, who had early on brought Hegel to English attention, influenced Green. Green coupled philosophy with championing social reform and radical political causes. Like many other idealists, he wanted to emphasise the ethical and spiritual nature of man and social life against materialistic interpretations, working from the spiritual and ethical insights offered by Christian belief. Bernard Bosanquet lived from 1848 to 1923. Influenced by Green at Balliol he held posts in philosophy at Oxford and St Andrews. He developed a philosophy of charity alongside of his and his wife's association with the Charity Organisation Society (COS) in London: his *Aspects of the social problem* was issued in1895. Henry Jones was born in 1852 and died in 1922. His career as a philosopher was spent in Wales and Scotland, and he sought to apply philosophy to practical concerns. He was on friendly terms with Lloyd George. His *The working faith of the social reformer* appeared in 1910. David George Ritchie lived from 1853 until 1903. Influenced by Green at Balliol, he went on to hold a chair at St Andrews. His political sympathies were with the socialists, rather than the liberals as was the case for the other idealists just identified. *Darwinism and politics* appeared in 1889, and *The principles of state interference* two years later. Owing intellectual debts to idealism but more often known as New Liberals were John Atkinson Hobson (1858-1940) and Leonard Hobhouse (1864-1929). Hobson was a journalist and editor in the cause of the reform liberal press, and was a critic of the social theory of the COS as he saw it; his *The social problem* was first published in 1901 (Hobson, 1996a). Hobhouse was the first holder of a chair in sociology in Britain (at the London School of Economics) and, like Hobson, sought to relate the idea of social evolution to social science and social reform; *Social evolution and political theory* and *Liberalism* both appeared in 1911 (1911a and 1911b). Hobhouse developed his ideas in reaction to Spencer and had an 'always ambivalent' relationship with idealist thought (Collini, 1979, p 162).

A different kind of observation should also be recorded at this point. In the interests of clarity it is best at the outset of the following discussion to indicate that non-idealist social thought can display ideals, but that such a feature does not transform it into idealist social thought. The case of the poor law reforms of 1834 illustrates the contribution of ideals to the plans: 'the royal commissioners offered an authentically original solution to the poor law problem, original in the crucial sense that administrative structure and relief procedures were carefully coordinated to form a single, universal system in support of a comprehensive vision of ideal socio-economic relationships' (Dunkley, 1982, p 179). Senior's opinion of the 1834 Act was that changes from previous practice would provide 'an administration by which ... subsistence shall be given in a way which shall be favourable, instead of destructive to the welfare of society' (in Levy, 1970, pp 90-1). And Chadwick saw the views behind the Act as going 'beyond measures of cure or alleviation or the repression of evil to prevention and by preventive measures to the improvement of the condition of the population' (in Dunkley, 1982, p 146). The concern here is with how *members of* a society will in the new circumstances be able to enhance their own well-being as judged by themselves, rather than what will bring into being the virtuous, organic republic, the hallmark of idealist social thought.

From Spencer to idealism via the social organism

A good place at which to begin to develop the discussion is by considering something elevated to high prominence by non-idealists and idealists alike, that society may be considered as an organism. At several points in his career Spencer drew analogies between biological organisms and societies, accompanying the identification of similarities with unlikenesses. A society was a kind of organic entity, because of the 'general persistence of the arrangements' displayed by its members

(Spencer, 1893b, p 436). Spencer did not draw the analogy between the human body and society; he criticises both Plato and Hobbes for doing exactly this. They both fall into 'the extreme inconsistency of considering a community as similar in structure to a human being, and yet as produced in the same way as an artificial mechanism – in nature an organism; in history, a machine' (Spencer, 1901, p 271). Spencer's main reasons for seeing society in both its nature and development as an organism are:

> It undergoes continuous growth. As it grows, its parts
> become unlike: it exhibits increase of structure. The unlike
> parts simultaneously assume activities of unlike kinds. These
> activities are not simply different, but their differences are
> so related as to make one another possible. The reciprocal
> aid thus given causes mutual dependence of the parts. And
> the mutually-dependent parts, living by and for one another,
> form an aggregate constituted on the same general principle
> as is an individual organism ... Though the two are
> contrasted as respectively discrete and concrete, and though
> there results a difference in the ends subserved by the
> organization, there does not result a difference in the laws
> of the organization: the required mutual influences of the
> parts, not transmissible in a direct way, being, in a society,
> transmitted in an indirect way. (Spencer, 1893b, p 450)

This discreteness of the parts is of vital importance to Spencer and presents the cardinal difference between individual organisms and social organisms. Language, though, has a unifying role, for, even when physically separated, individuals 'nevertheless affect one another through intervening spaces, both by emotional language and by the language, oral and written, of the intellect' (Spencer, 1893b, pp 447-8). In individual organisms consciousness is concentrated in a small part of the unit; in social organisms it 'is diffused throughout the aggregate' (Spencer, 1893b, p 449). All individuals can be happy and miserable. Thus Spencer declares:

> As, then, there is no social sensorium, the welfare of the
> aggregate, considered apart from that of the units, is not an
> end to be sought. The society exists for the benefit of its
> members; not its members for the benefit of society. It has
> ever to be remembered that great as may be the efforts
> made for the prosperity of the body politic, yet the claims

of the body politic are nothing in themselves, and become something only in so far as they embody the claims of its component individuals. (1893b, pp 449-50)

It may be that conceptions of societies as organisms have historically accompanied and perhaps been designed to encourage authoritarian and conservative social and political arrangements. There is, though, no necessary connection here: the analogy could be legitimately formulated to point in the opposite direction. This Spencer does, arguing that since social individuals have consciousness there is in society no social sensorium. On Spencer's position Tim Gray comments,

> Spencer enunciated a conception of individualism which was opposed to collectivism, not to social organicism; and he enunciated a conception of social organicism which was opposed to mechanism, not to individualism. The general consistency of Spencer's position is made clear by the additional facts that his 'true' model of individualism was opposed to mechanism, and his 'true' model of organicism was opposed to collectivism. At the root of the critics' misinterpretation of Spencer's theory was their mistaken assumptions that the 'opposite' of individualism was organicism, and that the 'opposite' of organicism was individualism. The truth is, however, that if there *is* an 'opposite' of individualism it is collectivism, not organicism, and if there *is* an 'opposite' of organicism, it is mechanism not individualism. Spencer consistently developed an individualistic/organicist theory, and consistently opposed it to a collectivist/mechanistic theory. (1996, p 233)

For Spencer the process of free adaptation was crucial. The 'artificial' manipulation of society endangered both freedom, in the sense of negative liberty, and voluntary organic cooperation by social individuals. 'The mechanistic/artificial/manipulative theory of the state not only threatened the natural growth model of society, but it also encouraged the spirit of collectivism which put negative liberty in jeopardy' (Gray, 1996, p 232).

Idealists criticised Spencer's conception of the social organism, as they took it to be, as a means to establish idealist tenets (for instance Jones, 1883; and Ritchie, 1895). For Ritchie, a society of one hundred individuals working 'for the promotion of a particular end is something more than the aggregate of a hundred individuals working towards this same end' (1895, p 110). Rights can be directly created by a state or a society:

> Suppose a company of persons meet together for the purpose of founding a society – let us say for the study of Mr Spencer's System of Synthetic Philosophy. They appoint a committee to draw up rules. These rules are accepted by a vote of all the units (or by a majority, to which the minority voluntarily gives way). The individuals, as members of the society, have now rights (and of course duties) which they did not have before – *e.g.*, they have to pay subscriptions, they may write after their names M.S.S.S.S.S.P., and they may have the crystal-grub-butterfly emblem stamped on their note-paper. The trick is done. A right is created out of nothing. (Ritchie, 1895, p 113)

Enjoyable mockery, but scarcely engaging with Spencer's serious point that the individual's right to justice has, for him, a basis in natural order and is in that sense a 'natural' right.

According to Ritchie, individuals considered separate from society can only be hedonistic; morality comes with seeing society and individuals as intimately interrelated and interdependent. Spencer thinks of the individual as if 'he had a meaning and significance apart from his surroundings and apart from his relations to the community of which he is a member' (Ritchie, 1895, p 106). Idealists accused Spencer of interpreting people as 'atomic individuals' rather than ethical and interdependent beings rooted in society. They argued for the centrality of the moral and the spiritual in understanding social life and society, and self-consciously reconceptualised the role of the state. For Henry Jones the real meaning of the doctrine that society is an organism is that

> an individual has no life except that which is social, and that he cannot realise his own purposes except in realising the larger purposes of society…Whatever the difficulties may be in finding the unity of the social organism, if we hold to the doctrine and make it more than metaphor, we must recognise that society and individuals actually form such a whole, and that apart from each other they are nothing but names; and we must cease to speak of individuals as if they ever could exist apart from society, or

could attain their purposes except by becoming its organs
and carrying out its purposes. It seems to me that the first
and last duty of man is to know and to do those things
which the social community of which he is a member
calls upon him to do. (Jones, 1883, p 9)

A life a man 'perverts' to selfish ends 'is not merely his own but that of
the moral organism which lives in him' (Jones, 1883, p 9).

It is, though, worth reflecting on what is logically required as opposed
to possibly morally desirable in 'social life' for it to count as such. The
presence and use of language, consciousness and a sense of self and
other persons as persons, relatively stable, applicable and adaptable rules
of conduct, and some means of regulation and arbitration all seem
essential. All the characteristics would be to at least some degree
malleable, permitting and reacting to change initiated by social
individuals. Some such view would embrace all that we conventionally
regard as 'social life', or 'living in a society', whether a society apparently
at the point of dissolution, at peace, diverse and affluent, or with
totalitarian moral and political enforcement of prescribed values. In a
sense a society is only 'dysfunctional' or collapsing when, to put it
figuratively, social individuals are being reduced to a state of nature.

Non-idealist thought on society, however, as earlier chapters have
shown, has no difficulty with such matters, though its accounts of
how they have arisen may be contested. It is simply not the case that
it is committed to an individualism that interprets the individual as
finding others a limit to rather than a source of fulfilment in life.
Idealists tended to run together the separate questions: 'what *is* a society,
or social life?' and 'what *ought* a society or social life to be like?'. They
underestimated seriously the coherence of the answers non-idealists
could generate, beguiled by metaphysical speculation that drew them
to what was in fact an 'ideal' image of society and social life. This
image idealists then tried to relate to actual society and how it might
realise the ideal, for the ideal society became morally ideal. Idealists
adopted an unnecessarily narrow view of what it was for a society to
count as 'organic' (and 'organic' is anyway a non-essential starting
point for the interpretation of social reality). They emphasised a unifying
'general will' for which might be substituted some contingently
complementary and relatively uncontested ways of living adopted
within by transient coalitions of willing social individuals, and they
emphasised an inessential predilection for the state, or government,
and voluntary organisations as beacons of moral authority and growth,
rather than an acceptance of dispersed, diverse and competing

awarenesses of 'how to live'. They may be said to have specified the conditions for social performance in an exaggerated manner. In his *Prolegomena to ethics* Green wrote:

> Social life is to personality what language is to thought. Language presupposes thought as a capacity, but in us the capacity of thought is only actualised by language. So human society presupposes persons in capacity – subjects capable each of conceiving himself and the bettering of his life as an end to himself – but it is only in the intercourse of men, each recognised by each as an end, not merely a means, and thus as having reciprocal claims, that the capacity is actualised and that we really live as persons. (2003, p 183)

There is nothing in this passage that a non–idealist would disagree with in substance, except perhaps the contrast implicitly behind the emphasis on what it is to 'really' live as persons. None of this is to claim that non–idealist positions were without fault. However, the faults attributed to them by idealists were mostly in idealist minds.

The language used by idealists is problematic as well as heady and rhapsodic. A key tenet, expressed typically by Henry Jones, was that, since society is an organism, it is impossible 'to separate the welfare of the whole from the welfare of the members, or the welfare of the members from the welfare of the whole. To separate the one from the other is to give independent existence to unreal abstractions and to empty the notion of organic unity of its distinctive content' (Jones, 1883, p 7). A little later Jones adds,

> He who has made the welfare of the race his aim, has done so, not from a generous choice, but because he regards the pursuit of this welfare as his imperative duty. The welfare of the race is his own ideal; what he must realise in order to be what he *ought* to be. The welfare of the race is his own welfare, which he must seek because he must be *himself.* (Jones, 1883, p 26)

The proposition 'the welfare of the race is his own welfare' is directly derived from the conception of society as an organic whole, and is defined as true rather than furnishing an (improbable) statement of fact. Knock away the foundation in organicism and it appears untrue, extraordinarily vague, or metaphorical. In similar fashion the force of the proposition as a moral injunction about how to live vanishes: for 'the good must be an organism really existing in the world and yet an ideal for every individual' (Jones, 1883, p 23).

Indeed, idealists tended to conflate expressions such as 'society *really* is...' (by which they did *not* mean what it actually is) with 'society *ought* to be ...'. For the Individualist, W.H. Mallock,[3] writers in favour of social reform use 'is' in a sense very different from the common one (1882, p 196): 'It is simply a short substitute for three other expressions – *ought to be, can be* and *will be*', that are as it happens not at all matters of fact but topics needing debate and investigation. Alasdair MacIntyre in his *Short history of ethics* (1968, p 247) similarly observes that Green's 'metaphysical mode enables him to pass from the view that society ought to be the locus of a rational general will of a Rousseauesque kind to the view that at bottom this is what society *really* is'. Idealist writers take the ideal to be implicit in the actual, at least in part because of their conception of the social organism, although it is also a reflection of their Aristotelian disposition to teleology. It is arguably an illusion that in the idealists' sense the morally good society is somehow singularly implicit in existing social individuals; other ways of living morally were possible which might be no less implicit, or not *implicit* at all, and anyway, as the idealists perfectly well saw, it had to be actively worked for by guiding people towards it, not quietly and smugly awaited.

Note too, as den Otter (1996) has explored, that idealists' attempts to specify the nature of society and social individuals often led to inferences about the direction in which social science should develop, along non-materialist and non-positivist lines that acknowledged the special collectively moral and willed status of social life (again Spencer's work, this time his sociology in particular, became a target). Bosanquet indeed called for a new subject, 'social therapeutics' (see Vincent, 1984). More generally, the idealists wanted sociology to locate empirical research into, for example, poverty, in a framework of the moral meanings, choices and hindrances they took to constitute the actions of responsible citizens. 'Raw' statistics were of limited value. According to den Otter:

> In arguing for a philosophical definition of poverty, for example, Hobson acknowledged that poverty must be defined not by the individual's physical environment, but by how the environment imposed a barrier to 'the attainment of a higher life' willed by the individual. Like Ritchie, Hobson argued that to recognize 'the moral import of a fact' was not to confuse 'fact' and 'value', or respectively

> 'is' and 'ought'. 'The "ought" is not something separable
> and distinct from the "is"; on the contrary an "ought" is
> everywhere the highest aspect or relation of an "is".' In his
> hands, social science became an essentially normative
> inquiry set within a moral framework of modified
> utilitarianism. (den Otter, 1996, p 81, quoting from Hobson,
> 1996a, p 66)

The devil is of course in the detail: the 'higher life' 'willed' might, to
non-idealists, be a matter of diverse interpretation and moral evaluation.

Many idealist thinkers felt, not without reason, that Spencer moved
too directly from biological to social evolution: a different conception
of how change occurred in social life, properly conceived, was required.
The issue of evolution and social life was generally seen as too important
to be ignored. Thus, for example, in 1889, James Seth, professor of
philosophy at the University of Edinburgh, declared:

> Self-conscious evolution is essentially different from
> unconscious evolution, and the former cannot be stated in
> terms of the latter. While all lower life evolves by strict
> unconscious necessity, man, as self-conscious, is free from
> its dominion; and has the power consciously to help on, or
> consciously to hinder, the evolution. Hence it is that we
> are at once conscious of the inadequacy of such categories
> as 'adaptation to environment', 'survival of the fittest' etc.,
> as applied to moral life ... they are only imperfect analogies
> drawn from a lower plane of existence. (Seth, 1889, pp 350-1)

A concise exchange of essays, written by the libertarian Auberon
Herbert, and Hobson, first published in *The Humanitarian* in 1898 and
1899, 'uniquely distilled into their bare essentials' many of the points
at issue over 'society' and the study of it between the Individualists
and their critics (Taylor, 1996, pp xiii-xiv: the essays are reprinted in
Taylor, and page references are to this edition). Herbert (1838-1906)
was the third son of the third Earl of Caernarvon, and much influenced
by Spencer.[4] In 'A voluntaryist appeal' (Herbert, 1898a), Herbert
championed a departure from 'the present Compulsory State, with its
usurped ownership of the minds, bodies and property of men, into
the Voluntary State, in which men would cooperate together for all
their needs, as free men and Self-owners, not as those who have sold
themselves into a bondage' (Herbert, 1996, p 228). A majority can
possess no power over an individual, so long as the individual respects

the rights of others to their freedom, unless an individual 'of his own free choice consents to make himself subject to the decisions of such a majority' (Herbert, 1996, p 229).

Hobson responded in 'Rich man's anarchism' (Hobson, 1898), claiming that for Herbert 'there is no such thing as Society' (Hobson, 1996b, p 241). For Hobson, it is the 'commonplace of most social philosophies' that 'society' is not the mere addition of its individual members but an organic system of the relations between individuals' (Hobson, 1996b, p 243). Indeed, the conscious person does not exist apart from his relations to other persons: to suppose these relations absent is to make a false abstraction. 'The organized action of Society through the State', Hobson adds, 'is one of the most important instruments of the growth of the positive freedom of the individual life' (Hobson, 1996b, p 242; the idea of positive freedom is discussed in the following section).

Herbert's first rejoinder was 'Salvation by force' (Herbert, 1898b), which homed in on a weakness and an omission in Hobson's analysis.

> We are all agreed probably that we are subject to innumerable influences, that we all act and re-act upon each other in the great social whole, that the environment constantly affects and modifies the individual. Marvellous indeed is the great subtle web of relations in which we are all bound together – man and nature, man and man, body and mind, nation and nation, each for ever interacting on the other. But what in the name of good logic and plain common sense have this universal interaction and interdependence to do with the fundamental dogmas of Socialism? Socialism rests upon the assumed rights of some men to constrain other men ... Socialism differs from other systems in this essential, that it recognises and, so to speak, sanctifies compulsion as a universally true and proper method ... It represents the belief that prosperity, happiness, and morality are to be conferred upon the world by force – the force of some men applied to other men. (Herbert, 1996, pp 249-50)

Elsewhere Herbert distinguished 'voluntary socialism' from 'force socialism' (Hutchinson Harris, 1943, p 317): here his target is 'force socialism'. The elevation of force over consent comes at the expense of valuing truth and respect for fellow men. Hobson has not addressed the harm caused by turning from the open field to the use of force in social life.

Herbert subsequently returned to the attack in 'Lost in the region of phrases' (Herbert, 1899). Hobson had attempted 'to reduce the individual to nothingness, and on the ruins of the individual to exalt and glorify "the social organism"'. Herbert poses the question 'when we oppose the Social Entity to the individual, are we not simply opposing some individuals to other individuals?' (Herbert, 1996, p 259). If the individual is moulded by society it can only mean that he is moulded by other individuals, for, according to Herbert, 'no literary phrases about social organisms are potent enough to evaporate the individual' (Herbert, 1996, p 263). Interdependence does not extinguish the individual.[5]

Indeed, there is a giant leap from the fact that we choose to engage in social relationships to satisfy our material wants in which, in part, mutual dependence features to a substitute universal system of compulsory organisation to meet our 'needs', a system 'amiably devised for us by Mr. Hobson's friends in their spare moments of abstract contemplation, and which may not in any way correspond to our own individual likings and requirements' (Herbert, 1996, p 265).

True social action is voluntary action, not forced action. In Herbert's view, the social entity can only be found in

> the whole mass of individuals ... it is vain to look for it in any faction or part of a nation overriding other factions or parts of a nation ... it can only be found where all bodies and minds are free, and each individual gives his contribution of bodily or mental labour voluntarily, after his own kind and his own fashion ... The unity of unrestrained difference is a far truer unity than the unity of compulsory sameness. (Herbert, 1996, pp 267-8)

Hobson has become the 'deadliest enemy' of his 'well-beloved Social Entity, just because he makes war upon the individual. In slaying the unit he slays the whole, that is compounded from the unit' (Herbert, 1996, p 304).

In Herbert, Mack discerned 'a model reply' to the '"new" Hegelian organicist Liberalism' (1978, p 304). More generally, Tame has celebrated Herbert's support of free market capitalism as 'the means for liberating the masses from their age-long burden of poverty', and bringing 'increasing productivity, high wages, innovation and progress ... Hayek's modern insights on the diffusion of knowledge, the market as the means of discovering and channelling such knowledge into the most urgent applications and the impossibility of efficient central planning, were all presciently suggested in Herbert'(Tame, 1980, p 2). Spencer, however, a normally staunch supporter of Herbert's arguments, dissented from his advocacy of voluntary taxation: the '*organic* badness of existing human nature' limited the liberty of which men were capable and a system of voluntary taxation was hence, at best, premature (Hutchinson Harris, 1943, p 310).

Idealist social thought, freedom and social intervention

The emphasis put by idealists on the modifiability of social and economic circumstances and the moral reform of 'character' through direct intervention deliberately fostered reformist programmes to be undertaken, on the one hand, by voluntary organisations (for Loch and Bosanquet) or, on the other hand, by the state (for Ritchie, and Hobson and Hobhouse). Unless they conformed with the dictates of justice or beneficent impulses, neither the modification of circumstances nor direct attempts at the reform of character could have a place in Spencer's framework, which stressed the law-like discipline of the process of character adapting to circumstances as the source of progress, and in which systematic intervention would be counter-productive. Within idealism there were tensions over the balance to be struck between individualism and collectivism, and the possibility of meaningful social science (on both of which see Collini, 1976 and 1978; and McBriar, 1987), and also over the importance of 'character' over 'circumstances' (see Hobson, 1896; and H. and B. Bosanquet, 1897). Within idealist thought 'individualism' and 'collectivism' stand for differences about means, not ends. Bosanquet, on the individualist wing of idealism, wrote:

> I believe in the reality of the general will, and in the consequent right and duty of civilised society to exercise initiative through the State with a view to the fullest development of the life of its members. But I am also absolutely convinced that the application of this initiative to guarantee without protest the existence of all individuals brought into being, instead of leaving the responsibility to the uttermost possible extent on the parents and the individuals themselves, is an abuse fatal to character and ultimately destructive of social life. (1885, p 52)

Henry Jones, a close contemporary of Bosanquet, but less hostile to state action, considered that (1883, in Boucher 1997, p 7): 'Society must exist for the benefit of its component parts, and the component parts must also exist for the benefit of society'. In these contexts the idea of freedom gained a special meaning; it was bound up with the idea of citizenship, of self-development as a person within a civilised state. Freedom meant acting in harmony with the 'good' or general will of society. The idealists who feature here would nearly all describe themselves as liberals, and they were not arguing that either the Charity Organisation Society or action by the state could force people to be moral, acts had to be willed, by persuasion if necessary, not forced:

> They endorsed the Kantian principle that volition was central to morality, and that, therefore, an act that is compelled or committed out of fear of penalty cannot be a moral act. None the less the state could provide an environment for all its members that would 'enable them to live as good lives as possible'. By defining in this way the moral function of the state, idealists provided a persuasive rationale for increased state intervention in new areas of social and political reform. Ritchie was instrumental in fusing this moral state to an agenda of political reconstruction which was adopted by Fabians and New Liberals. (den Otter, 1996, p 170)

Writers of liberal persuasion earlier in the century had attempted to find principles that set limits to how the state could legitimately intervene in individual lives. Hence Spencer's principle of justice in terms of equal freedom; and John Stuart Mill's more elastic proposition that the state should prevent an individual from being harmed by others (in his *On liberty* of 1859). The accent was on freedom in the sense of freedom from coercion. Green and the other idealists retained this concern but complemented it with a focus on hindrances, such as poor education, that detracted from the ability of individuals to be free to achieve certain goals, including 'self-realisation'. This contrast is often referred to as the distinction between 'positive' and 'negative' freedom.

Spencer was at pains to draw this distinction clearly in his *The man versus the state* of 1884. Spencer detected an increasingly paternalistic trend in the legislation of past and present Liberal governments, and characterised the Liberals as the 'new Toryism'. Unless legislators changed their stance, a 'coming slavery' of socialism was inevitable –

the Liberals would be bringing into effect the explicitly socialist goals of H.M. Hyndman's Social Democratic Federation, if unintentionally. Liberals originally set out in their legislative initiatives to abolish grievances suffered by the people (Spencer, 1884, p 69): 'This was the common trait they had which most impressed itself on men's minds. They were mitigations of evils which had directly or indirectly been felt by large classes of citizens, as causes of misery or hindrances to happiness.' However, Spencer continued, since, 'in the minds of most, a rectified evil is equivalent to an achieved good, these measures came to be thought of as so many benefits; and the welfare of the many came to be conceived alike by Liberal statesmen and Liberal voters as the aim of Liberalism'. This confusion has grave consequences:

> The gaining of a popular good being the external conspicuous trait common to Liberal measures in earlier days (then in each case gained by a relaxation of constraints), it has happened that popular good has come to be sought by Liberals, not as an end to be indirectly gained by relaxations of restraints, but as the end to be directly gained. And seeking to gain it directly, they have used methods intrinsically opposed to those originally used. (Spencer, 1884, p 69)

Some commentators, such as Isaiah Berlin, have suggested that 'positive freedom' is not really an idea of freedom at all, but of self-realisation, a different matter (see Gray, 1995, ch 7), while for David Millar (1989, pp 24-5) they are essentially indivisible. Non-idealists could accept that some people might make a voluntary choice to adhere to a version of idealist social thought that promoted a conception of positive freedom, as, for instance, in the form of life followed in an enclosed religious community, though doubtless they would point to problems involved in social closure, such as the limited possibilities of innovation, and also to the risks of coercion as the choice came to be made. Compulsion, though, would be a violation of liberty. It is, though, clear that idealists (the term encompassing here New Liberals) would seek to mould social individuals into responsible citizens who understood their relationship with the moral organism that was society and who would, through their enlightened performance of duties, bring themselves and at the same time their society closer to 'the good'. People would not be coerced or forced in making their choices, rather they would come to will the 'right' outcomes from 'within'.[6] A 'right' understanding of social relations as moral relations would lead to 'rational' choices to act in such a way as to foster one's higher interests.

Such ideas were the common currency of idealism, and had some resonance in the work of Durkheim with which, from the late 1890s, Bosanquet had a degree of familiarity – but he remained critical of a tendency towards 'materialism' in it (see Collini, 1978, p 23). However, materialist usurpation of the autonomy of rational agents was also threatened in Hobson's criticisms of the Charity Organisation Society:

> Only upon the supposition that environment affords equal opportunities for all can we possess a test of personal fitness. Then only should we be justified, after due allowance for accidental causes, in attributing the evil plight of the poor or the unemployed to personal defects of character; then only would the scientific treatment consist, wholly or chiefly, in the moral training of the individual. As matters actually stand, the philosophy which finds the only momentum of social reform in the moral energy of the individual members of the masses is just that smart sophistry which the secret self-interest of the comfortable classes has always been wearing in order to avoid impertinent and inconvenient searching into the foundation of social inequality. (Hobson, 1896, pp 726-7)

Helen and Bernard Bosanquet replied that 'though at any moment misfortune may make circumstances seem insuperable, yet, given time, character – if not thwarted – will re-assert itself, and mould circumstances to its own support' (1897, p 115).

This area of disagreement became associated with a further disagreement to emerge within idealist social thought, one called to our attention by Harris' broad definition. It is over the roles of charity and of the state in securing improvement in moral and social relations. It is appropriate to consider the case of those who championed charity first. Charles Loch and Bernard and Helen Bosanquet were prominent 'early' idealists and important in shaping the theoretical leanings of the COS. Bernard Bosanquet's thought was one of the cornerstones of COS thinking. Moreover, Loch and Helen Bosanquet were members of the royal commission on the poor laws, with Helen Bosanquet, as noted earlier, the main author of the majority report to which Loch's support went. Charity meant personal contact with poor people, allowing the understanding of personal and familial circumstances. Relief could be tailored to the capacity of recipients to develop themselves morally and socially into responsible citizens, with a sense of duty and obligation. This would only be achieved through trust and reciprocity between sources of charity and its beneficiaries. In contrast, the state would be impersonal in its dealings, and thereby likely to encourage dependency. Similarly the process of funding state action involved coercion (tax paying) rather than suasion (donations), not allowing the character of the giver to develop as it could through charitable activity. Overall, ties of obligation would be weakened, whereas voluntary action strengthened and deepened these ties. Charitable action fostered reciprocal ties of obligation, unlike state action, and involved self-sacrifice. Charity was a vital engine of social improvement. Central to charitable work for Loch, was, writes Lewis (1995, p 29), 'purposive striving. It was important not to look for results, but just to seek to "do right". By striving for the good life the means became the end.'

Lewis expresses the key relevance in the following comment, referring specifically to Bosanquet's article entitled 'Charity organisation and the majority' (1910):

> Bernard Bosanquet's idea of democratic citizenship was based on the idea of innumerable obligations of citizens one to the other. Citizens were independent and in a society founded on the principles of true charity gave service to one another voluntarily. In Bosanquet's view, the better off were performing their obligations as citizens when they (voluntarily) offered the poor help, not just in the form of alms, but of personal service designed to promote self-maintenance and fully participative citizenship. The poor fulfilled their duties as citizens by responding to whatever plan was proposed to restore them to self-maintenance. The principle of reciprocity guarded against purely selfish actions on the part of the rich. It lifted charity above the narrow concerns of political economy and gave it ethical purpose. It implied face-to-face interaction between giver and recipient that would, it was hoped, bring the social classes together and create a socially efficient society, and it made the practice of personal social work integral to social theory. (Lewis, 1995, p 31)

The Bosanquets' vision of social welfare was as the means to the goal of ethical rationality and spiritual growth, and hence admission to citizenship of the 'virtuous republic' (Harris, 1992, p 132). The inner meaning and context of a benefit was all important. Even a state benefit was allowable within 'a reciprocal personal relationship between the giver and receiver' and if its end promoted independent citizenship (Harris, 1992, p 132). But no mere mechanical and impersonal transfer of resources from one individual to another could expect their support. State intervention, by its usually impersonal nature, would undermine character in the recipient, leading to dependence and inactivity as a citizen; by cutting off opportunities for 'donors' to participate it would also deny them routes to self-fulfilment (for a discussion of 'working-class' attitudes to state intervention at this time, see Thane, 1984).

A strong view on the family was part of this perspective. For idealists, families should strive to promote a member's welfare; in so doing they became powerful agents for advancing the quality of life for all citizens. Where family members possessed this sense of mutual responsibility the family could present itself as the medium by which the public interest or general will would be combined with private welfare (see Lewis, 1995, p 42).

Towards a socialist turn

As has already been discussed, the idea of freedom in idealist thought is bestowed with the special meaning of a sense of self-development achieved through acting in socially and morally responsible ways, based on reason and understanding of the nature of social life. In particular, acting for the good of society and in harmony with its 'general will' were emphasised. Acting in this way one would be a good citizen and become a better one.

For Bernard Bosanquet and many idealists, the 'general will' was an important concept in shaping an approach to governance if difficult to pin down (see den Otter, 1996; and, on a later idealist, A. D. Lindsay, see Scott, 1971, p 223). Action informed by it would reduce barriers to personal freedom, such as poverty, and advance social cohesion and development. In an idealist worldview ordinary poor people need tutoring and guidance by example to improve their character, or moral natures, so as to become responsible citizens and hence 'free' to 'develop' and contribute to social relations in general. Their impulses are not to be trusted; indeed, they are responsible for their own predicament, combined in some way with their 'circumstances', the importance of which in shaping outcomes was a matter of disagreement between idealist thinkers.

For, as we have seen, some writers steeped in idealism were willing to argue that 'good' government should take direct responsibility for personal welfare, with material circumstances given greater but not unqualified importance in explaining problems (see for example S. and B. Webb, 1912. A recent general discussion is Humphreys, 1995). These social theorists were less sanguine that charity was a unique engine of social improvement and the best means to their ends (see Hobson, 1896, and the joint reply by the Bosanquets, 1897, to which reference was made in the previous section). Direct action by the state could guarantee the meeting of needs and force up the rate of self-development. The state and individuals could take control of the direction and pace of social evolution. D.G. Ritchie and L.T. Hobhouse effectively 'socialised' Spencer's idea of social evolution by an emphasis on what could be achieved by concerted, conscious agency. The Webbs as Fabian socialists may have been concerned with administrative rationalisation and faith in professional expertise, and eager to invoke depersonalised statistics to advance their arguments. But they also believed in 'social health' (see S. and B. Webb, 1910, p 319), and they wholly shared the Bosanquets' view that private and public virtue were interdependent, that 'state-conscious idealism' was the goal of citizenship, and that social welfare policies should be ethical.

By 1901 the Webbs, as already indicated, considered that Englishmen had had revealed to them a 'new world of relationships, of which they were before unconscious ... we have become aware, almost in a flash, that we are not merely individuals, but members of a community...'. Gladstonian liberalism 'thinks in individuals', but 'the opening of the twentieth century finds us all, to the dismay of the old-fashioned individualist, "thinking in communities"' (in Webb, 1948, pp 221-2).

Within this framework the Webbs sought to diagnose the causes of destitution and prescribe effective measures of prevention, which required the dismantling of the poor law. Perhaps the fullest statement comes in *The prevention of destitution* (1912). Most destitution for the Webbs is attributable to circumstances beyond an individual's control, that is to say, not the result of moral failings. Yet when they criticise Liberal proposals for compulsory insurance against the risks of sickness and unemployment, with the payment of a cash benefit as the result, rather than their preferred provision of preventive services, it is the moral weakness of beneficiaries that is most emphasised. Health insurance partly funded by sources other than the beneficiaries (through contributions from the state and employers), and available unconditionally to contributors, creates 'the utmost temptation, and, an inevitable tendency, to a great deal of malingering' (S. and B. Webb, 1912, p 175). The scheme inflicts 'psychological damage' (S. and B. Webb, 1912, p 183) by 'paying the people to be ill': there are 'innumerable people who would at any time prefer one-half of their income in idleness, rather than the whole of it in return for work' (S. and B. Webb, 1912, p 186). If insured persons are permitted a free choice of doctor, moral defects will multiply further, for the sick man 'naturally prefers the doctor who is "kindest" in giving him the necessary certificate' (S. and B.Webb, 1912, p 188) and least censorious about weaknesses of personal character: doctors will 'emulate each other in this laxness' (S. and B. Webb, 1912, p 187). The minority report on the poor law of 1909 failed to advocate compulsory insurance because the degree of 'collective responsibility for, and of authoritative interference with, the patient's own life that will be required if there is not to be ... an actual increase of sickness, and a gravely demoralising malingering, is more than is usually contemplated' (S. and B. Webb, 1912, p 202). Such Liberal measures would, for the idealist-minded Webbs, transform hitherto blameless persons into vicious parasites. Indeed, their idealist emphasis on the need for 'self improvement' and 'treatment' helps to account for what would otherwise be a perverse inconsistency in their view of ordinary people as agents: why else would a little extra money be charged with bringing such moral collapse in its wake rather than be applauded as an egalitarian measure?

However, as well as drawing on idealist thought, the Webbs tapped into the utilitarian tradition of Bentham and Chadwick (which itself had both non-idealist and idealist variants). From this source, according to Alasdair MacIntyre, in his *A short history of ethics*, sprang the fact that 'freedom was sacrificed to happiness in the history of Fabian socialism. For Fabianism socialism was a matter of schemes of reform initiated from above by the enlightened few for the welfare of the unenlightened many' (MacIntyre, 1967, p 238). The 'greater good' was to be attained regardless of what people chose or willed.

The utilitarian tradition noted by MacIntyre could be made to fuse with the illiberal potentiality of idealist social thought. MacIntyre's verdict is perhaps, though, just a little too severe. The Webbs at least recognised the distinction between 'positive' and 'negative' freedom. In their *Soviet communism:A new civilization?* (1935) they declared that those whose intellectual training 'has been unconsciously based on the hypothesis of a static universe almost inevitably think of freedom as the *absence of constraint*; those who assume that every part of the universe (including minds) is always in motion are apt to think of freedom as the *presence of opportunity* to act as they desire' (S. and B. Webb, 1935, p 1033). Equality of opportunity thus becomes an important idea in connection with freedom, one for them unrealised under capitalist conditions. Quoting from Tawney, they remark that, proportionally, as the capacities of some 'are sterilised or stunted by their social environment, while those of others are favoured or pampered by it, equality of opportunity becomes a graceful, but attenuated, figment' (S. and B. Webb, 1935, p 1034). Their downplaying, however, of the importance of freedom from constraint seems to compromise seriously their view that capitalist society

> which allows the British shipowner to treat himself and his family to a long and expensive holiday in Switzerland and Italy, whilst the hundreds of dock labourers who are unloading his ships, together with their families, get nothing more like a holiday than their wageless days of involuntary unemployment, not only injures them, but also diminishes the total aggregate of freedom within the community. (S. and B. Webb, 1935, p 1036)

Communist economic and social arrangements might arguably improve the dockers' range of opportunities, however, as Millar notes (1989, p 25), 'in the absence of negative liberty being positively free would be merely frustrating, because you would be unable to act on many of the choices that you might make'. Having the means to travel can be offset by the fact that many destinations are closed to you.

The Fabians also tended to have reservations about the value of democratic institutions, and in this respect their position was shared with others in the idealist tradition. Bertrand Russell thought the Webbs (and George Bernard Shaw) too prone to worship the state: they were

> fundamentally undemocratic, and regarded it as the function of a statesman to bamboozle or terrorize the populace. I realized the origins of Mrs. Webb's conceptions of government when she repeated to me her father's descriptions of shareholders' meetings. It is the recognized function of directors to keep shareholders in their place, and she had similar views about the relation of the Government to the electorate. (Russell, 1967, vol I, p 79)

In the late nineteenth century the Fabians preferred the communitarian and cooperative vision of social transformation of Robert Owen to the critique of capitalism offered by Marx. In 1820 Owen had written 'if there be one closet doctrine more contrary to truth than another, it is the notion that individual interest, as that term is now understood, is a more advantageous principle on which to found the social system, for the benefit of all, or of any, than the principle of unison and mutual cooperation' (1970, p 232). Later, though, in 1938, while reflecting on Fabian social analysis, Beatrice Webb felt they had been 'hopelessly wrong' in 'ignoring Karl Marx's forecast of the eventual breakdown of the capitalist system as the one and only way of maximising the wealth of nations' (Webb, 1948, p 488). However, H.M. Hyndman had read Marx in 1880 and went on to found the socialist Social Democratic Federation in 1884, the same year as his *Socialism and slavery* was published. Once again, this time from a Marxist perspective, Spencer was the target:

> Such an overturn of the whole bourgeois system Mr. Spencer evidently cannot bring his mind to contemplate. To him competition alone can mean freedom; the forfeiture by the labourers of the greater part of the labour value of their produce to the employing class and their hangers-on can alone prevent slavery for the workers. For, under Socialism, 'each member of the community would be a slave to the community as a whole'. Surely the word 'slave' is here misused ... The very definition which Mr Spencer himself has already given of slavery excludes the use of the word 'slave' under conditions where all co-operate in order that none should be the slave of an individual or of a class. (Hyndman, 1884, p 157)

Marxist theory, with its emphasis on rupture rather than social reform, does not figure much in the record of social policy in Britain except in analyses of the 'welfare state' in the 1970s and 80s (see Gough, 1979; and Ginsburg, 1979, and also Avineri, 1972). However, its relationship to the idea of idealist social thought requires some brief comment here, though in fact the issue is complicated by interpretative controversy over how to 'read' Marx, prompted by the re-evaluation of his early *Economic and philosophical manuscripts* (or *Paris manuscripts*) of 1844. Here Marx argues that, in capitalist social relations driven by the motive of profit, men are 'alienated' from the product of their labour, which is their 'species-being', from each other, and from nature. With the abolition of the private ownership of property under communism, society will no longer be a fixed abstraction opposed to the individual. The individual will be a social being: 'Man confirms his real social life in his species-consciousness' (Marx, 1971, p 151). To achieve authentic reform in individual lives one must work to this end. In this, Marx is writing in an idealist manner: he was deeply influenced as a student in Berlin by Hegel's writings, in which reality was a unity and purposive, moving towards self-knowledge. An intellectual debt is undeniable in terms of the structure of Marx's own subsequent thought, if not its content. The later Marx of *Capital* leaves 'alienation' and the 'ethical critique' of capitalism on one side; preferring the technical concepts of 'surplus value' and 'exploitation', it is not entirely clear if the earlier position remains assumed or is abandoned. The focus instead is on the formation of contrasting and conflicting social classes according to whether or not they control the means of production. Out of the motion of class conflict and escalating points of contradiction comes movement to a post-capitalist economic structure – from thesis to antithesis to synthesis. The question disputed by Marx scholars is whether or not in this fundamentally materialist analysis people can act as conscious agents working to an end of social revolution or are doomed to be passive vessels of an inexorable process. If the first then still we are in contact with a variant of idealist social thought, but if the second, an implausible deterministic scenario, then in a key sense we are not dealing with social thought at all, but a mechanistic and immutable non-idealist force.

Idealist social thought and 'New Liberalism'

It is important to consider with care the development of idealist thought and its relationship to New Liberalism. The exact relationship of influence between idealists and New Liberalism has been variously described. For den Otter, in the opinion of New Liberals, 'the idealists had tipped the balance too far in the direction of communal well-being, and had moved too far from the creed of individual autonomy' (1996, p 166). Idealism had entered popular discourse through 'prominent political figures like Haldane and Asquith and the New Liberal reformers Hobhouse and Hobson' (den Otter, 1996, p 206). However, according to den Otter, while 'Green, Ritchie, Jones and others are often viewed as representing the progressive, New Liberal face of philosophical idealism, Bosanquet's political colours have been more difficult to determine' (1996, p 175). For Bevir and O'Brien, idealism 'inspired many of those who laid the basis for the welfare state. While New Liberals, such as Hobhouse and Hobson were hostile to idealist metaphysics, they deployed themes from its social theory, often combined with a more prominent evolutionary motif, to reform liberalism so as to emphasise community, welfare rights and an activist state' (Bevir and O'Brien, 2003, p 308).

On the other hand, for Freeden (1978), New Liberalism had grown in a way that was not dependent on a reaction to idealism. Earlier liberalism is not fairly presented if seen as synonymous with laissez faire, and in the hands of both Mill and Spencer, though in divergent ways, sociality and the idea of community were mainstream liberal concerns. The state had a moral or ethical dimension, in part because a strict division could not be made between the individual, society and the state. This notion formed the basis of idealist views of the state as a moral force that so influenced late nineteenth-century socialism and New Liberalism. However, liberal thought had itself adapted in the face of social concerns such as poverty and unemployment, which were political issues any living ideology had to confront. For Freeden, neither British Idealism, in general, nor T. H. Green in particular, had the prime responsibility for the transformation of liberal ideas with which they are traditionally credited. 'Had Green not existed, liberalism would still have become collectivist and favourably oriented to progressive social reform. More influence on, and responsibility for, events and trends has been ascribed to him than he actually exercised' (Freeden, 1978, p 17). In Freeden's view, 'Ritchie, though also an Idealist, was much more of a key figure in the adaptation of liberal thought ... he went beyond Green in the importance he attributed to the state as reformer of human minds' (Freeden, 1978, p 58). 'Rather than Idealism giving birth to a new version of liberalism', Freeden adds, 'it was liberalism that was able to assimilate certain aspects of Idealism into its mainstream and thus bestow new meaning upon Idealist tenets' (1978, p 18). Freeden instead points to the impact of evolution as a theory, paying special attention to Ritchie and Hobson. He finds that the 'role of the organism model in making liberalism consonant with Idealism as well as with the biological variant of positivism was of special importance for liberal theory. Liberalism remained a viable theory for social and political thinkers because it could establish its legitimacy in relation to the two dominant idea-currents of the English academic world' (Freeden, 1978, p 97). Indeed, 'biological and evolutionary theories, grafted on to the liberal tradition itself, were an independent source of liberal philosophy – more sophisticated, more immediately concerned with the issues of the times, and almost certainly more widespread as well' (Freeden, 1978, p 18).

The example of Herbert Samuel lends substance.[7] In his *Liberalism* of 1902 Samuel found Spencer an important source to question in his espousal of New Liberal theory. Samuel saw Spencer as committed to what George Eliot had called in a letter of 1875 (in Cross, 1885, vol III, p 256) an 'enervating fatalism' and denied that evolution requires harsh social conditions in the struggle for survival; 'progress can be made by methods more humane, by using the powerful agencies within our reach that tend not to kill but to cure, not to destroy but to raise, that would enlarge the opportunities for becoming fit rather than overwhelm with penalties those who fail' (Samuel, in Greenleaf, 1983, p 158).

Since the present study is based on a broad definition of idealist social thought the precise contribution of particular British idealist philosophers to New Liberalism is not a central matter. Of this group, Ritchie probably had most impact. Versions of social evolution theory, to which Spencer himself would not have subscribed, were circulating and attracting substantial attention. These versions reworked the idea of social evolution into a form of idealist social thought in which social progress was an end to be striven for directly by active government. Benjamin Kidd expressed one such version (see Chapter Two earlier). Kidd was not closely linked to academic idealism, but some other exponents were, including Bosanquet, Ritchie and Hobhouse: it is, therefore, misleading to present social evolution and academic idealism as mutually exclusive in this connection. However, the key point for the present analysis is that both academic idealism and modified theories of social evolution, whether mixed together or not, provided modes of idealist social thought, defined broadly, that New Liberalism absorbed into its intellectual framework.

In an election speech in 1906, Winston Churchill declared:

> I do not want to impair the vigour of competition, but we can do much to mitigate the consequences of failure. We want to draw a line below which we will not allow persons to live and labour yet above which they may compete with all the strength of their manhood. We do not want to pull down the structure of science and civilization – but to spread a net over the abyss. (Churchill, in Greenleaf, 1983, pp 151-2)

Earlier, in 1901, the more orthodox Liberal John Morley[8] had drawn Churchill's attention to a book hot off the press. Soon after, Churchill spoke in Blackpool:

> I have been reading a book which has fairly made my hair stand on end, written by a Mr Rowntree who deals with poverty in the town of York. It is found that the poverty of the people of that city extends to nearly one-fifth of the

population, nearly one-fifth had something between one and a half and three-fourths as much food to eat as the paupers in the York Union. That I call a terrible and shocking thing, people who have only the workhouse or prison as the only avenues to change from their present situation.[9] (in Jenkins, 2001, p 81)

Seven years later, now at the Board of Trade in the Liberal government, Churchill made clear his dedication to New Liberal innovations in a letter to Asquith: 'We are organized for nothing except party politics. The Minister who will apply to this country the successful experiences of Germany in social organization may or may not be supported in the polls, but he will at least have left a memorial which time will not deface of his administration' (Churchill, in Jenkins, 2001, p 146). Churchill then lists six steps to take over two years, giving pride of place to his own interest: labour exchanges and unemployment insurance; national infirmity insurance; special expansive state industries – afforestation and roads; modernised poor law, that is, classification; railway amalgamation with state control and guarantee; education compulsory to the age of 17. 'I say,' he finished, 'thrust a big slice of Bismarckism over the whole underside of our industrial system, and await the consequences whatever they may be with a good conscience' (Churchill, in Jenkins, 2001, p 147).

Perhaps the quintessential New Liberal social reform was the introduction of compulsory schemes of health and unemployment insurance in 1911, though there was a stronger connection in logic between the unemployment scheme and Labour exchanges, introduced in 1908, than with health insurance (on the schemes see Hennock, 1987). Insurance was a 'slice of Bismarckism': the unemployment part was overseen by Churchill, with Lloyd George masterminding the politically more complicated health component (friendly societies had established interests in health, and needed to be placated: in the end they and a range of other institutions ran the scheme for government as 'approved societies'; government itself ran unemployment insurance where there were no toes to tread on). According to Gilbert, 'Social insurance directly contradicted the Fabian conception of "conditional relief". Churchill and Lloyd George never admitted that the function of the nation's welfare institutions was to teach cleanliness or providence or to attempt to improve in any way the character of the poor so that they would not need relief' (1966b, p 855). In Churchill's mind, contributions entailed entitlement to benefit irrespective of failings of 'character' that may have engendered unemployment. In 1909 he declared to H. Llewellyn Smith, his permanent secretary:

> I do not feel convinced that we are entitled to refuse benefit to a qualified man who loses his employment through drunkenness. He has paid his contributions; he has insured himself against unemployment; and I think it arguable that his foresight should be rewarded irrespective of the cause of his dismissal, whether he has lost his situation through his own habits of intemperance or through his employer's habits of intemperance. I do not like mixing up moralities and mathematics. (Churchill, in Gilbert, 1966b, p 856)

The effective alleviation of distress was paramount, rather than a social theory of prevention. Insurance properly deals with the average of risks and is blind to character defects:

> A disposition to overindulgence in alcohol, a hot temper, a bad manner, a capricious employer, a financially unsound employer, a new process in manufacturing, a contraction in trade, are all alike factors in the risk. Our concern is with the evil, not with the causes. With the fact of unemployment, not with the character of the unemployed. (in Gilbert, 1966b, p 856)

Gilbert is surely correct to describe insurance as free from the conditionality favoured by the Webbs. Nevertheless, key New Liberal policies, such as compulsory health and unemployment insurance, were idealist, with a non-idealist icing. According to Hay, 'social justice' was the force behind these policies, providing an answer to critics who preferred to play down 'the wider welfare of society' as a legitimate objective (1975, p 36). The icing was that money was given in the form of benefits, and without strings, a quintessential non-idealist feature. It is not surprising that expediency was the rule in these complex political times. Moreover, controversy over the content of social reform was being squeezed out of the headlines on account of the House of Lords deploying its powers to wreck the government's intentions (in which it eventually failed).

It is evident that in the ensuing years social policies have been characterised by migrating truces between idealist and non-idealist thought, with the truces themselves taking different forms in particular areas of policy, such as health and social security. The battleground between autonomy and choice on the one hand, and social justice and the virtuous republic on the other, did not disappear with the scrapping of the poor law in 1948. However, academic analysis of social policy remained pretty firmly idealist in orientation until a quarter of a century after the end of the Second World War. In time it was buttressed by the arguments for a lead role for governments in the management of financial and economic activity as delineated by John Maynard Keynes, and also by the more general political, economic and social merits of planning and intervention at a national level as a duty of governments argued for by, for example, Harold Macmillan in the 1930s (in *Reconstruction*, 1934, and *The middle way*, 1938).

Another and less commonly raised perspective on New Liberalism deserves a mention, since it places the 'novelty' of some of the reforms in the wider context of welfare provisions for ordinary people at the time. Some employers had already inaugurated extensive 'in-house' welfare arrangements for their employees and their families. The Rowntree cocoa works in York had a range of provisions: by 1904 there was a works doctor and dental surgeon, and by 1906 a contributory pension scheme. These were seen as enhancing the vigour and intelligence of the workmen, necessary for success when faced with keen international competition. Seebohm Rowntree's biographer, Asa Briggs, observed that 'Before the state adopted a social services policy the Rowntree company had started one, and for parallel if not identical reasons. The "new Liberalism" thus took shape in a business context before it modified national politics' (Briggs, 1961, p 101). A further illustration is provided by Hay, in connection with the introduction of health insurance by government in 1911. The Lanarkshire Coal Masters Association reacted to this development in an interesting way. They did not prune their existing medical benefits scheme. Instead, 'in conjunction with the doctors and the Miners Federation, they extended it to the wives and families of insured workmen, who were of course not covered by the Act. The scheme was financed by workers' contributions, with employers meeting the administrative costs' (Hay, 1978, p 115).

Idealism, non-idealism and social policy

It may be helpful at this point first to summarise the thrust of this chapter up to now. It has demonstrated, I hope, that the broad concept of idealist social thought embraces a perhaps unexpectedly large range of related theoretical positions and professional interests, often taken to have nothing in common. Thus it has drawn together key supporters and opponents of both the majority and minority reports on the poor laws, and also 'New Liberalism'. It has shown too that idealist social thought did not reject empirical research, but regarded facts as meaningless in the absence of a contextual framework derived from subjective experience and a priori reasoning. Crucially, it has substantiated the view that idealist social thought subordinated

> the analysis of specific social problems to a vision of reconstructing the whole of British society, together with reform of the rational understanding and moral character of individual British citizens. Social policy was not viewed as an end in itself, nor were the recipients of welfare ends in themselves; on the contrary, both policies and people were means to the end of attaining perfect justice and creating the ideal state. (Harris, 1992, p 126)

The chapter has, furthermore, tried to show the practical influence of idealist social thought in social policy in particular, from the late nineteenth century through to the writings of Richard Titmuss in the second half of the twentieth century. Idealist social thought is, it will be recalled, a wider and more enduring body of thought than the Idealist philosophical school from which it sprang. Differences within idealist thought as embodied in the majority and minority reports and elsewhere over the parts to be played by the state or by voluntary action, and to the weight accorded to freedom in achieving 'the good' are really differences over means, not ends. The logical structure shared by the Bosanquets and the Webbs is that a 'good society' can be achieved by enlightened intervention in ordinary lives to move them forward in a particular direction. This identification of a common mind-set pulls together positions often treated as discrete. It enables us to identify similarities and continuities in social policy thought that are otherwise overlooked. For example, idealist thinkers such as the Bosanquets, the Webbs and Titmuss all distrusted informal care as a means to welfare, seeking to have it supervised or replaced. Interest in informal care in policy and research only surfaced as social policy studies 'moved on' from a Titmussian (that is, idealist) framework in the 1970s and 1980s (see the following chapter).

However, 'idealism', as suggested above, implies a contrast with 'non-idealism' or perhaps 'materialism'. The contrast is not drawn or investigated by Harris, but it is a matter of key significance to this book: discussion of it returns us to Spencer. In so far as Spencer is an example of the contrasting style, 'non-idealist' is preferable to 'materialist' as a descriptor. It accords with Spencer's own views of the metaphysical basis of his work, and prevents an idealist-laden judgement from being seen as a fact. Antagonism between Spencer and idealism ran very deep. In 1902, just over a year before his death, he wrote to Professor Masson:

> I suppose Hegelianism is rife in Edinburgh as it is in Oxford and Cambridge. This is one of those inevitable rhythms which pervade opinion, philosophical and other, in common with things at large. But our Hegelianism, or German Idealism in England, is really the last refuge of the so-called orthodox. As I have somewhere said, what could be a better defence for incredible dogmas than behind unthinkable propositions? (Duncan, 1911, p 458)

Nevertheless, Spencer's work retained a substantial following well into the 1890s (see Taylor, 1992), but the pace of criticism had increased: his denial of freedom of the will, his opposition to religious belief, his conception of social explanation, and his political individualism attracted idealist hostility. Looking at matters from the idealist side, Collini has commented in respect of the relationship of Marx to idealism (1978, p 43): 'It is worth remembering that for Durkheim, as much as for Hobhouse or Bosanquet, Spencer's was a much more important ghost to exorcise'. The task of refuting Spencer involved formulating a rival account of social development, and was of much more immediate relevance to the central themes of political argument at the end of the century. R.G. Collingwood, who read philosophy at Oxford from 1910, and subsequently made distinguished contributions to studies of Roman history, the nature of historical understanding, and philosophy, regarded Green's philosophy as 'a reply to Herbert Spencer by a profound student of Hume (Collingwood, 1944, p 16). However, while there may indeed be difficulties in the logic of Spencer's theoretical sociology, he denied, as explored earlier in the chapter, that he viewed individual civilised men (and women) in the solipsistic, materialist manner attributed to him by Bosanquet, Ritchie and others. This denial was echoed by Auberon Herbert in his replies to Hobson.

The Webbs and the Bosanquets shared, whatever else divided them, a belief that 'society' or 'the state' had a real corporate identity, something Spencer, of course, repeatedly denied. If a vision of the ideal state was the driving force of social policy, both in terms of goals and methods adopted, then the expressed preferences of recipients would indeed be entirely subordinated to the larger objectives. Thus, informal care, in the face of such grand projects, was untutored care, care incorrectly focused. Idealist social thought would tend to ignore this area both in research and in the formulation of policy because it is defined as inferior or backward. For Spencer, as we have seen, informal care was absolutely central in his analysis of how welfare could be achieved. For both the majority and minority reports it was a secondary matter, though less so in the case of the majority. It needed to be enlightened by professional direction, or displaced. On this analysis, then, idealist social policy would seem to have little logical space for a serious concern with informal care per se, or for the views of service users. This would indeed explain the strangely muted interest in informal care in the majority and minority reports, and also the eclipse of Spencer's insights, deriving from non-idealism. More speculatively, it might also explain why social policy research ignored the topic in general for so long until the 1970s, as explored in the next chapter. This appears to have been when academic confidence in the idealist goals of social policy first appears to have faltered significantly. It might also explain why social policy itself was not reoriented towards a much greater focus on informal care until the 1980s, a time when idealist goals ceased to be seen as sustainable and/or desirable within social policy by the Conservative government, encapsulated in the new emphasis on a division between purchasers and providers of services, with services festooned with user charters. After all, as Harris has suggested, '(t)he social philosophy of Richard Titmuss, Urwick's apostolic successor as head of the department of social science at the London School of Economics, was full of muffled resonances of the idealist discourse of the Edwardian age' (Harris, 1992, p 137). Certainly Abrams in 1978 recognised that something novel and significant had happened at the beginning of the 1970s with the discovery of the independence and legitimacy of the client's point of view signposted by Mayer and Timms (1970) (Abrams, 1978, p 96).

The remainder of this book thus examines informal care and how the revival of interest in the subject in the 1970s can be related to renewed interest in non-idealist perspectives on how best to secure well-being, and also how the distinction and struggles for dominance between non-idealism and idealism can illuminate the intellectual history of voluntary action and voluntary organisations. It concludes with a consideration of a theme emerging from the discussion of voluntary organisations: idealist thought has not disappeared from social policy discourse. Barry, writing in 1990, pointed out an important connection between idealism and current justifications for state welfare that appeal to the idea of 'community' or 'citizenship'. These justifications, he declares, are echoing some familiar late nineteenth century philosophies.

> There was a definite revulsion (experienced in a particularly convoluted way in the thought of T.H. Green) against that individualism of classical liberalism which identified the citizen as merely an abstract agent, endowed with a set of legal and political rights, who owed no obligations to his society other than the recognition of the equal rights of others ... The contemporary theorists of citizenship are echoing Green in their claim that the notion extends beyond the idea of a mere judicial relationship to include claims on the economic resources of the community by virtue of membership of it and an identification with its goals.(Barry, 1990, p 4)

As before, it is claimed that in an important moral sense a reliance on exchanges in the market place will not produce 'an autonomous agent' (Barry, 1990, p 4). As before, too, it might be added, a market is not obviously any less moral than the persons – endowed by themselves with both appetites and constraints, for good or bad – who enter into it. Not markets, but the decisions people make in them, may be the problem to confront. Non-idealism recognises this; whereas idealism, usually with impeccable intentions, in effect craves monopoly power as a shortcut to utopia. Both sets of ideas entail risks, reflecting matters of fundamental political and moral judgement, over what is to count as either too much or too little freedom of choice, and for whom. In the contemporary world, particular social policies may be straightforwardly idealist or non-idealist, or made up of elements of both (as was the case with the New Liberal insurance schemes). In both kinds of context, idealists and non-idealists may each appeal to their divergent underpinning theories of the nature of society for support, but the comfort afforded may be illusory: for if either one possesses indisputable epistemological superiority, it cannot yet be counted as settled.

SIX

Idealist thought, social policy and the rediscovery of informal care

Introduction

Recent work in the history of welfare has placed question marks beside the status of some conceptual frameworks within sociology and social policy studies regarding the meaning of 'social welfare' and the 'welfare state'. This chapter argues in particular that the marked upswing of interest in informal care in the UK beginning in the 1970s reflected, at least in part, a reaction, itself not so far adequately understood, to some features of the work of Richard Titmuss and 'traditional social administration', work that, on examination, reveals a distinctive 'idealist' core, unsympathetic to research into familial patterns of caring. Similarities with 'classic' British idealism, broadly defined, at the end of the nineteenth and beginning of the twentieth centuries are reviewed. This idealist thought emerges too as unresponsive to informal care, even though contemporary non-idealist thought had discussed it.

This chapter concludes that the (unacknowledged) persistence and influence of idealist modes of social thought diverted attention away from informal care; informal care was in fact not 'discovered' in the 1970s, it was *re*discovered as idealist preconceptions about the nature of 'real' welfare were discarded. The sense of 'discovery' reflected prevailing and dubious historiographical interpretations of the meaning of 'social welfare' and the status of the ('classic') 'welfare state'.

This chapter begins by considering some of the new work in the history of social welfare. It will then explore how it can be built upon to help answer the question, itself sociologically interesting, of why the study of social policy appears to have developed research interests in informal care only since the 1970s.

In this new work, acceptance of a particular conceptual framework has been increasingly challenged, for, according to Lewis,

> British historians have begun to rethink the periodisation
> of the modern welfare state and to ask whether the period
> of what is coming to be called the 'classic welfare state'
> (from 1945 to 1976) should be seen as exceptional rather
> than some sort of culmination. More fundamentally still, it
> has become necessary to rethink the nature of the welfare
> state. Rather than seeing the story of the modern welfare
> state as a simple movement from individualism to
> collectivism and ever-increasing amounts of (benevolent)
> state intervention, it is more accurate to see Britain as always
> having had a mixed economy of welfare, in which the
> state, the voluntary sector, the family and the market have
> played different parts at different times. (Lewis, 1995, p 3;
> see also Digby, 1989)

For the sake of clarity here, the expression 'classic welfare state' needs
to be broken down so that 'classic' 'ideas of' the 'welfare state' are
distinguished from the 'practices of' or 'phenomena of' the 'welfare
state' for the period in question. If the (material) foundations of the
(classic) welfare state were, as alleged by Fraser (2003), laid by the 1911
National Insurance Act, a complementary claim in the realm of ideas
could be made in respect of idealist thought at much the same time.

The key problem for Lewis though is in essence the teleological
one of seeing as a 'culmination' the ideas and practices of the 'classic
welfare state'. This kind of difficulty has been identified before: Collini
observed, for example, the danger of, in trying to explain the
development of sociology (1978, p 5), 'the tendency to lapse into
teleology, wherein it is axiomatic that sociology is destined to "emerge"
or "be realized", and so the task of the historian becomes that of
explaining how, until the crucial moment, the "obstacles" prevented
this from happening'.

This approach to the past is not uncommon and is famous enough
to have a name (the Whig approach). Gilbert's study titled *The evolution
of national insurance in Great Britain* (1966a), presents the 'decline' of
the poor law, not as a historically intriguing phenomenon in its own
right, but as a semi-inevitable accessory to the 'main' story of the 'rise'
of the insurance principle. Digby (1978), Crowther (1983) and McBriar
(1987) provide corrective perspectives (as does Ashford, 1986, in his
comparative study of France, Germany and Britain). In a similar way,
the long-running elevation of the role of Edwin Chadwick in poor
law reform in the 1830s at the expense of the liberal Tories, or 'Noetics'
– often Oxford-educated, and ordained – may reflect an attempt to

minimise as 'complications' the 'obstacles' in the way of a narrative that presents the classic welfare state as an end state of history, and an attempt to maximise the role of a 'hero' in that story, whose time of greatest influence was to be a decade later, in public health (Mandler, 1990). In fact, as was shown in Chapter One earlier, the Noetics were numerically the strongest grouping on the royal commission and networked energetically to dominate the ensuing administrative body, the poor law commission (Chadwick was only its secretary) and the Irish royal commission, chaired by one of the most prominent Noetics, Richard Whately (with the Noetics splitting over Whately's advice that a workhouse-based poor law should not be introduced to Ireland, and the introduction of one in 1838).

Consonant points have recently been made about the historiography of voluntary action. In reviewing the Charity Organisation Society (COS), Lewis has remarked,

> it is mistaken to describe the nineteenth-century voluntary sector as something as big as or larger than statutory provision and as a wholly separate element from the state. This depiction consciously or unconsciously draws on the current conceptualisation of the voluntary sector as an alternative to the state and applies it to an earlier period. It is more accurate to see voluntary organisations in the late nineteenth-century as part of the way in which political leaders conceptualised the state. (Lewis, 1995, p 8 – see also Finlayson, 1994)

It appears that in a general context of historiographical revision one change in the study and practice of social policy coming in the last years of the so-called 'classic welfare state' has not yet been adequately considered, namely, the rise of concern in the UK with 'informal care'. After fitful interest in the topic in the 1970s it became a major concern from the mid-1980s. 'The "informal sector",' Ungerson has stated, 'has only been named as such since the 1970s' (1998, p 169). A working definition of 'informal care' would have to include reference to the unpaid care (ranging from round-the-clock tending to occasional acts of assistance), support and guidance which is provided mainly, but not only, by women to family members or others, such as neighbours, who are disabled, chronically sick, or frail older people. It has also been argued that the definition could be extended to cover the childcare and 'self-help' health care that individuals undertake for themselves (for example, Graham, 1991).

In the context of awakening interest in informal care, Philip Abrams, himself one of the twentieth century's pioneers of the study of informal care, pointed, as noted previously, to the occurrence of something unusually innovative in respect of the appearance of Mayer and Timms' *The client speaks* in 1970 (Abrams, 1978, p 96): 'The discovery of the independence and legitimacy of the client's point of view ... may well prove the most revolutionary development in the whole field of social care since 1950; its implications for both policy and research have still largely to be absorbed'. In a nutshell, Mayer and Timms had made central to their argument the claim that the availability of informal care meant that an untold number of people never came to the attention of social workers, and that for many who did their experiences of informal coping mechanisms decisively shaped their expectations of and reactions to social work, in particular whether or not they were dissatisfied with it. Abrams himself also emphasised that researchers should acknowledge the subjects' own views of what actually benefits them as well as those of various caring agents.

Townsend's contribution to Shanas et al's *Old people in three industrial societies* of 1968 appears to be an even earlier indication of change. However the status of informal care is, in this case, disparaged, and the legitimacy of its 'voice' disputed. According to Townsend,

> The evolution of professional skills sometimes results in society recognizing the inferiority of the 'equivalent' skills as practised by the family. Treatment from a professional doctor is preferred to patent family medicines prescribed by Aunt Jane. We are wrong to imagine that this is the same service being provided differently. It is an entirely different (and usually more comprehensive) service, displacing one that at best was very rough-and-ready. What seems to be true of medicine seems no less true of professional nursing and chiropody. (1968, p 117)

In an important sense, which will be developed later, this passage points 'backwards' not 'forwards'. Anticipating a change towards reduced home-based care McGregor and Rowntree had written in a similar vein (1968, p 205): 'the extent to which the collectively provided school, health and welfare services have reduced the compelling need for kinship ties has not yet been investigated'.

The novelty detected by Abrams in Mayer and Timms, and explored further in his own research (see Bulmer, 1986), showed through also in an influential 'theoretical' text of 1971, Robert Pinker's *Social theory and social policy*, ideas also pursued further in *The idea of welfare* (1979). In these texts the perspective of the user of services, and of the non-user, were emphasised, rather than the alleged aims and motives of the providers of services. Paramount for Pinker was the need to understand everyday, familial practices designed to enhance welfare, both through the market and within the domestic economy, practices which comprised a 'counter culture' to that of state welfare, with which they could collide. Thirty years on, it is still doubtful that his call for a 'sociology of morals' has been adequately responded to:

> One of the tasks of a sociology of morals would be to clarify the nature and consistency of individual and public attitudes towards the varieties of mutual aid which are practiced both within welfare institutions and within families. We need to know far more about the preferred and the actual forms of reciprocity and obligation which occur between strangers sharing a common citizenship and members of the same kin. A second task would be to re-examine the extent to which the values and assumptions which are implicit in social legislation support, weaken or modify the moral beliefs and practices of ordinary people. (Pinker, 1974, pp 8-9)

It is unnecessary here to tell the complete story of policy documents increasingly emphasising informal care and the need for voluntary and statutory action to seek to support it rather than replace it. Key components of the planning considerations behind the full introduction of welfare pluralism to community care policy are the Wolfenden Report (1978), the Barclay Report (1982), the Griffiths Report (1988) and *Caring for people* (HMSO, 1989). The development of a long list of research studies through these years within social policy studies has also been noted many times (for instance Parker, 1990; and Twigg and Atkin, 1994).

How has this new focus on informal care in social policy been accounted for? One factor advanced is that from the late 1970s onwards the effectiveness of public expenditure in areas of social provision has come under increasing scrutiny (in the area of social work services see Brewer and Lait, 1980; and Hadley and Hatch, 1981). A further factor is that expenditure on social policy has been challenged as contrary to the interests of economic policy and as encouraging dependency (for example, Anderson, 1980; and Barnett, 1986). Beyond doubt both factors have influenced policy in the years concerned, but neither points necessarily to serious, explicit concern with informal care.

Other factors advanced come a little closer to answering the question. From the early 1970s the major political parties, whether forming the government or not, have been particularly concerned to express what they take to be the principles defining the 'proper' scope of action by the state in relation to individuals and the family. In addition, there were calls for more 'consumer' consideration and participation in the provision of services. The idea of community care had also emerged as a matter of controversy. Feminist writers argued that 'community care and care by families were intrinsically exploitative of women' (Ungerson, 1998, p 170).[1]

These three factors have also been influential even if, as I propose, the original question is now narrowed to accounting for the new focus on informal care in social policy *research*. There is, though, a further and key factor to be kept in mind. Early on, interest in informal care as a research topic seems to have grown from within the subjects of social policy and administration and sociology, and in particular and initially within sociology as it happens, rather than as the result of external pressures.[2] Without this development it is conceivable that the pressures for change from the other factors could have proceeded along other conduits to quite different policy outcomes (as, in fact, the passage quoted earlier from Townsend illustrates).

The following sections excavate the role of British idealism in social policy thinking and relate changes in that role to changes in the status of informal care studies. The final section explicitly reintroduces problems associated with Whig interpretations of the 'welfare state' to account for the continuing neglect of material on informal care dating from the end of the nineteenth century.

Titmuss, social policy and idealist ways of thinking

Julia Parker remarked that 'problems selected for investigation will inevitably reflect ideologies and fashions as well as individual tastes and values' (1976, p 80). The aims of this section are to argue that interest in informal care was discouraged by Titmuss' conception of social policy as a subject, and that his conception was in fact idealist in nature in a way that needs to be made explicit.

I cannot here attempt a comprehensive history of research into informal care, but I do want to show that something more than a 'naive curiosity' in a hitherto ignored 'division of welfare' was involved. Social policy as a subject was indeed undergoing wider change at the time, with this new topic of interest as one manifestation. Claims of a Kuhn-like 'paradigm shift' in progress in the subject were common by 1980 (see for example, Rose, 1981; Taylor-Gooby and Dale, 1981; Wilding, 1983; and Carrier and Kendall, 1986). But a shift from what to what?

According to Wilding, the 1950s, 1960s and early 1970s formed a period of 'traditional social administration' (1983, p 5): 'a recognisable social administration evolved characterised by shared – and limiting – assumptions about subject-matter, by a shared approach which I have categorised as particular, prescriptive and parochial and by certain shared social values and assumptions about society'. For Wilding, the leading figures of social administration at the time were 'all implicitly or explicitly Fabians', united by a 'shared vision of a more equal, more just society, with "better" social services financed through redistributive taxation' (1983, p 5).[3] Titmuss was a central figure. As Pinker has claimed with care (1993, p 58): 'There were other eminent figures in the discipline, and the collectivist consensus with which Titmuss came to be identified was never total even during his lifetime. Nevertheless it made a lasting impression.'

For Taylor-Gooby and Dale, and Wilding, the shift was to a Marxist, sociological critique of welfare based on materialistic analyses of the impediments to social and political reform within capitalism. For others the shift was to a framework of analysis which argued that the intended beneficiaries of social welfare, and their experiences of social welfare and of family and economic life, needed to be taken into account to understand 'problems' in the legitimacy of and responses to social welfare services (for example, Pinker, 1971 and 1979; Hadley and Hatch, 1981; Rose, 1981; and also Abrams, in Bulmer, 1986). It is this second group with which I am most concerned of course.

Pinker, whose important *Social theory and social policy* of 1971 challenged the Titmuss vision of social policy on many fronts, earning him a rebuke from Titmuss in his *Social policy* of 1974,[4] later distinguished several features distinctive of Titmuss' approach. First, the ends and means of social policy were defined in terms of 'an egalitarian and moral purpose' that fostered social unity (Pinker, 1993, p 58). Second, the economic market and its competitive ethos were seen as morally inferior to the social market. Third, Titmuss was a welfare unitarist: the altruism in statutory social services united and elevated people, and thus 'the state should be the main funder and provider of social services, and only the state had the authority to implement, without fear or favour, the redistributive policies that he considered necessary' (Pinker, 1993, p 60). Fourth, while Titmuss had an active interest in translating his ideas to the circumstances of Third World countries, he viewed with dismay American welfare practice and was disdainful of arrangements in European neighbours: 'the social services in the member states were less comprehensive and less civilised than their British counterparts' (Pinker, 1993, p 60). Fifth, Titmuss' definition of the subject field of social policy in terms of its particular and quintessential moral nature led to awkward relations between social policy academics and the other social science subjects, particularly economics, sociology and law. The resources of these subjects were drawn on highly selectively, rather in the spirit of 'missionary visitations to heathen parts' (Pinker, 1993, p 60). Sympathy with the work of Durkheim is singled out by Pinker, a matter of significance to be developed below.

Three further points may be added that flesh out, in fact, Pinker's first three points. I take them from Titmuss' *Social policy* of 1974. Although Titmuss' swansong – he died in 1973 at the age of 65 – the book is not atypical of his postwar thought. First, the moral purpose of (British) social policy is seen as 'expressing the "general will" of the people' (Titmuss, 1974, p 24) or as embodying the idea of to each 'according to our ideas ... the will of society' (Titmuss, 1974, p 141). Second, Titmuss was committed to an idea of 'social growth' as being achieved in postwar policy. Reflecting on the treatment received by himself and others as patients in the Westminster Hospital, part of the National Health Service, Titmuss commented:

> In some of the things that I have said and in some of the things that I have written in some of my books, I have talked about what I have called 'social growth'. I believe that my experience at the Westminster provides some of the unquantifiable indicators of social growth. These are indicators that cannot be measured, cannot be quantified, but relate to the texture of relationships between human beings. (1974, p 150)

Third, Titmuss seems to have ignored informal care. There is a fleeting glimpse (Titmuss, 1968, pp 98-9), but it is in the context not of addressing carers' wishes but of the need to plan more services to replace carers. Even in the years immediately after Mayer and Timms (1970), a rare and oblique reference is telling in its form – social services, Titmuss writes, are concerned with 'providing services to meet publicly acknowledged needs which markets or the family cannot, or should not, or will not, meet' (1974, p 52). Titmuss simply forecloses on a consideration of what services might do to enable 'families' to meet needs themselves; and the references to what they 'should not' and 'will not' meet are left undeconstructed.

A final point may be added, one missing from Pinker's list. In several places Titmuss raises some concern related to 'users' of services, perhaps most notably in the essay 'The hospital and its patients' (1958, but see also 1968, pp 67-9). However, his interest is in changes in professional practice and forms of service delivery that may be judged as 'better' for recipients. The user's own view in this judging process is accorded at best a secondary status. Indeed, when Titmuss explicitly discusses consumer choice it is usually within a framework that decries it because of, for example, the likelihood of ignorance on the part of the 'user' jeopardising 'optimum' outcomes (for example, 1968, ch 21). Doctors, moreover, would be tempted to 'play the market' in circumstances where consumer choice rather than 'need' was the driving force: 'In embracing the market system, doctors would thus relinquish their role (as Durkheim put it) as "centres of moral life"' (Titmuss, 1968, p 250).

Titmuss consistently sought to show that social policy, as he conceived it, provided the means to securing the production of a particular kind of citizen as well as a particular kind of society. Social policy could, as he expressed it in *The gift relationship*, 'help to actualize the social and moral potentialities of all citizens' (1970, p 238). Before the Second World War he had held this to be something unrealised and to be desired; the war years he judged to have transformed the idea of social policy into the form he wanted. Thus he wrote in *Problems of social policy*,

> by the end of the Second World War the Government had, through the agency of newly established or existing services, assumed and developed a measure of direct concern for the health and well-being of the population which, by contrast with the role of Government in the nineteen-thirties, was little short of remarkable. No longer did concern rest on the belief that, in respect to many social needs, it was proper to intervene only to assist the poor and those who were unable to pay for services of one kind and another. Instead, it was increasingly regarded as a proper function or even obligation of Government to ward off distress and strain among not only the poor but almost all classes of society. (1950, p 506)

Much of Titmuss' writing after this date may be read as celebrating and defending the intrinsic 'goodness' of social policy so established; if it was not fully realising its aims (and Titmuss wrote at length – for example, 1962 – to demonstrate this point) the answer lay in better generic structures for services rather than altered principles. This main theme surfaces strongly in *The gift relationship* where Titmuss finds altruism in attitudes to the National Blood Transfusion Service associated with the altruistic characteristics of the 1948 National Health Service Act:

> The most unsordid act of British social policy in the twentieth century has allowed and encouraged sentiments of altruism, reciprocity and social duty to express themselves; to be made explicit and identifiable in measurable patterns of behaviour by all social groups and classes. In part, this is attributable to the fact that, structurally and functionally, the Health Service is not socially divisive; its universal and free access basis has contributed much, we believe, to the social liberties of the subject in allowing people the choice to give or not to give blood for unseen strangers. (Titmuss, 1970, p 225)

Thus, for Titmuss, postwar social policy as established had a fundamental moral nature and purpose (see also Lowe, 1993, p 21).

All nine elements of Titmuss' thought just discussed may be described as 'idealist'. His 'democratic socialism' or 'Fabianism' is, I think, secondary to the fundamentally idealist structure of his philosophy. This important point, which I have tried to substantiate, is often overlooked (see George and Wilding, 1985, and 1993). However, for Taylor-Gooby and Dale (1981, p 77), Titmuss' social philosophy had an 'idealist orientation' and, according to José Harris (1992, p 137), it resonated with earlier idealist discourse.[5]

In many circumstances, trying to account for the neglect of certain topics by an author may simply collapse into an account of what that writer was interested in, and thus not be of any analytical assistance. With Titmuss and informal care the case is different. As Collini has argued (1978, p 6), where 'past thinkers had access to the appropriate range of concepts and were interested in the relevant set of problems, then it can be illuminating to consider why their thought did not develop further in a certain direction, if only as a way of focussing on the limits and presuppositions of their actual thinking'. The neglect of informal care as a topic reflects, I want to argue, the limits and preconceptions of idealist social thought in general and what may be seen as its long period of not 'inevitable' dominance in social policy discussion, predating the specific influence of Titmuss. The precise claim is that 'British idealism', particularly its moral and social dimensions, had characteristics that selectively limited the range of vision of its followers, and these include, perhaps unawares to himself, Titmuss.

Let me now attempt to relate the discussion of 'classic' idealism in the two previous chapters to these main elements of Titmuss' thought. Clearly, both defined social policy in terms of the requirements of a larger moral purpose. Both also saw economic transactions as qualitatively different from social or moral transactions. Both are wedded to welfare unitarism, although Titmuss, unlike many idealists – though not to so great an extent the later ones – adhered to state action rather than voluntary action as the preferred mechanism. Both are marked by a sense of the moral superiority of British political structure and the general will expressed therein. Both have a markedly politicised and 'engaged' attitude towards the business of thinking about welfare. Both explicitly owe a similar debt to Rousseau's political philosophy. Both are committed to ideas of 'social growth' or 'social health' (for this concept in the Webbs' thought, see S. and B. Webb, 1910). Both presume that the family and informal care may well, without supervision, prove inadequate and may also need to be supplanted. Both are united on the point that 'users' of services should not have a decisive say about the availability, content and quality of those services. Lastly, both agree that the moral purpose of social policy entails that neither economics nor sociology has an approach appropriate to making full sense of the subject matter involved. One might note here the poignant corroboration provided in this context by a letter of 1935 from A.D. Lindsay, the idealist political philosopher and warden of Balliol College, Oxford, to the economist Roy Harrod, calling into question the foundations of the approach of economists to social research:

> I don't think from your argument you have ever faced the
> fact that the proposals I put forward are put forward for
> theoretical considerations of the same kind as yours. I think
> a proper [underlined twice in ms.] investigation into the
> working of the means Test would not perhaps be
> immediately practical but under several principles of social
> inquiry more important than or as important as anything

discovered about the Trade Cycle. Most students of politics
in this University agree with me. (Lindsay, 1935a)

Lindsay felt that for Harrod economics was 'quality', and disciplinary
pluralism 'quack' (Lindsay, 1935b).

All of these points together suggest strongly that to describe Titmuss
as an idealist is appropriate. However, now it is necessary to try to put
to the test, independent of the case of Titmuss, the claim that idealism
is by its nature, rather than contingently, averse to taking seriously
informal care. It is fortunate that it is not difficult to set such a test.

Idealist thought and the 'problem' of informal care

As noted in the previous chapter, Spencer was the most significant
intellectual figure at the time for the emerging idealists to wrestle
with, a paradigm non-idealist. This was true for Tönnies and Durkheim
no less than for Bosanquet and Hobhouse. A rival account of social
life and social progress would have to survive in a climate in which
the idea of evolution was rapidly gaining ground – and with which,
of course, Spencer's name was powerfully connected – and reach a
credible accommodation with it.

Spencer was some 18 years older than Bosanquet. By the time idealist
thought was establishing itself he had already set forth a comprehensive
account of the mechanism and direction of social and natural evolution
(maintaining the primacy of the inheritance of acquired characteristics
rather than Darwin's dynamic coupling of spontaneous variations plus
a struggle for existence, or 'natural selection' – which Spencer renamed
'survival of the fittest'). He had, he believed, provided utilitarianism
with a sound base in science. Politically he was an unyielding
individualist, and his view of justice censored action by the state to
promote welfare, except in the sense of preventing or punishing acts
by individuals that infringed the freedom of other individuals. He also
distrusted the effects of bureaucratic charitable action. To idealist eyes,
Spencer's thought was 'materialist', though he repudiated the epithet.
Although Spencer used the 'organic analogy' to describe society, idealists
found, as the previous chapter demonstrated, his interpretation
insufficiently holistic and purposive. Indeed, the 'materialism' that
idealists found in Spencer's substantial attempts to establish sociology
(1873, 1876, 1882 and 1896) was sufficient to make some of them
intolerant of the idea of man as a subject for science (see Collini,
1978).

From about the 1860s Spencer was a writer in demand. By the

1880s, however, his work was besieged by philosophical criticism, to which he on occasion gamely rose in reply. By the time he finished his *Principles of sociology* in 1896 (the third volume of which completed the definitive statement of his theory of evolution in the ten volumes of the 'System of synthetic philosophy') his intellectual isolation was a source of pain. Bosanquet was among those who signed a letter of congratulation; yet only a year earlier he wrote that 'a Dante of philosophers ought to grant him the distinction of the lowest circle in the inferno' (1885, p 57). In a more restrained vein, Bosanquet's review of Thomas Mackay's *The English poor* (Mackay was a Spencerian individualist) noted that 'the inheritance of acquired instincts on which the author rests a good deal of his case was always exaggerated by Mr. Spencer, and seems likely now to topple over altogether' (Bosanquet, 1889, p 465).

Bosanquet may have contrasted what he called the 'ethical individual' against the Spencerian 'atomic individual' (Vincent, 1984, p 353), but Spencer would reject this description of his position, arguing that individual life 'may and does go along with an elaborate form of mutual dependence' (in Duncan, 1911, p 354). (Durkheim's cognate criticisms of Spencer have been evaluated at some length in Jones, 1974 and 1975; Perrin, 1975; and Corning, 1982.)

'Positive private beneficence' is a topic to which Spencer gave considerable attention, as already shown. His discussion has its basis in a long tradition of concern about state–family relations. The poor law report of 1834, for example, declared,

> We have seen that one of the objects attempted by the present administration of the Poor Laws is to repeal *pro tanto* that law of nature by which the effects of each man's improvidence or misconduct are borne by himself and his family. The effect of that attempt has been to repeal *pro tanto* the law by which each man and his family enjoy the benefit of his own prudence and virtue. In abolishing punishment, we equally abolish reward. (Poor Law Report, 1974, p 156)

One focus of such analysis later in the century was on the likely impact of state-run insurance schemes to provide pensions in old age, an idea much discussed following the publication of Canon Blackley's proposal (1878). In this context Mackay pronounced, it would be the height of presumption for the rough hand of the law to interfere to coerce or cajole the workman into preferring the remote risk of his old age, which he may never live to see, to the more obvious claims of sickness, wife and children, more especially as a patient frugal attention to these will not leave his old age unprovided for. (1891b, p 296)

By 'private beneficence', to recap, Spencer means what is now called informal care, as his examples make clear, although the contextual framework in which he discusses it reflects both the concerns of the time and Spencer's own philosophical analysis. Matters of beneficence are not matters of justice as he defines it but matters of a different order of altruism, desirable in terms of personal and general development. The elevation of private beneficence over state action and voluntary action represents an important part of Spencer's vision of the future of welfare as the desirable alternative to idealist schemes. There are several distinctive points in Spencer's discussion. First, for the first time an explicit categorisation of means to welfare is made – statutory, voluntary and informal (Spencer, 1919, vol II, p 376). Second, within private beneficence, women have often been treated unfairly (Spencer, 1910, vol II, p 336), incurring costs to themselves that men must become aware of and rectify, as part of their obligations as beneficiaries of beneficence (Spencer, 1910, vol II, pp 356–7). Third, beneficence is already often spontaneous and common. Thus, whether a spouse or children are involved, illness or accident calls forth beneficence: the house becomes a hospital 'and its inmates nurses' (Spencer, 1910, vol II, p 355). Fourth, private beneficence, whether in terms of cash or service, should take account of the conduct and character of the beneficiary; the more direct the contact the less the risk of beneficence producing a de-moralising effect on the beneficiary. Fifth, Spencer identifies a moral hierarchy of obligations to care for those who are ill. This hierarchy is intended to be descriptive both of how care actually happens and is in practice justified, and as prescriptive in respect of moral reasoning in ordinary life. The care falls primarily to a family member and secondarily to remoter relatives. It is only when there are no relatives, or none available, that unrelated persons are under some obligation. Here is Spencer's statement of the hierarchy of the moral obligation to care:

If, as all will admit, the care of one who is sick devolves primarily on members of the family group, and devolves

> secondarily on kindred, it devolves only in smaller measure
> on unrelated persons. These may rightly limit themselves
> to indirect aid, where this is needed and deserved. Only in
> cases where there are no relatives, or none capable of
> undertaking relatives' duties, does it seem that beneficence
> demands from unrelated persons the requisite attentions.
> (1910, vol II, p 358)

This passage is one of considerable insight and significance. It is
intended to be read both as descriptive, of how care actually happens
and is in practice justified, and as prescriptive in respect of moral
reasoning in ordinary life. Such comments strikingly anticipate a debate
a century later (see Qureshi, 1990; and Finch and Mason, 1990).

Now, if idealist modes of thinking about welfare are intrinsically ill
at ease over the 'legitimacy' of private beneficence or informal care,
this should show through in some way. Clearly the topic was known
about, and any association of it with Spencer's work would not of
itself have been sufficient to explain exclusion of the topic from
discussion. Yet exclusion, or near enough, is its fate. Private beneficence
seems to have been viewed as 'atomised', private action, inherently
suspect because devoid of any monitoring of its 'moral' quality.

Idealist thought was powerfully present among the members of that
monumental Edwardian inquiry into policy, the royal commission on
the poor laws, established in 1905 and reporting in 1909. The report
of the majority (including Helen Bosanquet, Thory Gage Gardiner,
Octavia Hill, Charles Loch and Lancelot Phelps) represented the wing
of idealism most strongly committed to a prominent place for charity
in welfare provision, whereas the report of the minority (particularly
Beatrice Webb) represented that wing most strongly committed to
the primacy of the state in such provision, for one reason because it
provided the only way of guaranteeing a 'national minimum' of civilised
life for all citizens, a standard that would promote 'social health'. Above
this there was a limited place for voluntary organisations, as an 'extension
ladder' (S. and B. Webb, 1912).

Reading these reports today with informal care in mind it is notable
that the topic is raised in only a handful of paragraphs. Neither report
specifies as a primary role for social policy the promotion or support
of informal care per se. In respect of the need for an expansion of
home nursing provision 'where necessary', which both reports accept,
idealist values shine through, with the majority urging powers to
remove compulsorily to the infirmary cases where the recipient fails
to maintain 'a healthy domicile and good habits' (Poor Law Report,

1909, vol I, p 362) and the minority wishing such assistance to be withheld 'where the patient persistently malingers or refuses to conform to the prescribed regimen' (Poor Law Report, 1909, vol III, p 231). Such wording suggests that the majority report distrusted informal care as both insufficiently 'moral' and inadequately disposed to purposive or rational action once left to itself, and that the minority report distrusted the provisions of informal care because they were 'inexpert' (see also the discussion earlier in Chapter Four). Consequently, it was essential that the state adopted a vigorous tutelary role and displaced such care whenever 'expert' opinion so decreed. It is telling that the minority report dismisses peremptorily the idea, originating in Australia in 1908, of granting invalidity pensions to permanently incapacitated persons under 70 years old, who would thereby, says the report, receive 'fixed incomes which they can enjoy as of right, without obligation either to work or to live as may be medically most expedient for them'. Many, the report continues, could do some work, but will not 'under a lax and self-indulgent regimen' (in other words, living at home), and they may become 'the worst of parasites, capable of much mischief'. Institutionalisation, under medical superintendence, is advised instead (Poor Law Report, 1909, vol III, p 283).

Rediscovering informal care

Structural ingredients of idealist thought, as it became dominant, thus served to focus attention away from informal care in social policy planning and particularly in research undertaken in social administration and policy; this hegemonic state of affairs by and large endured into the early 1970s and the demise of Titmuss, when the idealist approach's moral premises and limited research horizons were increasingly challenged. It is significant, as was noted above and as Pinker (1990, ch 7) has underlined, that in social anthropology and sociology – subjects less indebted to idealist thought, at least in Britain, than social administration and policy – an interest was maintained through many of the relevant years in the helping networks formed in families and communities and in the impact of social policies upon them (see also Frankenberg, 1966; and Bulmer, 1985).

It should also be recalled that many areas of social service provision itself, for much of the period in question, were not notably idealist in character. Indeed, it was, for example, precisely the poor law's very lack of progressive 'idealist' principles that tended to dominate analysis of it (for example, the Curtis Report of 1946 on the care of children deprived of a normal home life, and the discussion of Gilbert, 1966a, and 1966b, earlier in this chapter). Harris has remarked,

> Progressive historians, following faithfully in the footsteps of the Webbs, have been inclined to treat the residue of the Poor Law as a mere pathological anachronism in twentieth-century British social policy. I would like to suggest that this view needs reconsideration: that on the contrary the underlying continuity between the Poor Law and the British version of the welfare state is much more tenacious and much more functionally and ideologically complex than is often supposed. (1990, p 194)

Whatever Beveridge may have argued for in 1942, and whatever commentators at that time and subsequently have wanted to find in his report, it is, says Harris (1990, pp 193-4), 'the continuing institutional inheritance of an absolute statutory right to non-contributory public relief, rather than the national insurance scheme, that has most markedly distinguished Britain's welfare state from that of most other parts of Western Europe'. The decisions of staff working under poor law rules (especially Poplar-style Unions) and public assistance, assistance board and national assistance legislation, often based on detailed knowledge of particular cases, quietly provided support as one would expect of 'informal carers' avant la lettre. The full story certainly remains to be told, but there are indications (Deacon, 1981, 1982; see also Chapter Eight later) that autonomy was protected rather than 'channelled' into idealist-approved directions under these provisions, with popular appreciation. People were allowed to be the experts about their own lives. In implementing Northern Ireland's 1949 Welfare Services Act, Antrim County Welfare Committee adopted the view that 'many of the problems of old and infirm people ... can best be met, in the majority of cases, in their own homes' (1949, p 7). It hoped to establish a domestic help service to help such persons, adding though, with admirable candour, that 'the longer such persons can remain in their own homes the better for them, and the less expense on the county' (Antrim County Welfare Committee, 1949, p 15). Nevertheless, it seems likely that in practice such sentiments were twinned with a stronger paternalistic predisposition to resort to placement in institutions than is now the case. Corroboration is provided by a Nuffield Foundation report of 1947 called *Old people*, which reported on an enquiry chaired by Seebohm Rowntree. This called for an adequate number of suitable homes (in other words, institutions), the provision of which (Nuffield

Foundation, 1947, p 96) 'will lessen the need for extensive plans of home help, home nursing, visiting and home meals services for old people who would be better off in a Home or Institution. The right sphere for such domiciliary services is in helping able-bodied old people in cases of temporary illness or during convalescence'.

Thus, although informal care naturally featured strongly in everyday life right through the period in question, it was only fleetingly noticed *in social administration and social policy studies*. When it was noticed, as the passage above suggests and in Townsend's work quoted earlier, service users' own perspectives were not uppermost. The Seebohm Report of 1968, the blueprint of the 1970 Social Services Act, and social work after 1971, had found itself 'unable to sound consumer reaction … in any systematic way' (Seebohm Report, 1968, para 43, n 1).

A further important lesson, therefore, is that social policy studies did not discover informal care in the 1970s, it rediscovered it (see Cecil, Offer and St Leger, 1987). And here I come back again to my starting point. The perception of informal care in the history of social policy has to be reconstructed before the sense of 'discovery' can be put into proper context. The rupture with Titmussian idealism is, then, only part of the process of the rediscovery of informal care. Two Whig biases have been operating together in existing accounts of the rise of informal care studies, first that 'non-progressive' thought in the nineteenth century (that is to say, thought not 'leading' to the classic welfare state, mostly non-idealist) has been air-brushed out of historical interpretation, second that a change in concerns 'after' the time of the 'classic welfare state' must be interpreted as a change to new concerns, rather than the taking up again of what should not have been put down (though see Offer, 1983, 1984 and 1985). It is these biases in the interpretation of the past, not themselves necessarily the product of idealist welfare thought (though often associated with it), that seem to have protected for so long the particular idealist nature of much social policy thinking and study from critical analysis; rather, indeed, made it seem the only 'real' way to conceive of things.

If my main argument holds water that a blind-spot over informal care accompanied idealist-influenced social thought and research, then some final comments on present circumstances may be helpful. At the level of policy practice, Conservative emphasis on consumer choice, market freedom and a purchaser-provider division in community care was non-idealist in character. Carers in principle gained some say in defining their needs and the ways in which they should be met. Resources being limited meant that preferred outcomes were not realised in many cases. Nevertheless, at a subjective if not material level, a difference remains between a policy in which carers' needs and preferences as expressed by them are considered and one in which the outcomes sought are designed solely to comply with values applied from outside. Recent Labour emphasis on the values of 'social inclusiveness' and 'empowerment' might be interpreted as signalling a revival of idealist thought and a shift to the second type of policy. Whether or not it will be appropriate to invoke again Popper's contrast in policy objectives between those of 'piecemeal social engineering' and 'utopian social engineering' (1966, vol I, ch 9) will, of course, very much depend on whether 'empowerment', for example, is taken to refer descriptively to what people wish to achieve, or prescriptively to what it is believed they ought to achieve or 'really' want to achieve.

In social policy research the intellectual turmoil of the 1970s and 1980s did not obliterate idealist concerns. Sometimes they took new forms. Informal care had quickly become too visible and too widely acknowledged to be sidelined for long in idealist thinking; instead it underwent interrogation from standpoints that may be described, broadly, as idealist in nature. The concept of 'carer', for example, emerged as a category of person distinct from, say, husband, or mother. In the 1990s, the development of social care on the community led, from a non-idealist perspective, the House of Commons Social Services Committee to go so far as to believe that in some circumstances, rather than a social worker, a carer, himself or herself, might be the most appropriate 'case manager' (1990, para 31). But an idealist perspective on 'carers' was also emerging in which new obligations on the state were proposed:

> What was new and distinctive about the term was not so much that it delineated more clearly a particular family relationship previously obscured or overlooked, but that it implied a new moral claim within public discourse. This moral claim rests on a recognition that there are relations of obligation that can have severe consequences for carers and in which they are not free to abandon caring once the burdens have become onerous or the tasks distressing... Carers are thus not free to act fully in their own interest and often continue to act against their own interest... It is this fact that that enables carers to lay claim to public consideration in their own right. Regarding someone as a carer rather than just a relative endows them a different status within public discourse. (Twigg, 1994, pp 290-1)

To a degree this had been foreseen in Rose's rereading of Titmuss (1981). The shape of the interrogation reflected and continues to reflect moral concerns of the time. Beyond doubt, foremost among these have been the goal of women's full social fulfilment of their capacities as citizens and the constraints on this that result from the gender inequalities revealed in familial care and the household division of labour, and from the replication of these inequalities under policies related to informal care (see, for example, Pascall, 1997, ch 3). Although Titmuss did not explicitly address these issues, they chime well with the authentic Titmussian commitment to the world of welfare.

SEVEN

Social theory and voluntary action in Britain since 1880

Introduction

Rethinking the history of welfare and the role of theories of society offers a new perspective on the 'classic' 'welfare state'. Idealist social thought had a dominant, though not unchallenged, influence from the 1880s to the 1970s: some idealists, including Bernard Bosanquet and Charles Loch, found organised charity to be the most ethical and indeed logical way by which to secure idealist social goals, others preferred action by the state. Whether charity or the state was the preferred conduit, reference to enhancing and realising the 'general will' of the society was a shared feature. The analysis up to this point has, it is hoped, shown that it is important to explore in some depth the contrast between idealist and non-idealist modes of social thought: the crux of the contrast concerns whether individuals are conceived of as agents who should seek *directly* or *indirectly* to achieve the good of society as a whole.

The present chapter is concerned with the application of this fundamental distinction to aspects of the history of voluntary action over the last hundred or so years. Throughout its treatment of substantive aspects of voluntary action it is designed to maintain a challenge to three historiographical assumptions about how to interpret voluntary action in the context of the history of welfare. Of these assumptions the first is that the 'welfare state' represented the climax of a 'natural' or 'inevitable' process, with earlier voluntary action studied merely as foreshadowing it, the second that, with the 'welfare state' established, voluntary action had become a secondary matter, and one to be approached from a state-centred point of view, and the third that idealist social thought, in a broad sense, tended to be taken for granted rather than to be seen as a topic for investigation. The explicit examination of idealist social thought, through the broad definition adopted, underlines the particular historical and moral concerns of the 'classic' 'welfare state' and effectively disposes of the view of that state as an inevitable and enduring evolutionary triumph. The contrast with non-idealist social theory can bring to our attention and account for, as the previous chapter reviewed, the neglect of informal care in social policy until the 1970s, particularly in social policy research. Non-idealists, such as Herbert Spencer, had given informal care considerable attention but idealists distrusted it and sidelined it as insufficiently 'ethical' and 'rational'. Only as the influence of idealism in general and Titmuss in particular waned in the 1970s was it rediscovered (and not 'discovered' as has often been suggested).

This chapter thus applies the contrast between idealist and non-idealist modes of thought to an analysis and interpretation of ideas and practices of voluntary action in Britain in the period from the 1880s to the 1990s. The chapter deals substantively with five particular themes. First, it considers idealism and non-idealism as properties of social theories about voluntary action. Second, it draws attention to idealist and non-idealist social thought *in* voluntary organisations themselves and their purposes. Third, it examines pro-state idealist social thought in 'official' or governmental circles concerning the perceived role of and relationships with voluntary action, and changes in such thought and in government relationships with voluntary action in the 1970s. Fourth, it considers the innovation of *classifying* voluntary organisations by the kind of social theory they profess in their own 'mission statements' and suggests this is helpful in considering voluntary action and the 'third way'. Fifth, it explores new approaches to the study of voluntary action in social life, sensitive to the theoretical orientations of all the parties concerned.

Idealism and non-idealism

Defined broadly, 'idealist social thought' encompasses a distinctive style of thinking about social and moral life which reached beyond a select group of universities into everyday political life: Seebohm Rowntree, Beatrice and Sidney Webb, E.J. Urwick, J.A. Hobson, L.T. Hobhouse, R.H. Tawney and R.M. Titmuss are among those sharing idealist views about the ideal state and society as a moral and spiritual organism. The previous chapter indicated that these features characterise, for instance, Bernard Bosanquet's thought as much as that of Titmuss: they may not always be saying the same things, but they are always saying the same *kinds* of things on the appropriate dimensions.

The broad conception of idealist social thought draws attention to the propositions shared by, for example, Fabian socialism and idealism whereas the two are typically treated as if there were no logical connections. 'Idealist social thought' thus gives us a powerful, because simplifying and economical, conceptual aid. On the other hand the conception directly implies a contrast with a rather unfamiliar but a very important world of non-idealist thought on welfare matters. It is usually only briefly mentioned even today in British social policy textbooks; often it appears at best as a wicked stepmother in a pantomime. As has been argued earlier, we need to revisit non-idealism and remove the blinkers that bracketed it off as 'unprogressive' in social policy scholarship in Britain, blinkers so long affixed by the dominance of idealism. Spencer was an important non-idealist and valuable as a source of 'voluntaryism'. Others, such as Auberon Herbert and Thomas Mackay, in varying degrees drew on aspects of his thought. More recently Robert Pinker, especially in his *Social theory and social policy* might well be described as a non-idealist, with his concern to uncover why ordinary people in everyday life define their needs as they do, and how they go about meeting them in family settings (Pinker, 1971, p 106). However large the difference between writers who might be described as non-idealists may be, they share opposition to the tenets of idealist thought identified in the previous chapter.

The dominance of idealist social thought was under pressure in the 1970s. Gradually changes came in service provision as attacks representing non-idealist social thought triumphed, and the pace quickened after the election of a Conservative government in 1979. These changes stressed greater accountability and exposure to public scrutiny, drives for the more efficient use of scarce resources, a separation of professional and managerial authority, enhanced autonomy in, for example, the field of primary health care, and a new emphasis, at least in principle, on placing first the needs of service users, rather than those of service providers.

The 'big' conceptual division in thinking between idealist and non-idealist social thought cannot but have resonances for making sense of voluntary action in the British Isles and beyond. The contrast recurs in a wide range of national contexts in connection with voluntary action, and has acquired fresh importance in Britain today in assessing the policy of Blair's Labour government towards voluntary action. However, it is important to emphasise that the picture is complicated. For both idealists (though *not* all) *and* non-idealists have been champions of voluntary action; this has to be borne in mind in respect of all five of the matters specified at the start for further comment and to which I now want to turn.

Social theories of the nature and effects of voluntary action

In the context of this chapter, a concern with *theories* of voluntary action is seen as separate from the rationales and ways of organising themselves adopted by actual organisations. In broad terms the focus is on political and academic views of the contributions of voluntary action to the nature of life in a society. As pointed out earlier, a potentially difficult point to grasp is that there can be both idealist and non-idealist theories of voluntary action: there are, though, important differences between them. (It might, of course, be argued that *all* voluntary organisations are in some broad sense 'idealist' or 'idealistic' but that is not the sense at issue now.) Non-idealists would stress that voluntary action benefits individuals or groups of individuals in respect of the aims being pursued; they might argue that, as an indirect result wider society benefits, but this feature would not be the basis for promoting voluntary action. Idealists, by contrast, if indeed they are idealists who favour voluntary action above state action (as they tended to be especially in the late nineteenth century), would champion 'charity' as *the* means of assistance of choice, whereby the character of all citizens would be enhanced, through voluntary and responsible giving and receiving thus securing, directly and deliberately, the overall elevation of the moral character of the social whole and its individual members. The gulf within idealism that was to open up between Helen and Bernard Bosanquet on the one side and J.A. Hobson and the Webbs on the other was not about 'social growth' as a goal directly to be sought, but how best to reach it. Action by the state could be more comprehensive in coverage and need not bring with it the habits of 'dependence' that the pro-charity lobby alleged, though pro-state idealists tended to retain a limited role for voluntary action in their schemes.

Non-idealist thinkers considered individual liberty of paramount importance. Idealist social thought and action, particularly by the state, threatened rather than enhanced this liberty and thus also threatened the innovations that stemmed from it. But individuals possessed a sense of altruism that could be expressed and developed in voluntary action to achieve desired aims for groups of individuals. Hiskes has seen Spencer, undoubtedly important in Individualist thought, although 'packaging' it in his distinctive theory of evolution, as the author of a liberal ideal of community (Hiskes, 1983). For Spencer, 'general happiness is to be achieved mainly through the adequate pursuit of their own happinesses by individuals; while, reciprocally, the happinesses of individuals are to be achieved in part by their pursuit of the general happiness' (Spencer, 1910, vol I, p 238). As has been shown in earlier chapters, at the heart of Spencer's thought was a principle of 'justice', and it is respect for justice to which the second part of this passage refers. A central role of government was to deal with acts of injustice, in a way readily accessible by ordinary people, thus removing impediments to individuals in securing their well-being and that of their families and of others with whom they identified. For Spencer it is one thing to secure to each man the unhindered power to pursue his own good; it is a widely different thing to pursue the good for him. To do the first well, 'the state has merely to look on while its citizens act; to forbid unfairness; to adjudicate when called on; and to enforce restitution for injuries. To do the last efficiently, it must become an ubiquitous worker – must know each man's needs better than he knows them himself – must, in short, possess superhuman power and intelligence' (Spencer, 1853, p 235). However, this position, as has been shown, could be complemented by a strong commitment to private beneficence, as it was by Spencer. For Spencer, there is scope for charitable assistance, given freely rather than by compulsion, to the victims of accidents in life (1851, p 327):'men who have failed for want of knowledge inaccessible to them, men ruined by the dishonesty of others, and men in whom hope long delayed has made the heart sink, may, with advantage to all parties, be assisted'.

On such matters Auberon Herbert was one of Spencer's most loyal followers. In the 1860s he aligned himself as a Liberal, and from 1870 to 1874 served as a Liberal representative for Nottingham in the House of Commons. By then he had become a controversial independent-minded politician who espoused republicanism. A meeting with Spencer and reading his work had changed him:

> I went into the House of Commons, as a young man, believing that we might do much for the people by a bolder and more unsparing use of the powers that belonged to the great law-making machine; and great, as it then seemed to me, were those still unexhausted resources of united national action on behalf of the common welfare ... I began to see that we were only playing with an imaginary magician's wand; that the ambitious work we were trying to do lay far out of the reach of our hands, far, far, above the small measure of our strength. It was a work that could only be done in one way – not by gifts and doles of public money, not by making that most corrupting and

demoralizing of all things, a common purse; not by restraints and compulsions of each other; not by seeking to move in a mass, obedient to the strongest forces of the moment, but by acting through the living energies of the free individuals left free to combine in their own way, in their own groups, finding their own experience, setting before themselves their own hopes and desires, aiming only at such ends as they truly shared in common, and ever as the foundation of it all, respecting deeply and religiously alike their own freedom, and the freedom of all others. (Herbert, 1908, pp 5-7)

It is the politician given to needless taxation who stands in the way of the efforts of the people, 'of their friendly co-operation, their discovery of all that they could achieve for their own happiness and prosperity, if they acted together in their free self-helping groups' (Herbert, 1908, p 51). These words encapsulate what Herbert called 'voluntaryism' and come from his Herbert Spencer Memorial Lecture given at Oxford on 7 June 1906, only a few months before his own death (Herbert, 1908, pp 5-7; for more on Herbert see Hutchinson Harris, 1943). In sharp contrast, idealists tended to see individuals as not fulfilling their potential unless they were in a process of being bound into a larger, spiritually interdependent social whole. To be 'free' was to act *in certain ways*, related to this vision. Fairly or not, Spencer's individual was seen as an asocial 'atomic individual', or 'anomic' in Durkheimian terminology, whereas the idealists believed their notion of the individual as an 'ethical individual' was superior, both epistemologically and morally. For Bernard Bosanquet charity, voluntarily offered and accepted,

and involving personal service designed to promote self-maintenance and fully participative citizenship, had a uniquely ethical, rational and civilizing purpose. It advanced the mutual understanding and moral awareness of all concerned, rich and poor alike. Charity was *the* engine of social improvement: properly conducted it alone discouraged dependency and fostered the growth simultaneously of independence and a sense of mutual interdependence in membership of an organic whole. Yet, at a deeper level, actual outcomes of charity were secondary: for C. S. Loch it was important just to strive to 'do right' rather than look for results. (see Lewis, 1995, p 29)

As already noted, later idealists tended to promote the idea of state action as the way to champion the growth of individual citizenship rather than voluntary action. The Webbs, as we have seen, clearly say exactly this. At this point, however, it is appropriate to turn to some recent statements in favour of voluntary action, considering them in the context of the framework of this chapter.

In a recent essay entitled 'The road to the good society', Etzioni has stated (2000, p 25): 'Mutuality is central to communities. A good society relies even more on mutuality – people helping each other rather than merely helping those in need – than it does on voluntarism. We see mutuality at work in, for example, crime prevention, childcare, care of the sick and in bereavement.' Etzioni's characterisation of 'mutuality' is unfortunately vague; it is not clear if it is directly or indirectly productive of the 'good society'. The passage is most likely to be intended as idealist in nature, although it is materially significant that we cannot be certain. In terms of theoretical and conceptual clarity, and the practical consequences for people, quite a lot is at stake: we do need to know if advocates of a 'third way' have idealist or non-idealist views of how to build the future. On this issue itself it seems unlikely that there can be a 'third way'. The two may of course be mixed in the detail of a policy, but the proportions can be identified. David Green in *Community without politics* has drawn attention to the same kind of neglected contrast in discussions of 'citizenship':

> We are now seeing a contest between two competing visions of citizenship: on the one hand the *equalised* citizen and on the other, the *morally-responsible* citizen. Under the former view, the 'good life' is determined by politicians in the political process; whereas under the latter, the role of the state is to facilitate the freedom of individuals to choose the 'good life' for themselves in mutual but voluntary association with other people. (1996, p 74)

Theories of voluntary action need careful interrogation on such matters to ensure clarity about moral and political ends and means. These matters are returned to in the penultimate section of this chapter.

Purposes and justifications in voluntary organisations

For many years Christian beliefs were often to be found at the heart of important voluntary organisations – a process of change away from this position in the twentieth century is outlined by Whelan in *The corrosion of charity* (1996). The idealism associated with such beliefs is expressed in the following passage from Hall and Howes, although in fact it is a comment on the nature of Christian commitment more generally in the field of welfare (the reference to Barry is to his *Asking the right questions* of 1960).

> As Bishop Barry has reminded us, while it may be accepted that Church and welfare state work together, the concept of 'welfare' itself presents Christians with a new challenge. 'In particular the Church must keep on asking the prior question "What is welfare?" It must always be keeping alive the protest that man is the citizen of another city, and the heir of an eternal destiny and that, therefore, no earthly policy can claim his total allegiance or satisfy the need of his whole being. Otherwise it will be failing in its own witness and no less in its essential contribution to the health and welfare of the community.' (Hall and Howes, 1965, p 267)

As will by now already be clear, the Charity Organisation Society (COS) (founded in 1869) tended to express its aims and rationale in terms of idealist thought: Lewis, drawing on the publications of C.S. Loch, the society's loyal secretary and himself an idealist thinker, has claimed that, for the society: 'the test of charity was the successful promotion of economic independence *and fully participative citizens* [emphasis added] ... Social work with individuals and families was the means of achieving this; no social advance was possible without individual improvement' (Lewis, 1995, p 34).

However, it is unlikely that this view was shared by all the leading figures in the COS. Certainly Thomas Mackay in his writing as a leading Individualist (for example Mackay, 1891a), and an enthusiastic Spencerian, eschewed idealist conceptions (on Mackay, see Taylor, 1992). Critics of the COS, who could themselves be idealist inclined, sometimes failed to perceive the vital idealist penumbra, seeing only its propensity for rather shrill opposition to 'indiscriminate' charity, the 'vetting' of those seeking help, and the devaluing of 'circumstances' as opposed to 'character' in understanding misfortune (see, for instance, Hobson, 1896).

An important empirical question today, as well as in the days of the COS, is what proportion of voluntary activity is idealist and what not. It is a complicated question because in differing socio-political contexts individual organisations may be Janus-faced. Nevertheless, if idealism in its religious form has indeed become weaker as a motive in voluntary action, one might speculate that idealism is now less common in the aims and rationales of organisations. Today, or at least until recent years, a focus on limited, precise objectives seems to be the norm, with the direct idealist aim of achieving 'social growth' largely absent. It may still flourish at the level of community groups, and may be in the course of flourishing more widely if adoption of the 'third way' really is ushering in a new wave of idealist mutuality as Etzioni was appearing to suggest.

As it happens, the particular case of Northern Ireland as it hesitantly emerges from violent social conflict is interesting in this context. A recent document produced by the Rural Community Network, *Reconciliation and social inclusion in rural areas*, notes that 'very few countries have made internal peace-building a goal of public policy' (Morrow, Wilson and Eyben, 2000, p 19). I think it can be argued that as a consequence Northern Ireland is developing voluntary organisations, and a range of other institutions as well, that are casting themselves into an idealist form. According to Morrow, Wilson and Eyben (2000, p 6), a serious search for reconciliation will 'entail change not only in personal behaviour and relationships but in the form in which institutions are organised and structured, in the way in which hostility and tension are dealt with in public and managerial contexts and in the political and social organisation of rural life'.

In other words, particular initiatives will need to be conducted in a generic (idealist) framework having the goals of social inclusion, reconciliation and peace at its heart (on related issues of government expectations of voluntary organisations in Northern Ireland see Acheson, 1995). It is interesting that an important funding body for research associated with voluntary action in Northern Ireland is the Joseph Rowntree Charitable Trust. With its overarching commitment to the promotion of Quaker values this trust embodies idealism.

In the main, though, even in the fields of social welfare and of concern with protecting the environment, non-idealism for the present seems dominant within the United Kingdom as a whole (but see the previous and the next sections on possible changes associated with the 'third way'). Thus the Child Poverty Action Group, for example, sought social change in a limited area; general, socialist, social change was not a direct motivation (see Field, 1972). Similarly the Landmark Trust, concerned with buildings mostly in the UK, describes itself (1999, p 6) as simply 'a charity with two purposes. The first is to rescue worthwhile buildings and their surroundings from neglect. The second is to promote the enjoyment of such places, mainly by letting them for holidays.' The rescue process seems to involve no retrospective idealist and Arcadian vision. There are no prescriptions about what should be done on the holiday or who should be having them (unless you wish to read sinister intent into the prices!).

Relationships between voluntary action and the state

As has already been discussed, within idealist social thought some thinkers favoured charity and others government and the state generally as the best means to advance the good of society. In Britain in the 1940s the idealists who favoured the state were in the ascendancy in social policy circles (Brenton, 1985, pp 20-2). However, such a generalisation does mask the fact that the thought of one key figure, William Beveridge, was more fluid in its nature. Subsequent to his Report of 1942, which championed the expansion of provision by the state in the fields of social security benefits, health care, and in the pursuit of policies to maintain full employment, he went on to advocate in his *Voluntary action* of 1948 a continuing role for voluntary activity. Nevertheless, he seems at the time of the Report to have played down its significance: his *Pillars of security* of 1943, a collection of articles, speeches and papers, concentrates on relationships between the state and individuals. It should be noted, though, that in the 1940s Beveridge was not himself consistently committed to *idealist* social thought, a feature fuelling his observation that, 'in Britain, we cannot find for the individual a moral aim as it is found in Germany, by subordinating the individual to the State ... There must be as many separate aims as there are separate lives in the State' (1943, p 93). Beveridge seems less concerned for the state in its interventions in individual and family life to reach towards some 'good society' than to empower individuals and families to reach for whatever it is that they themselves desire, a coherent enough non-idealist position.

However, by the 1970s, social policy analysis was beginning to consider seriously means of securing welfare other than those provided by the state (see, for example, Hadley and Hatch, 1981). The 'rediscovery' of informal care at this time has been discussed already. Here, the claim that a division between idealist and non-idealist thought is analytically important in the field of voluntary action needs to be demonstrated by considering the intellectual background to the renewed prominence accorded to voluntary action. In this instance it is useful to consider the 1970s and the case of the personal social services. Lowe has remarked:

> By the mid–1970s … formal voluntary care was almost
> wholly rehabilitated. A Voluntary Services Unit was
> established in the Home Office by the Conservative
> government in 1972 to coordinate policy and an increasing
> number of local authorities started to employ voluntary
> bodies on an agency basis to discharge their statutory
> responsibilities … Well recognised dangers, of course,
> attended this increasingly close identification of statutory
> and voluntary care … That such questions were being asked,
> however, represented a remarkable transformation in the
> position of voluntary organisations, whose very future had
> seemed in the 1950s to be under serious threat. (1993,
> pp 276-7)

The view that the 1970s ushered in a markedly enhanced regard by
government for voluntary action is echoed by Glennerster (1990, p 26):
'though voluntary or non-statutory non–profit organizations had long
been part of the academic study of social policy, the shift in the political
preferences in the 1970s and 1980s was to concentrate much more
attention on to the role they played and could play'. By the mid-
1970s, Glennerster adds, 'the welfare state began to be portrayed as a
rather old-fashioned concept. The wave of the future lay with care by
"informal networks", "voluntary action", and families as well as the
private sector' (1990, p 26).

If Lowe and Glennerster are correct in seeing something significant
as occurring in the 1970s in terms of more pluralistic relationships
between the state and voluntary action it could plausibly be accounted
for by the waning of the dominance of idealist preconceptions at that
time at least in respect of the state's role in the promotion of welfare,
as already noted. In particular both the Labour Party and the
Conservative Party, to the extent that there was a consensus on welfare
matters from the 1940s, had had a pro-state 'idealist' analysis with
impressive credentials available to them, placing voluntary action
essentially in a position of subservience. For Sidney and Beatrice Webb
state services alone could guarantee to all people the 'national minimum'
of civilised life that they had elaborated and promoted since before
the First World War. Voluntary action's role was to be that of an
'extension ladder':

> When we have once secured this solid foundation, our
> Voluntary Agencies will become what they ought essentially
> to be – pioneer endeavours to raise ever higher and higher

the standard of what human conduct can be made to be; by showing in this direction and in that, how and where it is possible actually to raise the 'National Minimum'; in this way pushing ever upward the conception of the order, the freedom and the beauty that it is possible to secure to and for every individual in this community. (S. and B. Webb, 1912, p 258)

The transcendent ideal present in A.D. Lindsay's slightly later advocacy of associations within the community, as a *complement* to action by the state, but again in a subsidiary role, should also be noted. Lindsay (1879-1952) was educated at Glasgow and Oxford universities. At Oxford the idealist Edward Caird was a formative influence and in Lindsay's own teaching and writing at Balliol Plato, Kant, Rousseau and Bosanquet shaped his contributions to political and social philosophy. Thus in 1943 he wrote:

Bosanquet has taken the hint conveyed in Rousseau's account of the general will as distinct from the will of all and has developed it into a masterly account of the elaborate system of institutions and mutual relations which go to make up the life of society. He has insisted on its complexity and richness and vitality – its transcendence of what any one individual can conceive or express. This, he declares, in all its elaborateness and multifariousness *is* the community. It is no less than that. That is the standard of legislation and what we ordinarily call state action. The business of politics is to take this elaborate complex of individuals and institutions for granted, try to understand the principles and fundamental ideas which inspire it, diagnose the evils from which it is suffering; and then by state action seek to remove the disharmonies which are threatening its life and checking its vitality. (in Scott, 1971, p 410)

Through his practical commitment to working-class adult education (through the Workers' Educational Association and associated tutorial classes), and also to the Labour Party, Lindsay sought to advance social inclusivity. In the 1930s he chaired a committee on employment for the National Council of Social Service, coordinating all the voluntary work for the unemployed at the behest of the Ministry of Labour and, with Beveridge and others, served on the Pilgrim Trust survey of unemployment that was published in 1938 as *Men without work* (see

Scott, 1971, p 158). When, in December 1942, the War Office hurriedly withdrew from circulation to the troops a summary that Beveridge had prepared of his Report for the Army Bureau of Current Affairs Lindsay went on the attack in Beveridge's support.

Lindsay had long had links with the Potteries through his commitments to adult education. In John Betjeman's *Summoned by Bells* (1960), undergraduates sprawl on Balliol's lawn

> While Sandy Lindsay from his lodge looks down
> Dreaming of Adult Education where
> The pottery chimneys flare
> On lost potential firsts in some less favoured town.

From 1949, freed from his duties as warden of the college (and earlier as vice-chancellor of the university), Lindsay immersed himself in founding a new University College at Keele Hall in North Staffordshire, whose grounds were once a picnic destination for workers' families, adjacent to but above and beyond the portly bottle-kilns, collieries and fiery furnaces encircling Stoke – a daunting challenge, but, as it happens, a success. Lindsay's irrepressible idealist fervour found expression in a degree structure in which, over four years, discipline specialisation was firmly embedded in a framework that made for an appreciation of the values of mutual understanding and interdependence he thought essential if responsible citizens were to make contributions of real value in the postwar world. Of this, Lindsay believed, other universities were losing sight. Keele was to have a foundation year of lectures covering major topics in the arts, sciences and social sciences to be attended by *all* students. The second-year structure ensured that an unusual breadth in the subjects studied continued, and in the next two years the structure ensured that each student chose *two* 'principal' disciplines as the core of his or her degree. The better to nurture the vision, staff and students were to reside on the campus.

This innovative project depended crucially on government approval and financial support, eventually forthcoming, lobbied for through the backing of free associations in the district and local government that Lindsay helped to coordinate. Within the community he, as ever, underlined the practical value of free associations, including trade unions. Nevertheless, in one important sense, as the philosopher, Dorothy Emmet, emphasised, Lindsay 'was not a political pluralist, in that he thought that the State had a unique directing role (though not necessarily a superior moral authority)' (in Scott, 1971, p 408).

For the Webbs, at least, voluntary agencies shared the predicament of Sisyphus, forever losing out and being asked to do it all anew. Lindsay's brand of idealist thought, although more sympathetic to voluntary action, also gave to the state the main responsibility of removing 'disharmonies' in social life. The 'welfare state' of the 1940s had certainly moved towards guaranteeing some kind of national minimum, with voluntary action often either nationalised, as with the voluntary hospitals, or otherwise regulated to comply with statutory service aims, as in the case of voluntary children's homes and the 1948 Children Act. However, by the 1970s it seems clear that idealist values and their legacy in terms of social policy were in retreat; rosier prospects for voluntary action beckoned as the welfare state came under 'political, popular and philosophical attack' (Lowe, 1993, p 304). A useful study of over a century of shifting relationships between informal care, voluntary action and the state is Finlayson (1994). Some further related discussion appears in the following section.

Categorisations of voluntary action

In principle there is no end to the ways in which we may try to categorise voluntary organisations. We may classify by purpose – pressure group or service provider; by relationship to the state – financially dependent or independent; by membership – mutual or philanthropic; and so on. A classification in terms of idealism and non-idealism serves to differentiate voluntary organisations according to the kind of theory of society and the place of individuals therein to which they themselves hold. To seek to classify voluntary organisations in this manner is no less legitimate than to classify them by, say, their kind of relationship to the activities of the state, such as whether they 'complement' or 'supplement' state provision, or by the other criteria just listed. It all depends upon the kind of feature in which we are interested. Classifications of this kind by intellectual orientation seem, though, to have received little attention. If, as at present, we are seeking to develop an understanding of the history of ideas and diversity of philosophical orientations embedded in voluntary organisations the development of a particular version of such an approach is indispensable.

However, two further points may be helpful. First, it would not appear that there is an isomorphic relationship between the idealist/ non-idealist and mutual aid/philanthropic categorisations. Mutual aid organisations can be either idealist or non-idealist, and so can philanthropic organisations. There is no necessary connection between the kind of organisational structure and the presence or absence of a 'holist' vision in the work done. Second, the concept of 'paternalism' and the distinction between idealist and non-idealist thought requires some comment. The Wolfenden Report, for example, drew a contrast between organisations 'based on mutual benefit rather than benevolent paternalism' (1978, p 185). How does this category or description of 'paternalism' relate to the idealist/non-idealist distinction? It seems to me that idealist organisations clearly lay claim to a 'better' moral vision than held in ordinary life (and, to be clear, some mutual benefit organisations may be idealist). That paternalism should accompany their actions is unsurprising. However, non-idealist organisations (again some mutual benefit organisations may be non-idealist) may also be experienced as paternalistic, but for a different reason. They may simply claim to have expertise or experience superior to what is available to ordinary people, rightly or wrongly (something that, of course, idealist organisations may also claim). 'Paternalism' as a descriptor applied to the results of voluntary action does not appear to have been sufficiently refined to discriminate between different sources of the feature.

It is often pointed out (for example Acheson, 1995; and Whelan, 1996) that governments are now increasingly seeking both to work in partnership with voluntary organisations, including the provision of substantial funding support, and to influence the direction of their operations. It does seem probable that the distinction between idealist and non-idealist social thought, as applied to the self-confessed rationales of different voluntary organisations, serves to sharpen our ability to conceptualise the dilemmas faced by the voluntary sector (note too the specific circumstances pertaining in Northern Ireland to which reference was made above). Governments, Labour and Conservative, seem, perhaps unintentionally, to have adopted idealist modes of thought in their attitudes to the voluntary sector in general (and beyond in respect of the idea of a 'third way'). The Chancellor of the Exchequer in Britain, Gordon Brown (2001), has written recently of the need for government to focus on 'enabling and empowering voluntary action. Increasingly, the voluntary sector will be empowered to play a critical role ranging from under-five provision and preventive health to adult learning and the war against unemployment and poverty.' And Brown referred also to 'the great British society founded on a new civic patriotism that we seek to build' (2001). For Tony Blair, writing in 1998, participants in voluntary action 'promote citizenship, help to re-establish a sense of community' and crucially contribute to a 'just and inclusive society' (cited in Lewis, 1999, p 265). Lewis, indeed, remarks that this vision of voluntary action 'has much in common with the much earlier ideas of C.S. Loch and Bernard Bosanquet, and

Hewitt (2001) has pointed to the revival of the 'social organic' model of human nature in New Labour, with reference to Blair (1994).

Voluntary organisations that themselves have an idealist orientation of whatever sort may be so structured as to respond with greater facility than non-idealist organisations to such governmental priorities. Of course it is important to keep in mind that in everyday life organisations and individuals may draw arguments from both camps in a pragmatic manner in order to favour themselves. Nevertheless, the analysis here highlights the fact that *non-idealist* organisations, in which the sentiments of the individuals concerned already may reasonably be said to strike a chord with the values that government seeks to foster – such as a commitment to social inclusion – may be disadvantaged in negotiations with government. The two may well misunderstand each other and their objectives: they do to a degree speak different tongues. This may well be a matter to be regretted: there are many pathways to 'empowerment' and 'social inclusion' (or to 'social growth' or 'social capital') and many outcomes that may be described as representing these goals.

Conclusion: interpreting voluntary action in the history of welfare

Research into voluntary action in the UK has historically been hampered by three dubious assumptions (see Harris, 1992; Himmelfarb, 1995; and Lewis, 1995). The first is that the 'welfare state' represented the climax of a 'natural' or 'inevitable' process, with earlier voluntary action studied merely as foreshadowing and yielding to it. The second is that, with the welfare state established, voluntary action had become a secondary matter, to be studied from a state-centred point of view (as in 'complementing' or 'supplementing' it). The third is that the dominance of, in a broad sense, idealist social thought tended to be taken for granted rather than be seen as a topic for investigation. To the comparatively limited extent that non-idealist social thought was recognised, whether in theory or in practice and whether in the state as related to the voluntary sector or in the voluntary sector itself, it tended to be viewed as a dinosaur. Naturally, this is not the place to take sides on the theoretical and practical strengths and weaknesses of idealist and non-idealist social thought relating to voluntary action. It does matter, though, if we wish to understand, to make explicit what seems to have been left implicit.

The present chapter rejected these three assumptions. The author is acutely conscious that at many points it is unduly speculative and open-ended in nature. Nevertheless, an analytic framework has to be laid out before it can be tested (to destruction if need be). What has emerged so far relating to the world of welfare will be seen, I hope, to represent a useful way of (1) clarifying theoretical contributions on the nature and effects of voluntary action; (2) depicting the differing 'models' of social life that voluntary organisations may themselves embody; (3) analysing changing relationships between the state and voluntary organisations; (4) categorising voluntary organisations according to their models of social life; and (5) perceiving some of the implications that may ensue from the differences between them for voluntary/statutory interaction.

It should be added that the framework might be of use beyond the field of welfare matters to which it has largely been confined in this chapter. For obvious professional reasons academics involved in the study of social policy are indeed prone to focus on this field. However, there is much to learn from analysing a much wider range of voluntary activity (and collaborative social action in general), not least because some 'non-welfare' organisations evoke a response from an unexpectedly large number of people – the National Trust in Britain, for example, has a membership of over 3 million (and 40,000 affiliates in the USA). The analytical framework sketched here might help to explain such popularity. The founders of the National Trust had ideals but did not display idealist social thought as interpreted in this analysis. The trust may have provided 'patrician protection' (Hewison, 1995, p 74) of country houses, but if, as seems the case, it has avoided interpreting its founding principle of overall 'benefit of the nation' in a unitary, idealist sense when determining which buildings, coastline and countryside to protect, the potential for schisms has been minimised and at the same time popular appeal enhanced. The absence of a commitment to wholesale social engineering has left it relatively immune to political conflict. Couple this to the constitutionally limited position of its large membership in decision making (see Lansley, 1996) and the Trust, even in the face of minorities of the membership who were in support of ideological campaigns that would otherwise have proved deeply fissiparous, could maintain flexibility, unity and support.

As has been said already, the framework advanced in this chapter requires extensive trials in rough empirical waters to assess its seaworthiness. It is clear that the framework could not have been constructed unless the three assumptions listed at the start of the section had been abandoned. If this chapter does no more than advance the demise of those assumptions, with their pernicious impact on the historiography and general interpretation of voluntary action, the effort will have been worthwhile.

EIGHT

Epilogue: from poor law to Labour's 'new idealism'

Reinterpreting the end of the poor law

One matter to which the contrast between idealist and non-idealist social thought serves to draw attention is the persistence of non-idealist thought in policy well into the twentieth century, concealed, as it were, below the Plimsoll line. This was touched on in Chapter Six, but deserves further attention.

Support for people in their own resolves and thus in exercising their own liberty, rather than subjugation to idealist tutelage, retained a wide appeal. Alfred Marshall (see Chapter Two) acknowledged Spencer's substantial influence as did parti pris Fabian H.G. Wells who in 1914 felt that we then emerged 'from a period of deliberate happy-go-lucky and the influence of Herbert Spencer who came near raising public shiftlessness to the dignity of a national philosophy' (1914, p 69). Both the 1908 Old Age Pension Act and 1911 National Insurance Act delivered cash benefits to people without serious supervisory strings attached. Health insurance in particular jarred with Beatrice Webb: 'I fear the growth of malingering and the right to money independently of the obligation to good conduct. I cannot dismiss my rooted prejudice to relief instead of treatment' (1948, p 474). She was also scathing of the 'insistence on free choice of doctors by the beneficiaries of state insurance – an obvious administrative absurdity' that favoured 'the pecuniary interests of the worst type of medical men' (Webb, 1948, p 472). Financial partnership between the state, the employer and the employee in National Insurance meshed well with idealist concerns, cash benefits without social obligations much less so.

The Liberal government politely declined the invitation to change the poor law, either on majority or minority lines after the poor law reports in 1909. It was largely left alone until 1929. But, lacking any idealist-inspired revolution, the poor law had been quietly changing and the guardians mounted a credible defence, through the National Committee for Poor Law Reform, which sought a via tertis, 'third way', between the reports (for which Sir William Chance wrote *Poor law reform – via tertis – The case for the guardians*). Two members of the commission, Booth and Downes rallied to this cause, as did Mackay. Asquith opined (in McBriar, 1987, p 330): 'I think you will find the Boards of Guardians will die very hard. They are powerful bodies. With all their defects and shortcomings they after all represent an enormous amount of gratuitous and public spirited service ... we could ill spare from the sphere of local administration. I confess I am old-fashioned in that matter.'

Already use of poor law infirmaries no longer entailed the label 'pauper'. More considerate relief was in place for older people. The majority report attributed increases in old-age pauperism since 1900 to the 'growing attractiveness of Poor Law institutions' (Poor Law Report, 1909, vol I, p 232). On 11 December 1906, Dr Cecil Stephens, district medical officer and workhouse medical officer for the North Witchford Union in Cambridgeshire, had given evidence to the commission. Asked by Downes if the workhouse is as deterrent as formerly, Stephens replied,

> Not nearly. The workhouse has got a bad name very often, I think, from the fact that the inmates of the workhouse go outside and they are very anxious to get money, and they say how badly they are treated in the workhouse, in order to get people to give them 2d, and that quite gets around in the place. (Poor Law Report (Evidence), 1909, vol III, app: 34808-10)

Stephens then adds that the bad name is not deserved, and to Charles Booth's question regarding feeling against the workhouse decreasing he replied, 'Yes, it is decreasing a great deal, I am sure of that.'

Other evidence pointing in this direction is furnished by what has become known as 'Poplarism' 'because of the defiant example set by the Poplar Board of Guardians both in the Edwardian and in the post-war period'[1] (McBriar, 1987, p 365; see also Gilbert, 1970, ch 5; and Ryan, 1978). By the mid-1920s between 100 and 200 boards were administering outdoor relief in times of high unemployment on scales of relief extravagantly high in the view of poor law officials at the Ministry of Health, and in a lax manner. Bruce reported that John Wheatley, who had been Minister of Health in the first Labour government of 1924, saw as one of the brightest results of the growth of the Labour movement 'that the control of the poor has passed into the hands of popular boards of guardians' (cited in Bruce, 1968, p 237).

Indeed, according to Bruce, Wheatley suggested that, rather than Poplarism, '"Popularism" would be a more appropriate term' (1968, p 237). As, however, McBriar notes, the policy has often been 'attributed to "Labour" initiative, although it was by no means confined to Boards which had majorities of Labour members' (1987, p 365). In 1926 the Conservative government secured the Board of Guardians (Default) Act empowering the Minister of Health to replace with a board of his own nominees any board apparently not fulfilling its legal obligations: these powers were used against the guardians at West Ham in London, Chester-le-Street, County Durham, and Bedwellty, South Wales.

In short, it may be that well before the poor law was officially abolished it was by no means as loathed as we are led to believe. 'Where workhouses evolved into quiet and comfortable old people's homes, cottage hospitals, and high-quality infirmaries, then in some areas at least people began to "queue up" to get into them' (Harris, 2002, p 436). In the absence of majority-style tutelage towards ideal citizenship or Webbian surveillance an approach that took people for what they were – thus non-idealist – became practical poor law social theory and appreciated as such by those needing support. It may be time to distinguish demonising the poor law from understanding its social reality. Instead of viewing the nineteenth-century poor law as merely an unsubtle mechanism for pushing people into the market, it may be seen as representing Noetic and hence liberal Tory social and moral theory, theory that fused later with non-idealist social thought and survived, unsung, as practical poor law philosophy into the twentieth century. Quelling at least initially powerful idealist-inspired onslaughts, this philosophy helped the poor law to a position where its nature as less manipulative than the other radically reformist options on offer won it popular support. In the process this analysis illustrates that 'ideas about "social welfare" can migrate unexpectedly across the political spectrum, such that preconceived assumptions about the left/ right implications of particular policies are often false' (Harris, 1992, p 119). Clearly related, then, to the rediscovery of informal care, and to interpreting voluntary action, is the question of how far actual social policy, rather than its academic study, was 'idealist' in the 1950s and 1960s. Public assistance and then national assistance derived directly from the patently non-idealist poor law. For Harris, the shift from poor law to universal insurance never really happened: 'The vast majority of claimants for relief were nearly always women, children, the disabled and the aged, whereas those entitled to social insurance benefits were always predominantly adult males' (2002, p 436). Titmuss argued against the 'social divisiveness' of an over-reliance on means tests in these years.

The National Health Service, on the other hand, certainly set objectives in its performance in line with a vision of the 'social good': the pursuit of 'territorial justice' (see Davies, 1968; and Forder, 1974, ch 4) through the Resource Allocation Working Party (see Allsop, 1995, ch 4) was intended to divert resources from certain areas and thus reduce the health care available to individuals in them. It may be that idealist thought in and about the NHS, in respect, say, of its ability to promote 'social growth' in the 'texture of relationships' between human beings (Titmuss, 1974, p 150) provided (and still provides) underlying theoretical 'respectability' to decisions on who to treat, and how and when (how much weight must you lose before you will be operated on?), which are presented as matters of clinical judgement or financial necessity, but might not be, or not solely. A patient-driven non-idealist NHS would be unable to bring into play this kind of justification for failure to treat or to treat promptly at the time illness presents. The point here is not about advocating policy change, but to indicate some potential practical dispositions when particular social theories are embedded in policy. It can be argued, as we have already seen, that whether bodies such as voluntary organisations theorise about themselves as idealist or non-idealist in their objectives and methods is of considerable importance in understanding them, and their financial relationships with governments depending on governmental disposition towards or against idealist social theories.

Towards an idealist future in social policy? Social capital and New Labour knights

Given the central concerns of this book it is of value to consider the increasingly common idea of 'social capital'. Social capital refers to the networks of ties and contacts people have through their occupations, leisure pursuits, religious and political commitments and family and residential situations. These ties and associated networks provide privileged opportunities to contribute to and draw upon flows of information, assistance, support and, ultimately, trust, thus enhancing the resources available to participating individuals and groups. The idea is particularly associated with the studies of Pierre Bourdieu, Robert Putnam and James Coleman, and has appeal both to non-idealists and idealists or, in other words, across a wide political spectrum. The idea itself is not new: in this study Spencer's comments on beneficence reflect an awareness of the concept and its value in social life, and Durkheim's pivotal concern with social solidarity is in tune with it. Putnam (2000) has seen the advocacy of social capital as a means for rescuing the USA from what he sees as a decline in social connectedness in everyday life, though the strength of the evidence of decline is a matter of dispute (Field, 2003).

Social capital is seen as 'bonding' and 'bridging'. Bonding refers to the strengthening of individuals with shared interests and maintaining their distinctiveness from those on the outside; bridging refers to the bringing together of people with diverse rather than similar interests. Ties can be of variable strength; a weak tie may introduce the unfamiliar, and particularly useful, more readily than a strong tie based, say, on family membership. Social capital is thus presented as a source of value to those involved: 'it brings to social theory ... an emphasis on relationships and values as significant factors in explaining structures and behaviour ... it contributes new insights by focusing on family, neighbourhood, voluntary associations and public institutions as integrating elements between individuals and wider social structures' (Field, 2003, p 139).

Romantic sentiments and a sense of nostalgia seem to have inspired an assumption that social capital is a good thing, a conduit to the 'good society'. Because it oils the wheels of cooperation it is seen as good, 'particularly for the individuals or groups concerned directly, but also for the wider society as a whole' (Field, 2003, p 72). However, it can also produce negative results, buttressing criminal activity or perpetuating social divisions and gender inequalities. Another matter to consider is to what extent promoting social capital should be an objective of government policy. One risk here is that, since the key to social capital is the outcome of the work of free individuals, it might collapse as individuals withdraw, bridling at external constraints. For Field,

> The promotion of social capital depends on other actors than the state's own agents; it can only be built by engaging civic society. This means that policy must act at a distance, working through partners and intermediaries who may then act in unanticipated ways. For example, a policy aimed at promoting volunteering by providing funds to voluntary bodies may end up by encouraging competition rather than cooperation among those who are applying for funds, and displacing civic activists with paid professionals. Policies designed to mobilize voluntary bodies may inadvertently

> suppress their capacity to nurture social capital. (Field, 2003, p 120)

In the 1980s non-idealists took the more limited but plausible view that government 'should remove those interventions of past governments which hinder or prevent the optimal operation of informal welfare', removing the 'laws, taxes, regulations and social benefits which obstruct individuals' ability, willingness or confidence to care for their fellows' (Anderson, 1985).

It is clear that New Labour finds the idea of social capital appealing (Field, 2003, p 117), but it is less apparent exactly why this is the case. Individuals drawing on their social capital may well not, in so doing, promote a substantive vision of the virtuous republic, but promote their own happiness and wealth. Success in attempts to mould actions directly towards a particular social outcome cannot be assumed. Champions of social capital may hold to either idealist or non-idealist social thought, but their expectations of it will differ accordingly. The distinction thus matters in this context, and policy proposals on social capital deserve to be analysed with it in mind.

This observation leads to a final comment on the nature of the current Labour government's thinking about aspects of welfare. It has been noted in the previous chapter that speeches by Gordon Brown and Tony Blair on voluntary action as promoting citizenship and social solidarity appear to be a reiteration of idealist modes of social thought. Bevir and O'Brien (2003) add substantial weight to such a claim. Their analysis reveals tangible connections between Blair, the idealist philosopher John Macmurray[2] – who placed a strong emphasis on action and social humanism to promote social solidarity and enhance our common life – and earlier idealist thinkers such as Henry Jones who had taught Macmurray's own tutor at Oxford, A.D. Lindsay (on Jones and T.H. Marshall, see Low, 2000). Personal and conceptual connections

> locate Tony Blair ... within a tradition of social humanism ... Indeed, Blair himself has acknowledged such an influence repeatedly. In 1994, he said: 'If you really want to understand what I'm all about you have to take a look at a guy called John Macmurray. It's all there.' In 1996, he praised Macmurray specifically for delineating the starting point of a modern concept of community through his rigorous location of individuals in social settings such that they

cannot properly ignore their obligations to others. (Bevir
and O'Brien, 2003, p 326. See also Heron and Dwyer, 1999)

The practical expression of this idealism in Labour thought is that
government should adopt social policies that enable people 'to develop
themselves through their own activity', but that development should
be so directed as to enhance a sense of interdependence and community
(Bevir and O'Brien, 2003, p 327). Bevir and O'Brien note the closer
proximity of this position than earlier idealist and ethical socialist ones
to an individualistic vision of community: communitarian critics could
argue it to be a 'capitulation to the individualism of neo-liberalism'
(2003, p 328). Into this jungle the contrast between idealist and non-
idealist modes of social theory penetrates: individual agents are here
ultimately, in the Le Grand (2003) lexicon, pawns. They are still to be
constrained, in knightly fashion, by the designers of the good society.

Conclusion: idealism, non-idealism and policy: the record

This book has endeavoured to argue a strong case for a broad
conception of idealist social thought and a contrast with non-idealist
thought as furnishing a fruitful way of interpreting the relationship
between social theory and social policy in Britain and Ireland since
the 1830s.

Revisiting the social theory involved in poor law developments in
the 1830s has drawn attention to the formative role of Noetic theology
and political economics associated in practice with the politics of the
liberal Tories. A distinctive emphasis on virtue, and the economic and
social arrangements that help rather than hinder it in progressively
squeezing out vice was clearly associated with the reforms. In a largely
secular time it is easy to underestimate how important a part may be
played in earlier times by religious perspectives in achieving social
change: while there was a Benthamite contribution to events it was
present on Noetic conditions. Crucially, virtue could only be created
through personal effort, not by government provision; though
government could encourage vice and hinder virtue. The question of
precisely what constituted the conditions under which virtue could
blossom, what sort of action by government counted as hindering
virtue, were hotly contested in the case of Ireland and whether or not
to introduce a poor law, and, if so, with what features. However, the
disagreements between the principal figures remained within a
recognisably Noetic framework. Whately had relatively mild differences

with Senior; Lewis and Nicholls took stronger exception to Whately's proposals. Even so, their alternative perspective concerned matters of interpretation of the material circumstances affecting Ireland rather than fundamental principles of theory. These differences could have surfaced over reform in England, though more favourable economic circumstances there seem to have prevented this from happening. Nevertheless, an enhanced appreciation of the underlying theoretical logic present in English reform is gained by comprehending the response once it was confronted by the challenges offered by Irish circumstances.

Spencer's principle of justice indicated that a poor law was unjust; for Spencer relief of the poor was a matter for private beneficence, not justice, and hence not a legitimate concern of government. It should be noted that Spencer distinguished between 'family ethics' and 'state ethics'. In rearing the young it is essential to survival that benefits and rewards are provided to the young according to their needs. However, on reaching adulthood, benefits must be in accord with merit and rewards with desert. Society in its corporate capacity courts disaster by disrupting the natural process of adaptation to circumstances if it interferes with the play of these two principles. By 1884 Spencer was complaining that in spite of such arguments there is 'continual advocacy of paternal government. The intrusion of family-ethics into the ethics of the State, instead of being regarded as socially injurious, is more and more demanded as the only efficient means to social benefit' (1884, p 127). Spencer had idealist thought, and Hyndman's socialism, in mind.

Nevertheless, Spencer saw that the abolition of the poor law was not practicable, and he admitted as much in the *Ethics*. Indeed, in one of his very earliest publications he had championed the 1834 reform and the workhouse, pointing out that without them the 'whole system of man's responsibility, and of his future reward or punishment, depending upon his being "diligent in business, fervent in spirit, serving the Lord"' would be set aside (Spencer, 1836, p 181).

At that time Spencer was 16, receiving tuition, as explained earlier, from his uncle, Thomas, parish clergyman, poor law reformer and pamphleteer. The nephew's Noetic tone is not surprising. In his later works Spencer very seldom referred to other theorists, still less quoted from them: Whately, though, is an exception. Spencer championed individualism in political and social life and invoked in his support the philosopher and archbishop of Dublin, Richard Whately (Whately was widely read at the time), quoting from him in his essay 'Specialized administration' of 1871: 'Many of the most important objects are accomplished by the joint agency of persons who never think of them, nor have any idea of acting in concert; and that, with a certainty, completeness, and regularity, which probably the most diligent benevolence, under the guidance of the greatest human wisdom, could never have attained' (Spencer, 1871, p 423). By such means London was supplied daily with provisions with which no 'State-manufacture' could compete. The unplanned, eventually beneficial, but remote outcome of cooperative acts for mundane purposes was a shared emphasis, alien to both the Bosanquets and the Webbs. Placing undue pressure on individuals to change their living styles accorded neither with 'justice' nor how adaptation to circumstances and progress could be securely achieved.

Poor laws came under close scrutiny again from 1870 to the outbreak of the First World War. New thought crystallised in the royal commission appointed on the poor law in 1905. It divided, issuing separate majority and minority reports in 1909. In addition to the reports for England and Wales there are separate majority and minority reports for Scotland and Ireland.

The majority reports largely reflected the social theory of the COS with which many of the commissioners were associated, while the minority reports represented the Fabian socialism of Beatrice Webb (and her husband Sidney, not a commissioner). Neither the COS nor the majority reports had a social theory that was 'individualist' in a 'selfish' or 'atomic' sense. Spencer's social theory was characterised in this way by Bernard Bosanquet within the COS, but in so doing he disingenuously underplayed Spencer's emphasis on altruistic sentiments in civilised life. Since the only prominent COS figure who owed an intellectual debt to Spencer was Thomas Mackay, the social theory embedded in the COS and the majority reports is best considered as idealist, not 'individualist'.

Brutally condensing highly complex thought, idealists can be taken to focus on the unity of a society with individuals organically related to each other. Freedom and fulfilment as a citizen was not possible unless individuals, with the family as a powerful moral force, recognised that they were citizens of this wider society towards which they had responsibilities to act according to the general will, and which itself had responsibilities to them. The more these reciprocal moral ties were acknowledged and fulfilled the greater the moral advancement of the whole society. Bernard Bosanquet suggested that a 'defect in the citizen character' was revealed by destitution, ignorance and dependence. Idealist thought subordinated, observes Harris, both particular policies and people as 'means to the end of attaining perfect justice and creating the ideal state' (Harris, 1992, p 126).

The Noetic focus on a natural order and atonement was thus compelled to yield to the empowerment of incarnation; orthodox Noetics would have blenched at the attempt to second-guess Providence and to front-load how specific virtues might best be given expression (see Hilton, 1988). In practical terms, many idealists insisted that reform processes had to treat the individual as a 'whole' person, taking into account his or her ensemble of social and moral relationships. Rich and poor could have a defect of the 'citizen character', although the poor had no cushion of affluence to soften the consequences of their social shortcomings. Painstaking personal work was required, given the uniqueness of each individual, to empower expression as a full citizen of an individual's capabilities. Through example, tutelage and supervision, personal independence and a sense of responsibility, and thus the progress of society as a whole, could be achieved. Merely awarding relief failed to incorporate into the transaction the vital ingredient of personal service; worse, it perpetuated a dependent state of mind. Organised correctly, charity could do this work, state officials not.

The minority reports of course parted company with the majority over the parts to be played by the state and charity in future reform. It was shown earlier, though, that idealist social thought provided the intellectual framework in which minority ideas were cast.

In the last two chapters matters of more recent concern were considered. Initially, the nature of the social theory of Titmuss was reconsidered with an exploration of the theme that his social philosophy 'was full of muffled resonances of the idealist discourse of the Edwardian age' (Harris, 1992, p 137). Idealist thought was embraced by Tawney, himself read with enthusiasm by Titmuss, and by many others in the first half of the century including A.D. Lindsay who founded what was to become Keele University with an overtly non-specialist degree structure, and John Reith, committed to public broadcasting as a means to improve popular taste. Describing Titmuss' thought as 'idealist' captures and explains his accentuation of 'social growth', the NHS as enhancing 'the texture of relationships between human beings' (Titmuss, 1974, p 150), the moral purpose of (British) social policy as 'expressing the "general will" of the people' (Titmuss, 1974, p 24), and doctors as 'centres of moral life' (Titmuss, 1968, p 250). It also chimes in with his views of a 'social market' as morally superior to the economic market, of social policy as possessing 'an egalitarian and moral purpose' (Pinker, 1993, p 58) that encouraged social unity, and of the need for a dedicated academic subject to study social policy, uniquely in tune with its 'moral' nature, unlike 'positivist' economics or sociology (strongly reminiscent of Bernard Bosanquet's desire for a focus on 'social therapeutics'). Finally, it draws attention to two matters neglected alike by Titmuss and the Edwardian idealists. First, choice among service users in terms of the form of service they wished to receive was a low priority: those with the appropriate 'moral' expertise knew best, nudging out any significant place for user choice. Second, informal care received very little attention. In one significant reference Titmuss points to the need for *more* service provision in the care of older people, but the wishes of carers and those they care for are not included in the picture (Titmuss, 1968, pp 98-9). Revealing intellectual continuities were noted: neither the majority report nor the minority report gave informal care serious attention, differing simply over whether its deficiencies were likely to be of a 'moral' or 'inadequately professional' nature. It was Spencer, the non-idealist, who drew attention to informal care and the urgent need to strengthen it.

This discussion led into the topic of the phenomenon of the 'rediscovery' of informal care in social policy studies in the 1970s. By then there were non-idealist dissenters within the subject that Titmuss had done a great deal to establish (Pinker, 1993). Something radical was afoot when Pinker himself observed that 'we still lack adequate explanations of the causes of ... why individuals define their needs as they do, and why these definitions so often appear to be at variance with those of the social scientists' (1971, p 108, see also Mayer and Timms, 1970; and Robinson, 1978). In this new climate policy-related documents also adopted a hitherto unfamiliar interest in informal carers' experiences and preferences (Wolfenden Report, 1978; Barclay Report, 1982) – a dimension almost entirely absent from the Seebohm Report of 1968, in which important conceptual continuities with the majority report (on England) have been noted by Harris (1982; see also Offer, 1999b). A parallel expansion in empirical research into informal care in social policy studies in the 1980s and 1990s developed. This reorientation within social policy studies predated the premiership of Mrs Thatcher and, while feminist concerns about the burdens of care falling disproportionately on women certainly swelled the research effort immensely, its origins seem to be in a critical dissatisfaction with idealist normative assumptions about what social policy should be like and how it should be studied. As with any paradigm certain questions become the centre of attention at the expense of others. Shift the paradigm and new (or old) concerns come into view. The rejection of idealist modes of thinking about social policy and welfare seem to be at the heart of these changes, releasing the conceptual space for informal care to be rediscovered.

Voluntary action was also reviewed in the light of the master distinction between idealist and non-idealist social thought. Divergent conceptions of the role of voluntary organisations, of the relationship between them and action by the state, and of the social theories held by voluntary organisations themselves about their activities were examined. The orientation of the present Labour administration towards voluntary action emerged as tending towards idealist social thought in the sense that a substantive conception of the social good framed expectations of their objectives.

It may be helpful to conclude with some comments on the framework that Le Grand has advanced. Le Grand's view is that in the last 30 or so years there have been shifts in policy makers' perceptions of the motivation of the providers of services and of the powers of agency of the users of services. Service providers are seen to have moved from being selfless 'knights' to self-interested 'knaves', and users from being passive 'pawns' to active, sovereign 'queens' (Le Grand, 2003).[3] The central concerns of this study rub shoulders with Le Grand's categories; theories of social policy cannot but take positions on motivation and agency, though there may be ambiguities and complications in the face of which Le Grand's categories may need some reconsideration. Perhaps the clearest outcome is that the two varieties of idealism we have encountered, champions of voluntary action and champions of state action, agree that service providers in their schemes would be of knightly motivation, whether because of their awareness of the 'moral' interdependence of people, or their professional expertise. Users of services are destined to be pawns; either insufficiently moral to make choices, or inadequately knowledgeable. They may become queens tomorrow, but tomorrow is deferred indefinitely; it is by definition hard to gain recognition as ideally 'moral' or 'rational'. The position of the varieties of non–idealist thought encountered, that of the Noetics and liberal Tories, Spencer, the later years of the poor law, and the thought associated with the rediscovery of informal care, is more intricate. At first sight it might seem, in the case of theory concerned with the poor law, that able-bodied paupers are pawns. Yet on reflection they seem to be more like what may be termed 'lapsed queens'. The expectation is that they will regain independence and discover the rewards of virtuous living, and with their disappearance from the poor law they would simultaneously reacquire their queenly status (according to his critics a process likely to be protracted had Whately's proposals been adopted in Ireland with their commitment to want being not the result of individual fault). Guardians were seen as knights by governments; but they could become knaves in the eyes of idealists, and of government itself faced with Poplarism (though for those then receiving relief, guardians would have newly acquired a knightly status). Simpler again is the non-idealist rediscovery of informal care: clearly carers and those they cared for had or should have queenly status as agents, able to curb the knavish proclivities of professionals with whom they might be in contact.

At the core of this book has been the attempt to sustain two related claims: first that idealist social thought, broadly defined, dominated the history of social policy in Britain from the 1870s to the 1970s, and in fact continues to be influential, and, second, that the contrasted idea of non-idealist social thought which stalks it is also important in the history of policy up to the present. Traditionally non-idealist thought has had a raw deal from social policy studies and its own accounts of the history of policy, seen at best as unfashionable, or even irretrievably passé, to at worst discredited on theoretical grounds as an approach to understanding social life. However, the prevailing intellectual fashions of one time are never likely to provide the perfect springboard for plunging into other waters, many outside the fashions would disagree that personal liberty had ever ceased to be a benchmark by which to assess policy, and politically motivated objections to a theoretical approach may not invalidate its arguments or show as false its premises, especially if an interest in individuals is just assumed to rule out any kind of space for sociality from the picture.

It has not been my task to advocate a political position; unless an appeal for understanding that non-idealism can generate ideas of welfare is taken as such, for I am, I suppose, entering into the politics of historiography. Neither was the main task that of generalising historically about idealism and non-idealism. No linear progression is proposed; I am not suggesting a sociological dichotomous model of movement over time from the hegemony of one theoretical approach to another, whether past or future. The intention has not been to postulate a trend at all, as Dicey did from individualism to collectivism, or as Spencer did from a militant to an industrial form of society. Certainly, though, I hope I have demonstrated successfully that a particular veering away from idealist social thought did occur in the 1970s, but if that analysis were to prove unsustainable it would not torpedo the book's core mission. That has been to highlight conceptual and analytical differences between idealist and non-idealist thought on social life and the attainment of well-being. The most evident difference between them is about the status accorded to the choices made by an individual; in idealist thought the pursuit of the good society requires individuals to act in certain ways, to make one kind of choice rather than another; for non-idealist thought it is not an end to be directly engineered but is, if it has any meaning at all, whatever results from the uncoerced actions and choices of individuals, subject to some equal liberty principle. The actions and choices are not necessarily unsocial or 'selfish'. In a non-idealist world people are 'queens', or perhaps sometimes 'lapsed queens'; in an idealist world they are 'pawns', with the distant prospect that one day they will have qualified for the queenly status of fully responsible citizen. Another difference emphasised was over the status of informal care. Whereas non-idealists recognised informal care as a significant constituent of promoting welfare in everyday life, idealists did not; the structure of idealist thought militated against finding merit in or even accurately perceiving the status quo. Against this, non-idealists find it difficult to accord legitimacy to a distributional ethic in the form of the Rawlsian principle of social justice, challenging rather the view of a society as an organisation on which they see it as founded (on Hayek's argument to this effect see Millar, 1989. For a non-idealist critical perspective on Rawls' account of social justice see Flew, 1981, chs 3 and 4). In this study, then, it has been the divergent implications for policy when the logical differences between idealist and non-idealist social thought are distinguished that has served as the master key to the selection and interpretation of topics for investigation.

In spite of trying to find a theoretical position that would in some way transcend and thus call into question this master distinction I have failed. There is, of course, ultimately a fine line between what may be deemed hindrances to (negative) freedom and the requisites of (positive) freedom. The removal of one may appear much like the provision of the other, although the underpinning arguments would reveal the ultimate theoretical difference. Certainly, I think that the argument could be made in particular that T.H. Green's concern that individuals themselves have to choose freely to act so as to promote the New Jerusalem makes him more of a non-idealist than the opposite, but that is not the same thing at all. Moreover, Green had every expectation that 'reason' would govern the choices made. Similarly, New Liberal old-age pensions and health and unemployment insurance benefits were primarily designed to deliver 'social justice' and 'economic and social growth': the choices made in spending the new income by ordinary people were of course free, but again 'responsibility' was expected. Indeed, these schemes clearly placed an element of non-idealism in an idealist envelope. The envelope, though, is all-important.

In these matters there is no choice but to start from either idealist or non-idealist premises.

If we are to understand social policy today we need to understand, not caricature, our social policy past; and in that the poor law, familial welfare, and voluntary action loom very large indeed. The fundamental contrast between idealist and non-idealist social thought, once brought to the surface and examined in detail, commands us to assess the past afresh. It also assists, as has been shown, in the analysis of more recent policy-related matters. On occasion, a tour d'horizon may have merit, but, in dealing with a wide range of philosophers and theories, others must decide if this book escapes Swift's wise caution:

> All philosophers, who find
> Some favourite system to their mind,
> In every point to make it fit,
> Will force all nature to submit.

Notes

Chapter One – 'Virtue' and the poor law in Britain and Ireland in the 1830s

[1] Pinker describes Chadwick as Benthamist in his sharp distinction between indoor and outdoor relief, the efficacy of a workhouse test and his desire for a central inspectorate (1971, p 57). Pinker also cites J.R. Poynter's claim that 'the onus of proof is surely on those who would deny Bentham's influence on the Act which created the new Poor Law' (1971, p 57). This chapter points indeed to a relatively limited influence of Benthamite thought in comparison with Noetic viewpoints.

[2] The conventional and familiar distinction in literature on the poor law between 'able-bodied' and 'non able-bodied' persons is retained in this book in preference to less 'dated' alternatives.

[3] By reason of its set of simple propositions, welded into an argument and directed at a large concern, the report has important structural affinities with T.R. Malthus' *An essay on the principle of population* (1798) and Charles Darwin's later *On the origin of species* (1859).

[4] See Bicheno (1824) for his views more generally on poor relief.

[5] See MacIntyre (1965, p 211). MacIntyre provides a useful discussion of Whately in the context of thought on Ireland's 'problems'. See also Akenson (1981).

[6] Finer (1952, p 146) omits the important *Remarks* as an achievement in his assessment of G.C. Lewis.

[5] Finer (1952, p 142) apparently confuses the reports on Ireland by Whately and Nicholls.

[6] In 1836, Thomas Spring Rice, Chancellor of the Exchequer, described the proposed reforms of Whately as 'draining everything including patience'. A year later Melbourne wrote to Spring Rice about Whately's views: 'This comes of appointing university professors to great offices'

(in MacIntyre, 1965, p 213). A more positive view of Whately's influence on government on other issues is provided by Brent, 1987, p 142.

[9] Chadwick's memorandum, probably of 1841, entitled *Practical Christianity vs. professing Christianity but practical infidelity* contrasts James Kay's 'practical' contributions to reform with the 'false pharisaical charity which creates the misery it pretends to alleviate' (in Finer, 1952, p 151). G. C. Lewis, who had by now succeeded his father as a permanent commissioner, was in repeated conflict with Chadwick and marginalising him as the commission's secretary.

[10] From 1834 in England previously autonomous parishes were, for poor law purposes, grouped into 'unions' under the control of elected 'boards of guardians'. Typically about 20 or so parishes would be grouped together with a market town at the hub, but there were myriad local variations depending on geography and local politics. Today's district council boundaries sometimes still shadow them. In fact, in some areas, unions had been formed earlier under Gilbert's 1782 Act (on these unions in East Anglia see Digby (1978)). Unions were intended to bring administrative uniformity and a rationalisation of institutional provision, and were themselves accountable to a newly established permanent body in London, the poor law commission. In Ireland, after 1838, unions and guardians were also instituted, but of necessity with a rapid and distinctive new build of workhouses, designed by one architect (George Wilkinson).

Chapter Two – Spencer and a liberal road to welfare

[1] It may be helpful here to list Spencer's chief publications in order. *The proper sphere of government* appeared in 1842 followed by *Social statics* of 1851. The first edition of the *Principles of psychology* came out in 1855, before the 'System of synthetic philosophy' was conceived. According to his *An autobiography* (1904b, 2 vols), by early 1858 he had sketched out the structure of the 'System' (1904b, vol II, p 18). After the statement of his general evolutionary theory in *First principles* (1862) came the two volumes of the *Principles of biology* (1864 and 1867), and then the two volumes of the extensively revised and reorganised second edition of the *Principles of psychology* (1870 and 1872). The three volumes of the *Principles of sociology* appeared in 1876, 1882 and 1896, and the two volumes of the *Principles of ethics* in 1892 and 1893. Note that in 1878 Spencer decided to write the *Ethics*

before completing the *Sociology* to avoid the risk of failing to complete, through illness or death, the 'System' as a whole (which had the aim overall of being a 'basis for a right rule of life, individual and social' (Spencer 1904b, vol II, p 314)). In addition to the 'System', Spencer published *The study of sociology* in 1873 and *The man versus the state* in 1884, a revised and abridged edition of *Social statics* in 1892 to take account of changes in his thought and the contents of the *Ethics*, three volumes of collected *Essays*, and two late-in-life volumes of short essays, *Various fragments* (1897) and *Facts and comments* (1902). There is also the *Autobiography* (1904b) and Duncan (1911). The Spencer papers at the University of London Library contain little of substance not available in Duncan, but see also Spencer (1904a). Duncan (1911) contains a full listing of Spencer's publications. See also Perrin (1993). Virtually all of Spencer's major works are in print today with Routledge/Thoemmes or Liberty. In the case of *The man versus the state* the version in Offer (1994) may be preferred since it amplifies and corrects Spencer's frequently inadequate footnotes.

[2] 'Informal care' is usually now understood as care provided by relatives, neighbours or friends for infirm older people, or people with serious disabilities or chronic illness. 'Care' may involve cash as well as periodic or continuous nursing-type care. Its boundaries are not without contention – self-help care by an individual, for example, seems excluded for no clear reason (see Graham, 1991). The contrast is with 'formal' care, which is that provided by an organisation, statutory, voluntary or private. Spencer's examples of 'private beneficence' illustrate that equating the expression with 'informal care' is not unreasonable (see also Finlayson, 1994, p 7). However, discussion of 'informal care' today has to deal with at least two aspects not salient in Spencer's time, namely, that much informal care *depends upon* financial support from the state and on the 'consumption' of other forms of formal support such as respite care facilities, and that community care policy following the Griffiths Report (1988) is now officially committed to supporting informal care.

[3] Quoting from evidence received on the effects of outdoor relief on labourers actually relieved, the report records the comment: 'Why should I tend my sick and aged parents, when the parish is bound to do it? Or if I do perform the service, why should I excuse the parish, which is bound to pay for it' (Poor Law Report, 1974, p 178).

[4] The royal commission was announced on 2 August 1905. In the

absence of direct evidence as to why A.J. Balfour and the Conservative government established it, a number of interpretations have appeared (see McBriar, 1987, p 176). Perhaps most persuasive is K.D. Brown's suggestion that it was a response to a riot of unemployed workers in Manchester the previous day. The Unemployed Workmen Bill, which had already run into difficulties over the financial arrangements for providing the high number of the unemployed with work (outside of the poor law), was also hastily revived the same month (K.D. Brown, 1971a, and also 1971b). Unemployment and poverty were, of course, closely linked, and the commission was asked in their terms of reference to look not only at the relief of poor persons but specifically also at 'the various means which have been adopted out side of the Poor Laws for meeting distress arising from want of employment, particularly during periods of severe industrial depression'. However, J. Brown has cautioned that there is 'no direct evidence ... that it was intended as a sop to a disillusioned labour movement' (1971, p 322).

[5] See Poor Law Report (1909, vol III, pp 248-54, and 259-60. The minority report rejects the idea, proposed in Australia in 1908, of granting invalidity pensions to the permanently incapacitated under 70 years old. This is discussed in Chapter Four.

[6] It has been argued that the social aims and the social situation of past theorists are different from those prevailing today, and hence that using their products in the present day may not be 'proper extensions of their original theoretical urges' (Fuller, 1995, p 162). In fact, this argument indicates the need for caution rather than for a relativist-inspired embargo. I would contend that the (suspect) evolutionary context of Spencer's theoretical and practical analysis of 'private beneficence' can be identified and bracketed off quite explicitly, leaving insights that in principle are useful. This is particularly likely to be the case if now, as with Spencer, there is a non-idealist heart to social policy discourse. Note, however, that to make this point is emphatically not itself to make a relativist point about the nature of truth. Non-idealist times may be times more receptive to making use of Spencer, but statements that are true statements, and arguments that are valid arguments are so, regardless of the social circumstances of the theorist who produced them or of the predispositions of audiences who listen to them – or ignore them (these matters are explored further in Offer, 1996).

[7] Tönnies himself is reported as having declared that it was his

opposition to Spencer's sociology that became the starting point of his sociological work (see Offer, 1991). Tönnies' *Gemeinschaft und Gesellschaft* first appeared in 1887, ahead of his four main critical articles on Spencer, of which his 1889 article is perhaps the most important. Bulmer (1987) provides a recent discussion of Tönnies' book in relation to the study of informal care. On the contemporary use of dead theorists see note 6, above.

[8] A further early example is provided by his essay 'Over-legislation' of 1853: 'In the case of bad house-building … it is obvious that a cheap, rigorous, and certain administration of justice, would make Building Acts needless. For is not the man who erects a house of bad materials ill put together, and, concealing these with papering and plaster, sells it as a substantial dwelling, guilty of fraud? … And if the legal remedy were easy, prompt, and sure, would not builders cease transgressing?' (Spencer, 1853, p 275).

[9] Benjamin Kidd (1858-1916) was a policeman's son, born in County Cork. He gained his education outside of the universities, and became a civil servant in England. His *Social evolution* (1894) was widely read and translated into many languages. His *Principles of Western civilisation* of 1902 and *The science of power* (1918) should also be noted. Kidd sided with Weissman's rejection of the inheritance of acquired characteristics and accepted in effect genetic variation, a large rupture with Spencer (see also the next chapter). For Kidd this meant that individuals and social life were in perpetual conflict, rather than moving to a harmony as Spencer envisaged. However, religion, not (individual) reason, is a force making for a new order in which a socialist equality of opportunity (Kidd was familiar with Marx's work) will become a state duty, allowing all persons to compete efficiently and fairly in social life. Kidd's version of social evolution found limited support from Bernard Bosanquet (see Boucher, 1997, pp 52-3) but strong criticism from Ritchie (see den Otter, 1996, pp 130-3). His acceptance of state intervention placed him close to a New Liberal position, and a variant of idealist thought. In certain respects, though, he must be counted an outsider.

Kidd declared that it

> must ever remain an incalculable loss to English science and English philosophy, that the author of the *Synthetic Philosophy* did not undertake his great task later in the

nineteenth century. As time goes on, it will be clearer what the nature of that loss has been. It will be perceived that the conception of his work was practically complete before his intellect had any opportunity of realising the full transforming effect in the higher regions of thought, and, more particularly, in the department of sociology, of that development of biological science which began with Darwin, which is still in full progress, and to which Professor Weissman has recently made the most notable contributions. (1894, p 87)

Nevertheless, Kidd's own contribution on this front failed to convince critics such as Ritchie that it was a coherent application of biological science to social and ethical thought.

Chapter Three – Free agent or 'conscious automaton'?

[1] The selectionist paradigm of explanation in social science refers to the application of Darwin's theory of variations being produced, only some of which survive a struggle for existence, and hence being those that are 'naturally selected'. By this mechanism new species could originate. There is considerable and complex debate about how that biological theory can most coherently be worked through in the context of understanding social life, in which people purposefully strive to achieve ends. Neither Darwin's theory itself, nor its use in social science, in any way requires that what survives counts as in any *moral* sense the 'fittest'. Nor do the purposes behind novelty in social life directly guarantee survival, that outcome reflects the openness of society to the novelty, and its suitability to circumstances. No assumptions about design or direction are made. However, Spencer's in fact very different emphasis on change as produced by the inheritance of acquired characteristics, acquired through progressive adaptation to circumstances, with those not adapting perishing, is often confused with Darwinian selectionism. Spencer's mechanism was discredited during his lifetime as one outcome of Darwin's work. Darwin died in 1882 but subsequent work in what we would call genetics by August Weismann and Gregor Mendel vindicated his theory. However, the phrase 'survival of the fittest' (Spencer's) is so indiscriminately used as to disguise the difference. Hence clarifying Spencer's position may help to free attempts to relate Darwinian selectionism to understanding social life from some of the misconceptions associated with it. Spencer

tended to present some (government) actions as 'interfering' with the process of 'adaptation'; applying selectionism to social life would not permit this contrast since *whatever* happens to be produced or extinguished in social life is in the appropriate non-evaluative sense 'natural'.

[2] Weinstein incorrectly gives 'will' (1998, p 8).

[3] On the distinctions being made here relating to 'nature' see Mill, 1965, pp 400-1, and also Webb, 1926, pp 292-3. Mill's essay was completed in 1854, but not published until 1874.

Chapter Four – The case of older people

[1] It should be noted that this chapter deals with one of two separate stories in the period in question in respect of older people: a theoretically based literature on the care of older people, and a story about cash provision – pensions (on which in general see Macnicol, 1998). The two seem to overlap seldom, although the idea of pensions triggered reflection on the practices of the poor law in respect of indoor and outdoor relief to the 'deserving' aged poor. However, the attitudes of Spencer and the two reports to pensions provided by the state are noted below as appropriate. Beatrice Webb's husband was not a member of the commission, though he assisted in the preparation of the minority report.

[2] Spencer here is not concerned with older people whose children may have predeceased them, or with those who are childless. The beneficence that he believes can be demanded of non-relatives in such circumstances is discussed later in Chapter Six.

[3] Since Spencer proscribed the state from acting other than to protect justice he opposed schemes for old-age pensions to be a responsibility of the state. In 1878 the Rev. W.L. Blackley had published 'National insurance: a cheap, practical and popular means of abolishing poor rates' that required 'all young persons from the age of eighteen to twenty-one to contribute to a fund, State-collected and State-secured, a sufficient amount to entitle each contributor, when physically unable to earn wages, to a weekly sick pay of 8s. per week and to an old age pension of 4s. per week' (Blackley, 1892, p 382). The scheme was to be a compulsory and universal one with the post office as the agency and paying the pension at the age of 70.

Spencer flayed it in 1884: 'Habits of improvidence having for generations been cultivated by the Poor Law, and the improvident enabled to multiply, the evils produced by compulsory charity are now proposed to be met by compulsory insurance' (1884, p 90). H.M. Lynd described Blackley as a follower of Spencer (1968, p 73), but the passages given in support of this claim are unconvincing. I know of no passage in Blackley's writings specifically acknowledging a debt to Spencer, or displaying such a debt.

[4] Blackley's pension proposal had continued to be topical. It was scrutinised by a parliamentary committee in 1885-6 and 1887 that decided against its establishment. Competing schemes duly surfaced, a voluntary state-subsidised pension in association with friendly societies (advocated by Chamberlain) and a non-contributory state-funded pension (for those over 65, advocated by Charles Booth). Eventually the non-contributory, state-funded model of provision won the day in the form of the means-tested benefit introduced by the 1908 Old Age Pension Act associated with Lloyd George. In this form pensions were supported by Sidney and Beatrice Webb, but opposed not only by the Individualists but by Helen and Bernard Bosanquet, Octavia Hill and C. S. Loch within the context of their leadership of the COS (Hill and Loch were also associated with the majority report). It may be added that Meadowcroft (1995) notes 'expediency', 'gratitude' and 'national charity' as concepts that the Conservative Hugh Cecil invoked in his acceptance of pensions.

[5] The Irish reports record notable majority exasperation with the minority. In a memorandum from the Bishop of Ross and Sir Henry Robinson minority criticisms on the ground of the Irish majority report being the result of an inquiry as hasty and perfunctory as that which they describe as Sir George Nicholls' 'celebrated scamper' through Ireland in 1837 are roundly rejected.

> This criticism comes somewhat badly when accompanied by an alternative scheme prepared by four members of the Commission, two of whom did not visit Ireland at all, while the time spent in the country by the only member who accompanied the Commissioners on their visits was even shorter than that occupied by Sir George Nicholls' visit, which, on account of its brevity, has called forth such a severe condemnation from the Minority. (Poor Law Report (Ireland), 1909, p 87)

[6] Harrison (2000, p 35) notes the particular influence of 'Roman Collectivism' rather than 'Greek Individualism' on Sidney Webb in the 1880s. Roman law's systematic jurisprudence promoted 'national welfare at any cost of individual sacrifice'.

[7] A refrain repeated by a further idealist philosopher, J. H. Muirhead in 1939, ironically in the annual Herbert Spencer Lecture of that year entitled 'The man versus the state as a present issue', one of a series of lectures instituted after his death. According to Muirhead, Spencer's conception

> both of the Individual, and the State, was inherited from a philosophy and from circumstances which by the time of his book with the above title was published in 1884 may be said to have no longer existed except as a survival. The freedom of the individual was no longer conceived of as merely freedom from State-control. State-action was no longer conceived of as 'interference with natural liberty', but as itself a natural attempt to limit the excesses of such liberty in the interest of the physical and moral welfare, and so of a truer kind of freedom, in the mass of the people. (1939, p 5)

Chapter Five – Social policy and idealist versus non-idealist thought

[1] Idealists, according to Quinton, were ready to endorse

> a substantial degree of state regulation of the conditions of work of the industrial population, Herbert Spencer, who defended unrestricted economic competition on evolutionary grounds, was a direct object of Green's polemics and the political theory of Green and his followers is certainly one of the sources of present-day assumptions about the proper sphere of state activity, of the conception of the welfare state introduced into political practice by the Labour party but now widely embraced by all but the most unbending adherents of inalienable natural rights. (1972, p 132)

[2] It seems appropriate here to note also the case of Morris Ginsberg (1889-1970) who, as professor of sociology at the London School of

Economics (in succession to Hobhouse) 'carried the torch for Hobhouse into the 1950s' in Bob Pinker's view (personal communication). Certainly Ginsberg (1947) wrote in a notably sympathetic manner about Hobhouse's humanitarianism and intellectual orientation, indicating his debts to idealist thought. Ginsberg's own interests often seem indebted to an idealist perspective with moral and sociological interests entwined, and his 'The individual and society' of 1954 retains a place for 'a social or common good ... distinguishable from the good of individuals' (1954, p 66).

[3] W.H. Mallock (1849-1923) was a writer known best for his satirical *The new republic* of 1877. He was a critic of socialist theory and defended conservatism. In Eccleshall's view (1990, p 157) Mallock was 'the most original and prolific Tory publicist between 1880 and 1920'. In his *Aristocracy and evolution* he criticised Spencer for neglecting the role of great men as innovators in social evolution. However, Mallock read Spencer through the distorting lens of Benjamin Kidd, who had made societies as wholes, rather than in terms of their component individuals, the key to understanding social evolution. Indeed, in times of external aggression there was for Spencer a warrant for a society to adopt a 'militant' or coercive form of internal organisation at the expense of liberty for individuals. However, the difference between Spencer and Mallock was thus less significant than between Spencer and Kidd: Kidd saw social evolution as leading to *nationally organised* competition (and conquest), with individuals as means rather than ends in thinking of society, and had thus lost sight of his fundamental libertarian analysis. There had been no hiatus between Spencerian social evolution and liberty of the kind Mallock contended (see Duncan, 1911, pp 407-9).

[4] Through Spencer, Herbert met Beatrice Potter in 1888, before she had encountered Sidney Webb. Bringing her ponies, she rode with Herbert at his home in the New Forest and enjoyed his hospitality. They also met the following year in Scotland and planned a joint Individualist novel, 'Looking forward'. However, the cooperation bore no fruit (see Hutchinson Harris, 1943, pp 287-8). In 1890 she met Webb and her social thought crystallised into socialism, placing her and Herbert at loggerheads over social philosophy. Her diary records that she believed Herbert intended to propose marriage (see Harrison, 2000, p 142).

[5] Note that at this point Herbert has moved from essentially political arguments in favour of individualism to more fundamental arguments

about how social life is made up. A careful analysis of the many contexts in which 'individualism' occurs is Lukes (1973), who in particular distinguishes political individualism from methodological individualism.

[6] According to Letwin, 'Green's teaching insisted too much on the importance and reality of the individual to allow any simple reconciliation of individual with social ends'. Bernard Bosanquet went further by suggesting that individual minds should be moulded to public purpose, because he believed that 'every man possessed individuality only as part of a whole, and only to the degree that he identified himself with the "real will" of the individual, that is, with his will to fulfil his highest capacities as a rational being. It was not something external to the individual, but his higher self' (1965, pp 228-9).

[7] Samuel (1870-1963) was responsible for the 1907 Probation of Offenders Act and the 1908 Children Act, which gave children a range of legal protections. He worked with John Maynard Keynes and others on the Liberal 'Yellow book' of 1928, *Britain's industrial future*. In philosophy he is best known for *Belief and action* of 1937.

[8] Morley (1836-1923) in fact was on cordial terms with Spencer and in fundamental agreement with him as a free-thinker and over many matters of politics, including opposition to militarism, state intervention and ecclesiastical privileges. In 1908 (while in the Liberal cabinet as secretary of state at the India Office) he commented (1917, vol II, p 255), 'I'd rather have parliamentary rule with all its faults than Prussian bureaucracy' (with which Bosanquet's ideas were later sometimes associated). Morley combined journalism with a parliamentary career editing the influential *Fortnightly Review* and *Pall Mall Gazette*. In the autumn of 1903, shortly before Spencer died, Morley had accepted his invitation to give an address at his cremation. In the event Morley was in Palermo and unavailable: the day of the funeral found him (1917, vol I, p 116) 'pondering ... upon an indefatigable intellect, an iron love of truth, a pure and scrupulous conscience, a spirit of loyal and beneficent intention, a noble passion for knowledge and systematic thought'.

[9] The reference is to B.S. Rowntree's *Poverty: A study of town life*, first published in 1901. One of its key achievements was to demonstrate that wage levels in York were often below the level necessary to maintain

minimum physical efficiency, that is to say, to avoid what he called 'primary poverty' (51.96% of people in primary poverty were poor for that reason). No amount of change in habits of spending could lift a family in these circumstances out of poverty. Rowntree largely refrained from explicit political or theoretical comment, though he concluded the main part of his book with the claim that the 'dark shadow of the Malthusian philosophy has passed away, and no view of the ultimate scheme of things would now be accepted under which multitudes of men and women are doomed by inevitable law to a struggle for existence so severe as necessarily to cripple or destroy the higher parts of their nature' (1902, p 305). The precise meaning of Rowntree's concept of 'secondary' poverty and its contribution to the figure of 27.84% of the total percentage of poverty in York given by him has been discussed by Williams (1981, ch 9) and, without reference to Williams, Veit-Wilson (1986) and Townsend (1986).

Chapter Six – Idealist thought, social policy and the rediscovery of informal care

[1] It is beyond dispute that feminist analysis has done a great deal to promote research and political interest in informal care. However, as the evidence cited here would suggest, to say that the 'naming of the informal sector arose out of "second wave feminism" – that is, the feminism of the late 1960s and early 1970s' (Ungerson, 1998, p 170) is to risk two weaknesses in analysis. The first is that, as the discussion so far shows, academics who would not be conventionally described as feminist were also involved. The second and main one is that, as my subsequent analysis is intended to show, it was non-idealist modes of thinking about welfare matters, whether feminist or not, that were crucial in opening up informal care as a topic for research.

[2] Abrams, after all, was primarily a sociologist, as was Mayer, while Pinker was explicitly drawing on sociological theory to make his points. Townsend (1976) is perhaps best understood as having moved from sociology to social policy; early work at the Institute of Community Studies (Townsend, 1963) was a sociology of the family life of old people. However, chapters 14 and 15 reviewed how social policy might support informal care. These comments do not appear to have been taken up by social policy writers at the time. On sociology and social administration and policy as subjects and their logical relationships, see Offer (1990).

[3] There were close links to sympathetic Labour governments (see Hall, 1976, on the case of Titmuss).

[4] Quoting from Pinker (1971, p 175), Titmuss wrote that it was not necessarily true 'that "Public services may have a greater propensity to stigmatise." Greater than what? Private enterprise? Private markets? We are not told. What may be true is that "Public services have a greater propensity to be criticised" …' (1974, pp 45-6). For a recent discussion of the conception of agency in Titmuss, especially his early writings, see Welshman, 2003.

[5] It may be noted that although Titmuss was an active member of the Eugenics Society for many years, and addressed it on occasion, this fact, in the light of the nature of its membership, both radical and conservative, furnishes no reason, as Freeden (1979) has observed, to deny such a view of his work (see also Thane, 1990).

Chapter Eight – Epilogue

[1] Poplarism is particularly associated with George Lansbury as a Poplar guardian. He was briefly imprisoned in a campaign to equalise the burden of poor relief over London. His socialism was seen as 'sentimental' by Beatrice Webb (1948, p 337) – Lansbury had served alongside her on the 1905-9 royal commission and supported the minority report. He was leader of the Parliamentary Labour Party from 1931 to 1935.

[2] Macmurray was born in 1891 near Dumfries and died in Edinburgh in 1976. Between 1928 and 1958 he held chairs in philosophy, first in London at University College and then, from 1944, at the University of Edinburgh. Much of his career as a broadcaster and moral philosopher was spent in Edinburgh. Two significant books were *The self as agent* (1957) and *Persons in relation* (1961). Christian thought and Marxist ideas both flowed into Macmurray's writings, which rejected a Cartesian dualism between mind and body and emphasized agency in the world. There is currently a revival of interest in his work, reflected in Fergusson and Dower, 2001; and Costello, 2002.

[3] An earlier version of Le Grand's analysis of agency and motivation was presented in Le Grand, 1997.

References

Abrams, P. (1978) 'Community care', in J. Barnes and N. Connelly (eds) *Social care research*, London: Bedford Square Press, pp 78-99.

Acheson, N. (1995) 'A partnership of dilemmas and contradictions: unresolved issues in government-voluntary sector relations', in N. Acheson and A. Williamson (eds) *Voluntary action and social policy in Northern Ireland*, Aldershot: Avebury, pp 33-45.

Akenson, D. (1981) *A protestant in purgatory*, Hamden, CT: Archon.

Allen, G. (1904) 'Personal reminiscences of Herbert Spencer', *Forum*, pp 610-628.

Allsop, J. (1995) *Health policy and the NHS*, London: Longman.

Anderson, D. (ed) (1980) *The ignorance of social intervention*, London: Croom Helm.

Anderson, D. (1985) 'How the Tories can show they care', *The Times*, 13 February.

Antrim County Welfare Committee (1949) *Initial proposals for the performance of functions under the Welfare Services Act (NI)*, Belfast: Antrim County Welfare Committee.

Ashford, D. (1986) *The emergence of the welfare states*, Oxford: Blackwell.

Avineri, S. (ed) (1972) *Marx's socialism*, New York: Lieber-Atherton.

Bamford, T. (1990) *The future of social work*, Basingstoke: Macmillan.

Barclay Report (1982) *Social workers: Their role and tasks*, London: Bedford Square Press.

Barnett, C. (1986) *The audit of war*, London: Macmillan.

Barry, F.R. (1960) *Asking the right questions*, London: Hodder and Stoughton.

Barry, N. (1990) *Welfare*, Milton Keynes: Open University Press.

Barton, R. (1990) '"An influential set of chaps": the X-club and Royal Society politics 1864-85', *British Journal for the History of Science*, vol 23, pp 53-81.

Bennett, A. (1906) *Sacred and profane love*, Leipzig: Tauchnitz.

Bennett, A. (1971) *The journals*, Harmondsworth: Penguin.

Betjeman, J. (1960) *Summoned by bells*, London: John Murray.

Beveridge, J. (1954) *Beveridge and his plan*, London: Hodder and Stoughton.

Beveridge, W. (1942) *Social insurance and allied services*, Cmd 6404, London: HMSO.

Beveridge, W. (1943) *The pillars of security*, London: Allen and Unwin.

Beveridge, W. (1948) *Voluntary action*, London: Allen and Unwin.

Bevir, M. and O'Brien, D. (2003) 'From Idealism to Communitarianism: the inheritance and legacy of John Macmurray', *History of Political Thought*, vol 24, no 2, pp 304-29.

Bicheno, J.E. (1824) *An inquiry into the poor laws: Chiefly with a view to examine them as a scheme of national benevolence, and to elucidate their political economy*, London: Hunter.

Bicheno, J.E. (1830) *Ireland, and its economy*, London: John Murray.

Bicheno, J.E. (1836) 'Remarks on evidence', in *Third report of the commissioners for inquiring into the condition of the poorer classes in Ireland*, Appendix H, Part 2, London: HMSO.

Blackley, W.L. (1878) 'National insurance: a cheap practical and popular means of abolishing poor rates', *Nineteenth Century*, November, pp 834-57.

Blackley, W.L. (1892) 'Mr Chamberlain's pension scheme', *Contemporary Review*, March, pp 382-96.

Blair, T. (1994) *Socialism*, Fabian pamphlet 565, London: Fabian Society.

Bosanquet, B. (1885) 'Socialism and natural selection', in Boucher (1997), pp 50-67.

Bosanquet, B. (1889) 'Review of T. Mackay, *The English poor*', *Charity Organisation Review*, vol 5, September, pp 460-6.

Bosanquet, B. (ed) (1895) *Aspects of the social problem*, London: Macmillan.

Bosanquet, B. (1910) 'Charity organisation and the majority', *International Journal of Ethics*, vol 20, pp 395-408.

Bosanquet, H. and B. (1897) 'Charity organisation: a reply', *Contemporary Review*, vol 71, pp 112-16.

Boucher, D. (ed) (1997) *The British Idealists*, Cambridge: Cambridge University Press.

Boucher, D. and Vincent, A. (1993) *A radical Hegelian: The social and political thought of Henry James*, Cardiff: Wales University Press and New York: St Martin's Press.

Brent, R. (1987) *Liberal anglican politics: Whiggery, religion and reform 1830-1841*, Oxford: Clarendon Press.

Brenton, M. (1985) *The voluntary sector in British social services*, London: Longman.

Brewer, C. and Lait, J. (1980) *Can social work survive?* London: Temple Smith.

Briggs, A. (1961) *A study of the work of Seebohm Rowntree*, London: Longman.

Brown, G. (2001) 'Let the people look after themselves', *The Times*, 11 January.

Brown, J. (1971) 'The poor law commission and the 1905 Unemployed Workmen's Act', *Bulletin of the Institute of Historical Research*, vol 44, pp 318-23.

Brown, K.D. (1971a) 'The appointment of the 1905 poor law commission – a rejoinder', *Bulletin of the Institute of Historical Research*, vol 44, pp 315-18.

Brown, K.D. (1971b) 'Conflict in early British welfare policy: the case of the Unemployed Workmen's Bill of 1905', *Journal of Modern History*, vol 43, pp 615-29.

Bruce, M. (1968) *The coming of the welfare state* (3rd edn), London: Batsford.

Brundage, A. (1978) *The making of the new poor law*, London: Hutchinson.

Bulmer, M. (1985) 'The rejuvenation of community studies', *The Sociological Review*, vol 33, no 3, pp 430-48.

Bulmer, M. (1986) *Neighbours: The work of Philip Abrams*, Cambridge: Cambridge University Press.

Bulmer, M. (1987) *The social basis of community care*, London: Allen and Unwin.

Burke, H. (1987) *The people and the poor law in 19th century Ireland*, Dublin: Workers Education Board.

Cairnes, J.E. (1875) 'Mr Spencer on social evolution', *Fortnightly Review*, reprinted in Offer (ed) (2000), vol III, pp 125-145.

Carrier, J. and Kendall, I. (1986) 'Categories, categorizations and the political economy of welfare', *Journal of Social Policy*, vol 15, no 3, pp 315-35.

Cecil, R., Offer, J. and St Leger, F. (1987) *Informal welfare: A sociological study of care in Northern Ireland*, Aldershot: Gower, and Vermont: Brookfield.

Chadwick, E. (1842) *Report to Her Majesty's Principal Secretary of State for the Home Department from the Poor Law Commissioners on an inquiry into the sanitary conditions of the labouring population of Great Britain*, London: HMSO (reprinted by Edinburgh University Press, 1965).

Cohen, P. (1968) *Modern social theory*, London: Heinemann.

Collingwood, R.G. (1944) *An autobiography*, Harmondsworth, Penguin.

Collini, S. (1976) 'Hobhouse, Bosanquet and the state: philosophical idealism and political argument in England 1880-1918', *Past and Present*, no 72, pp 86-111.

Collini, S. (1978) 'Sociology and idealism in Britain, 1880-1918', *European Journal of Sociology*, vol 19, pp 3-30.

Collini, S. (1979) *Liberalism and sociology*, Cambridge: Cambridge University Press.

Corning, P.A. (1982) 'Durkheim and Spencer', *British Journal of Sociology*, vol 33, no 3, pp 359-82.

Costello, J. E. (2002) *John Macmurray: A biography*, Edinburgh: Floris.

Cross, J.W. (1885) *George Eliot's life as related in her letters and journals*, 3 vols, Edinburgh and London: Blackwood.

Crowther, M.A. (1983) *The workhouse system 1834-1929*, London: Methuen.

Curtis Report (1946) *Report of the care of children committee*, Cmd 6922, London: HMSO.

Darwin, C. (1859) *On the origin of species by means of natural selection*, London: John Murray.

Davies, B. (1968) *Social needs and resources in local services*, London: Michael Joseph.

Deacon, A. (1981) 'Thank you God for the means test man', *New Society*, vol 25, June, pp 519-20.

Deacon, A. (1982) 'An end to the means test: social security and the Attlee government', *Journal of Social Policy*, vol 11, no 3, pp 289-306.

den Otter, S. (1996) *British idealism and social explanation*, Oxford: Clarendon Press.

Digby, A. (1978), *Pauper palaces*, London: Routledge and Kegan Paul.

Dugdale, B.E.D. (1939) *Arthur James Balfour*, London: Hutchinson.

Duncan, D. (ed) (1911) *The life and letters of Herbert Spencer*, London: Williams and Norgate.

Dunkley, P. (1982) *The crisis of the old poor law in England 1795-1834*, New York: Garland.

Eccleshall, R. (1990), *English conservativism since the Reformation*, London: Unwin Hyman.

Etzioni, A. (2000) 'The road to the good society', *New Statesman*, 15 May, pp 25-7.

Fergusson, D. and Dower, N. (eds) (2001) *John Macmurray: Critical perspectives*, New York: Peter Lang.

Field, F. (1972) 'A pressure group for the poor', in Bull, D. (ed) *Family poverty* (2nd edn), London: Duckworth, pp 145-57.

Field, J. (2003) *Social capital*, London: Routledge.

Finch, J. and Mason, J. (1990) 'Filial obligations and kin support for elderly people', *Ageing and Society*, vol 10, no 2, pp 151-78.

Finch, J. and Mason, J. (1993) *Negotiating family responsibilities*, London: Routledge.

Finer, S.E. (1952) *The life and times of Sir Edwin Chadwick*, London: Methuen.

Finlayson, G. (1994) *Citizen, state and social welfare in Britain, 1830-1990*, Oxford: Clarendon Press.

Fiske, J. (1894) *Life and letters of Edward Livingston Youmans*, London: Williams and Norgate.

Flew, A. (1967) *Evolutionary ethics*, London: Macmillan.

Flew, A. (1981) *The politics of Procrustes*, London: Temple Smith.

Flew, A. (1983) 'Good Samaritans become Procrusteans', in C. Jones and J. Stevenson (eds) *The year book of social policy in Britain 1982*, London: Routledge and Kegan Paul, pp 13-31.

Flew, A. (1985) 'Do-gooders doing no good?', in M. Brenton and C. Jones (eds) *The year book of social policy in Britain 1984-5*, London: Routledge and Kegan Paul, pp 225-40.

Forder, A. (1974) *Concepts in social administration*, London: Routledge and Kegan Paul.

Frankenberg, R.J. (1966) *Communities in Britain*, Harmondsworth: Penguin.

Fraser, D. (2003) *The evolution of the British welfare state* (3rd edn), London and Basingstoke: Macmillan (first published 1973).

Freeden, M. (1978) *The new liberalism*, Oxford: Clarendon Press.

Freeden, M. (1979) 'Eugenics and progressive thought: a study in ideological affinity', *Historical Journal*, vol 22, pp 645-71.

Fuller, S. (1995) 'Is there life for sociological theory after the sociology of scientific knowledge?', *Sociology*, vol 29, no 1, pp 159-66.

George, V. and Wilding, P. (1985) *Ideology and social welfare*, London: Routledge.

George, V. and Wilding, P. (1993) *Welfare and ideology*, Hemel Hempstead: Harvester/Wheatsheaf.

Giddens, A. (1971) *Capitalism and modern social theory*, London: Hutchinson.

Gilbert, B.B. (1966a) *The evolution of national insurance in Great Britain*, London: Michael Joseph.

Gilbert, B.B. (1966b), 'Winston Churchill versus the Webbs: the origins of British unemployment insurance', *American Historical Review*, vol 71, no 3, pp 846-62.

Gilbert, B.B. (1970) *British social policy 1914-1939*, London: Batsford.

Ginsberg, M. (1947) 'The contribution of Professor Hobhouse to philosophy and sociology', in M. Ginsberg (ed) *Essays in sociology and social philosophy*, vol 2, London: Heinemann.

Ginsberg, M. (1954) 'The individual and society', in M. Ginsberg (ed) *Essays in sociology and social philosophy*, Harmondsworth: Penguin, 1968.

Ginsburg, N. (1979) *Class, capital and social policy*, London: Macmillan.

Glennerster, H. (1990) 'Social policy since the Second World War', in J. Hills (ed), *The state of welfare*, Oxford: Clarendon Press.

Gough, I. (1979) *The political economy of the welfare State*, London: Macmillan.

Graham, H. (1991) 'The informal sector of welfare: a crisis in caring?', *Social Science and Medicine*, vol 32, no 4, pp 507-15.

Graves, C.L. (1926) *Hubert Parry: His life and works* (2 vols), London: Macmillan.

Gray, J. (1982) 'Spencer on the ethics of liberty and the limits of state interference', *History of Political Thought*, vol 3, no 3, reprinted in Offer (ed) (2000), vol IV, pp 234-249.

Gray, J. (1995) *Liberalism* (2nd edn), Buckingham: Open University Press.

Gray, T.S. (1981) 'Herbert Spencer's theory of social justice – desert or entitlement?', *History of Political Thought*, vol 2, no 1, pp 161-86.

Gray, T.S. (1996) *The political philosophy of Herbert Spencer: Individualism and organicism*, Aldershot: Avebury.

Green, D. (1993) *Reinventing civil society*, London: Institute of Economic Affairs.

Green, D. (1996) *Community without politics*, London: Institute of Economic Affairs.

Green, T.H. (1883/2003) *Prolegomena to ethics*, Oxford: Clarendon Press.

Greenleaf, W.H. (1983) *The British political tradition*, vol 2: *The ideological heritage*, London: Routledge.

Griffiths Report (1988) *Community care: Agenda for action*, London: HMSO.

Hadley, R. and Hatch, S. (1981) *Social welfare and the failure of the state*, London: Allen and Unwin.

Haggard, R.F. (2001) *The persistence of Victorian liberalism: The politics of social reform in Britain 1870-1900*, Westport, CT, and London: Garland.

Hall, M.P. and Howes, I.V. (1965) *The church in social work*, London: Routledge.

Hall, P. (1976) *Reforming the welfare: The politics of change in the personal social services*, London: Heinemann.

Harris, J. (1982) 'The partnership of the Webbs', *New Society*, 25 November, pp 340-3.

Harris, J. (1989) 'The Webbs, the Charity Organisation Society and the Ratan Tata Foundation: social policy from the perspective of 1912', in M. Bulmer, J. Lewis and D. Piachaud (eds) *The goals of social policy*, London: Unwin Hyman, pp 27-63.

Harris, J. (1990) 'Enterprise and welfare states: a comparative perspective', *Transactions of the Royal Historical Society*, vol 40, pp 175-95.

Harris, J. (1992) 'Political thought and the welfare state 1870-1940: an intellectual framework for British social policy', *Past and Present*, no 135, pp 116-41.

Harris, J. (1993) *Private lives, public spirit: A social history of Britain, 1870-1914*, Oxford: Oxford University Press.

Harris, J. (2002) 'From poor law to welfare state? A European perspective', in D. Winch and P. K. O'Brien (eds) *The political economy of British historical experiences 1688-1914*, Oxford: Oxford University Press, pp 409-38.

Harrison, R.J. (2000) *The life and times of Sidney and Beatrice Webb 1858-1905*, Basingstoke and London: Macmillan.

Hay, J.R. (1975) *The origins of the Liberal welfare reforms, 1906-1914*, London and Basingstoke: Macmillan.

Hay, J.R. (1978) 'Employers' attitudes to social policy and the concept of social control, 1900-1920', in P. Thane (ed) *The origins of British social policy*, London: Croom Helm, pp 107-25.

Hennock, E.P. (1987) *British social policy and German precedents: The case of social insurance 1880-1914*, Oxford: Clarendon Press.

Heraud, B.J. (1970) *Sociology and social work*, Oxford: Pergamon.

Herbert, A. (1898a) 'A voluntaryist appeal', *The Humanitarian*, vol 12, pp 313-29.

Herbert, A. (1898b) 'Salvation by force', *The Humanitarian*, vol 13, pp 265-72.

Herbert, A. (1899) 'Lost in the region of phrases', *The Humanitarian*, vol 14, pp 320-30.

Herbert, A. (1908) *The voluntaryist creed*, London: Oxford University Press.

Herbert, A. (1996) 'A voluntaryist appeal', 'Salvation by force' and 'Lost in the region of phrases', in M. Taylor (ed) *Herbert Spencer and the limits of the state*, Bristol: Thoemmes Press, pp 221-39 and pp 249-69.

Heron, E. and Dwyer, P. (1999) 'Doing the right thing: labour's attempt to forge a new welfare deal between the individual and the state', *Social Policy and Administration*, vol 33, no 1, pp 91-104.

Hewison, R. (1995) *Culture and consensus*, London: Methuen.

Hewitt, M. (1991) 'New labour, human nature and welfare reform', in R. Sykes, C. Bochel and N. Ellison (eds) *Social Policy Review 13*, Bristol: The Policy Press.

Hilton, B. (1988) *The age of atonement*, Oxford: Clarendon Press.

Himmelfarb, G. (1995) *The de-moralization of society*, London: Institute of Economic Affairs.

Hiskes, R.P. (1983) 'Spencer and the liberal idea of community', *Review of Politics*, vol 45, pp 595-609, reprinted in Offer (2000) vol 3, pp 44-55.

HMSO (1989) *Caring for people*, Cm 849, London: HMSO.

Hobhouse, L.T. (1911a) *Social evolution and political theory*, New York: Columbia University Press.

Hobhouse, L.T. (1911b) *Liberalism*, London: Williams and Norgate.

Hobson, J.A. (1896) 'The social philosophy of charity organisation', *Contemporary Review*, vol 70, pp 710-27.

Hobson, J.A. (1898) 'Rich man's anarchism', *The Humanitarian*, vol 12, pp 391-7.

Hobson, J.A. (1996a) *The social problem*, Bristol, Thoemmes Press.

Hobson, J.A. (1996b) 'Rich man's anarchism', in M. Taylor (ed) *Herbert Spencer and the limits of the state*, Bristol: Thoemmes Press, pp 240-8,

House of Commons, Social Services Committee (1990) *Community care: Carers*, Fifth Report, HC410, London: HMSO.

Hudson, W.H. (1904) 'Herbert Spencer: a character study', *Fortnightly Review*, vol 75, reprinted in Offer (ed) (2000), vol I, pp 5-11.

Hughes, K. (1998) *George Eliot: The last Victorian*, London: Fourth Estate.

Humphreys, R. (1995) *Sin, organized charity and the poor law in Victorian England*, London: Macmillan.

Hutchinson Harris, S. (1943) *Auberon Herbert: Crusader for liberty*, London: Williams and Norgate.

Hutton, W. (1996) *The state we're in*, London: Vintage.

Hyndman, H.M. (1884) *Socialism and slavery*, London: Modern Press, reprinted in Offer (2000, vol 4, ch 8).

Jenkins, R. (2001) *Churchill*, London: Macmillan.

Jensen, J.V. (1970) 'The X club: fraternity of Victorian scientists', *British Journal for the History of Science*, vol 5, pp 63-72.

Jones, H. (1883) 'The social organism', in D. Boucher (1997), pp 3-29.

Jones, H. (1910) *The working faith of the social reformer and other essays*, London: Macmillan.

Jones, R.A. (1974) 'Durkheim's response to Spencer', *Sociological Quarterly*, vol 15, pp 341-58.

Jones, R.A. (1975) 'Durkheim in context: a reply to Perrin', *Sociological Quarterly*, vol 16, pp 551-9.

Kidd, B. (1894) *Social evolution*, London: Macmillan.

Kidd, B. (1902) *Principles of Western civilisation*, London: Macmillan.

Kidd, B. (1918) *The science of power*, London: Methuen.

Landmark Trust (1999) *The Landmark Trust handbook*, Maidenhead: Landmark Trust.

Lansley, J. (1996) 'Membership participation and ideology in large voluntary organisations: the case of the National Trust', *Voluntas*, vol 7, no 3, pp 221-40.

Le Grand, J. (1997) 'Knights, knaves or pawns? Human behaviour and social policy', *Journal of Social Policy*, vol 26, no 2, pp 149-69.

Le Grand, J. (2003) *Motivation, agency and public policy*, Oxford: Oxford University Press.

Lees, L.H. (1998) *The solidarities of strangers*, Cambridge: Cambridge University Press.

Letwin, S. (1965) *The pursuit of certainty*, London: Cambridge University Press.

Levy, S.L. (1970) *Nassau W. Senior, 1790-1864*, Newton Abbot: David and Charles.

Lewis, G.C. (1837) *Remarks on the third report of the Irish poor inquiry commissioners*, London: HMSO.

Lewis, G.F. (ed) (1870) *Letters of Sir George Cornewall Lewis*, London: Longman, Green.

Lewis, J. (1995) *The voluntary sector, the state and social work in Britain*, Aldershot: Edward Elgar.

Lewis, J. (1999) 'Reviewing the relationship between the voluntary sector and the state in Britain in the 1990s', *Voluntas*, vol 10, no 3, pp 255-70.

Lewis, J. and Meredith, B. (1988) *Daughters who care*, London: Routledge.

Lindsay, A.D. (1935a) 'Letter: A. D. Lindsay to Harrod, 13 February, no. 430', in D. Besomi (ed) *The collected interwar papers and correspondence of Roy Harrod*, 3 vols, Cheltenham: Edward Elgar.

Lindsay, A.D. (1935b) 'Letter of A.D. Lindsay to Harrod', 14 February, no 431, in D. Besomi (ed) *The collected interwar papers and correspondence of Roy Harrod*, 3 vols, Cheltenham: Edward Elgar.

Linton, L. (1984) 'Professor Henry Drummond's discovery', *Fortnightly Review*, vol 56, Sept, pp 448-57.

London, J. (1910) *Martin Eden*, London: Heinemann.

Low, E. (2000) 'Class and the conceptualisation of citizenship in twentieth-century Britain', *History of Political Thought*, vol 21, no 1, pp 114-31.

Lowe, R. (1993) *The welfare state in Britain since 1945*, Basingstoke and London: Macmillan.

Lukes, S. (1973) *Individualism*, Oxford: Basil Blackwell.

Lynd, H.M. (1968) *England in the eighteen eighties*, London: Cass.

McBriar, A. M. (1987) *An Edwardian mixed doubles: The Bosanquets versus the Webbs*, Oxford: Clarendon Press.

McGregor, O. R. and Rowntree, G. (1968) 'The family', in A. V. S. Lochhead (ed) *A reader in social administration*, London: Constable, pp 185-215.

MacIntyre, A. (1965) *The liberator: Daniel O'Connor and the Irish Party, 1830-1847*, London: Hamish Hamilton.

MacIntyre, A. (1967) *A short history of ethics*, London: Routledge and Kegan Paul.

Mack, E. (1978) 'Voluntaryism: the political thought of Auberon Herbert', *Journal of Libertarian Studies*, vol 2, no 4, pp 299-309.

Mackay, T. (1889) *The English poor*, London: John Murray.

Mackay, T. (ed) (1891a) *A plea for liberty*, London: John Murray.

Mackay, T. (1891b) 'The interest of the working class in the poor law', in *Proceedings of the Poor Law Conference for the South East District*, London: Knight.

Macmillan, H. (1934) *Reconstruction*, London: Macmillan.

Macmillan, H. (1938) *The middle way*, London: Macmillan.

Macnicol, J. (1987) 'In pursuit of the underclass', *Journal of Social Policy*, vol 16, no 3, pp 293-318.

Macnicol, J. (1998) *The politics of retirement in Britain, 1878-1948*, Cambridge: Cambridge University Press.

Mallock, W.H. (1882) 'The functions of wealth', *Contemporary Review*, vol 41, pp 195-220.

Malthus, T.R. (1798) *An essay on the principle of population*, reprinted in A. Flew (ed) (1970) *Malthus: An essay on the principle of population*, Harmondsworth: Penguin.

Mandler, P. (1990) 'Tories and paupers: Christian political economics and the making of the new poor law', *Historical Journal*, vol 33, pp 81-105.

Marshall, A. (1925) *Memorials of Alfred Marshall*, ed A.C. Pigou, London: Macmillan.

Marsland, D. (1996) *Welfare or welfare state?*, Basingstoke: Macmillan.

Marx, K. (1971) *Early texts*, translated and edited by D. McClellan, Oxford: Basil Blackwell.

Mayer, J. and Timms, N. (1970) *The client speaks*, London: Routledge and Kegan Paul.

Meadowcroft, J. (1995) *Conceptualizing the state: Innovation and dispute in British political thought 1880-1914*, Oxford: Clarendon Press.

Mill, J.S. (1965) 'Nature', in *Essential works of John Stuart Mill*, ed M. Lerner, New York: Bantam, pp 367-401.

Mill, J.S. (1970) *Principles of political economy (1848)*, reprinted in D. Winch (ed) (1970) *Principles of political economy, by J.S. Mill*, Harmondsworth: Penguin.

Millar, D. (1989) *Market, state and community*, Oxford: Clarendon Press.

Modernising social services (1998) London: Stationery Office, Cm 4109.

Mivart, St. G.J. (1873) 'Herbert Spencer', *Quarterly Review*, reprinted in Offer (ed) (2003), vol III, pp 201-27.

Moffatt, K. and Irving, I. (2002) '"Living for the brethren": Idealism, social work's lost enlightenment strain', *British Journal of Social Work*, vol 32, pp 415-27.

Morley, Viscount (1917), *Recollections*, New York: Macmillan (2 vols).

Morrow, D., Wilson, D. and Eyben, K. (2000) *Reconciliation and social inclusion in rural areas*, Cookstown, N. Ireland: Rural Community Network.

Muirhead, J.H. (1939) *The man versus the state as a present issue*, London: Allen and Unwin.

Murray, C. (1990) *The emerging British underclass*, London: Institute of Economic Affairs.

Neuman, M. (1982) *The Speenhamland County*, New York: Garland.

Nicholls, G. (1837) *Report of Geo. Nicholls, Esq. to His Majesty's principal secretary of state for the home department on poor laws, Ireland*, London: HMSO.

Nicholson, P.P. (1990) *The political philosophy of the British Idealists*, Cambridge: Cambridge University Press.

Norman, E. (1987), 'Legacies of an age of faith', *History Today*, October, p 56.

Nuffield Foundation (1947) *Old people: Report of a survey committee on the problems of ageing and the care of old* people under the chairmanship of B. Seebohm Rowntree, London: Oxford University Press.

Offer, J. (1983) 'Spencer's sociology of welfare', *The Sociological Review*, vol 31, no 4, pp 719-52.

Offer, J. (1984) 'Informal welfare, social work and the sociology of welfare', *British Journal of Social Work*, vol 14, no 6, pp 545-55.

Offer, J. (1985) 'Social policy and informal welfare', in M. Brenton and C. Jones (eds) *The year book of social policy in Britain 1984-5*, London: Routledge and Kegan Paul, pp 193-209.

Offer, J. (1990) 'Social administration and its relationship to the sociology of welfare', *International Journal of Sociology and Social Policy*, vol 10, no 1, pp 15-26.

Offer, J. (1991) 'Tönnies and Spencer', in L. Clausen and C. Schlüter (eds) *Ausdauer, Geduld und Ruhe: Aspekte und Quellen der Tönnies-Forschung*, Hamburg: Rolf Fechner Verlag.

Offer, J. (ed) (1994) *Herbert Spencer: Political writings*, Cambridge: Cambridge University Press.

Offer, J. (1996) 'Sociological theory and the sociology of scientific knowledge: a reply to Steve Fuller', *Sociology*, vol 30, no 1, pp 159-62.

Offer, J. (1999a) 'Idealist thought, social policy and the rediscovery of informal care', *British Journal of Sociology*, vol 50, no 3, pp 467-88.

Offer, J. (1999b) *Social workers, the community and social interaction*, London: Jessica Kingsley.

Offer, J. (1999c) 'Spencer's future of welfare', *The Sociological Review*, vol 47, no 1, pp 136-62.

Offer, J. (ed) (2000) *Herbert Spencer: Critical assessments*, London: Routledge, (4 vols).

Offer, J. (2003a) 'Free agent or "conscious automaton"? Contrasting interpretations of the individual in Spencer's writings on social and moral life', *The Sociological Review*, vol 51, no 1, pp 1-19.

Offer, J. (2003b) 'Idealism versus non-idealism: new light on social policy and voluntary action in Britain since 1880', *Voluntas*, vol 14, no 2, pp 227-40.

Offer, J. (2004) 'Dead theorists and older people', *Sociology*, vol 38, no 5, pp 891-908.

Offer, J. (2006) '"Virtue", "citizen character" and "social environment": social theory and agency in social policy since 1830', *Journal of Social Policy*, vol 35, no 2.

Owen, R. (1970) *A new view of society*, edited by V. A. C. Gatrell, Harmondsworth: Penguin.

Parker, G. (1990) *With due care and attention*, London: Family Policy Studies Centre.

Parker, J. (1976) 'Social policy', in A. H. Halsey (ed) *Traditions of social policy*, Oxford: Blackwell, pp 177-96.

Pascall, G. (1997) *Social policy: A new feminist analysis*, London: Routledge.

Passmore, J. (1968) *A hundred years of philosophy*, Harmondsworth: Penguin.

Peel, J.D.Y. (1971) *Herbert Spencer: The evolution of a sociologist*, London: Heinemann.

Peel, J.D.Y. (2004) 'Galton Lecture 2003: Spencer in history: the second century', in C. Jones and R. A. Peel (eds) *Herbert Spencer: The intellectual legacy*, London: Galton Institute, pp 125-49.

Perrin, R.G. (1975) 'Durkheim's misrepresentation of Spencer: a reply to Jones', *Sociological Quarterly*, vol 16, pp 544-50.

Perrin, R.G. (1995) 'Émile Durkheim's *Division of labour* and the shadow of Herbert Spencer', *Sociological Quarterly*, vol 36, no 4, pp 791-808.

Phillipson, C. (2001) 'History and historical sociology: divergent paths in the study of ageing', *Ageing and Society*, vol 21, pp 507-22.

Pinker, R.A. (1964) *English hospital statistics 1861-1938*, London: Heinemann.

Pinker, R.A. (1971) *Social theory and social policy*, London: Heinemann.

Pinker, R.A. (1974) 'Social policy and social justice', *Journal of Social Policy*, vol 3, pp 1-19.

Pinker, R.A. (1979) *The idea of welfare*, London: Heinemann.

Pinker, R.A. (1990) *Social work in an enterprise society*, London: Routledge.

Pinker, R.A. (1993) 'Social policy in the post-Titmuss era', in R. Page and J. Baldock (eds) *Social Policy Review*, 5, Canterbury: Social Policy Association, pp 58-80.

Poor Law Report (1909) *Report of the royal commission on the poor laws*, Cd 4499, London: HMSO, 3 vols.

Poor Law Report (Evidence) (1909) *Minutes of evidence, report of the royal commission on the poor laws*, Appendix Vol III, London: HMSO.

Poor Law Report (Ireland) (1909), *Royal commission on the poor laws: Report on Ireland*, C 4630, London: HMSO.

Poor Law Report (Scotland) (1909) *Royal commission on the poor laws: Report on Scotland*, C 4922, London: HMSO.

Poor Law Report (1974) *The poor law report of 1834*, edited by S.G. and E.O.A. Checkland, Harmondsworth: Penguin.

Popper, K.R. (1966) *The open society and its enemies* (5th edn), London: Routledge and Kegan Paul, 2 vols.

Poynter, J.R. (1969) *Society and pauperism*, London, Routledge and Kegan Paul.

Pringle Pattison, A. (1904) 'Life and philosophy of Herbert Spencer', *Quarterly Review*, July, pp 240-67.

Putnam, R.D. (2000) *Bowling alone*, New York: Simon and Schuster.

Quinton, A.M. (1972), 'Social thought in Britain', in C.B. Cox and A.E. Dyson (eds) *The twentieth century mind*, London: Oxford University Press, vol 1, ch 4, pp 113-35.

Qureshi, H. (1990) 'A research note on the hierarchy of obligations among informal carers: a response to Finch and Mason', *Ageing and Society*, vol 10, pp 455-58.

Report of the select committee on the state of the poor in Ireland (1830), London: HMSO.

Report of the Select Committee, Minutes of Evidence (1830) *Minutes of evidence before select committee on the state of the poor in Ireland*, London: HMSO.

Ritchie, D.G. (1889) *Darwinism and politics*, London: Sonnenschein.

Ritchie, D.G. (1891) *The principles of state interference*, London: Sonnenschein.

Ritchie, D.G. (1895) 'Mr Herbert Spencer's political philosophy', *Time*, vol 2, reprinted in Offer (2000), vol 4, pp 103-21.

Robinson, T. (1978) *In worlds apart*, London: Bedford Square Press.

Rose, H. (1981) 'Rereading Titmuss', *Journal of Social Policy*, vol 10, no 4, pp 477-502.

Rowlandson, P. (2000) 'Herbert Spencer and discrimination', *The Sociological Review*, vol 48, no 3, pp 473-5.

Rowntree, B.S. (1901) *Poverty: A study of town life*, London: Macmillan.

Runciman, W.G. (1998) *The social animal*, London: Harper Collins.

Russell, B. (1967) *Autobiography*, vol 1, London: Allen and Unwin.

Ryan, P.A. (1978) '"Poplarism" 1894-1930', in P. Thane (ed) *The origins of British social policy*, London: Croom Helm, pp 56-83.

Samuel, H. (1902) *Liberalism: An attempt to state the principles and proposals fo contemporary liberalism in England*, London: Richards.

Scott, D. (1971) *A. D. Lindsay: A biography*, Oxford: Basil Blackwell.

Seebohm Report (1968) *Report of the committee on local authority and allied personal social services*, Cmnd 3703, London: HMSO.

Senior, N.W. (1837) *Letter from Nassau W. Senior Esq. to His Majesty's principal secretary of state for the home department on the third report from the commissioners*, London: HMSO.

Seth, J. (1889) 'The evolution of morality', *Mind*, vol 14, reprinted in Offer (2000), vol 3, pp 333-51.

Sidgwick, H. (1880) 'Mr Spencer's ethical system', *Mind*, vol 5, reprinted in Offer (ed) (2000), vol III, pp 360-9.

Sidgwick, H. (1892) 'Critical Notice of *Justice*, by H. Spencer', *Mind*, vol 1, pp 107-18.

Smith, C.U.M. (1982) 'Evolution and the problem of mind: part 1 – Herbert Spencer', *Journal of the History of Biology*, vol 15, no 2, reprinted in Offer (ed) (2000), vol III, pp 238-66.

Spencer, H. (1836) 'Poor laws – Reply to "TWS"', reprinted in Offer (1994) pp 179-81.

Spencer, H. (1843) *The proper sphere of government*, London: Brittain, reprinted in Offer (ed) (1994), pp 1-57.

Spencer, H. (1851) *Social statics*, London: Chapman.

Spencer, H. (1853) 'Over-legislation', *Westminster Review*, July, reprinted in H. Spencer, *Essays: Scientific, speculative and political*, vol III, 1901, London: Williams and Norgate, pp 229-82.

Spencer, H. (1855) *Principles of psychology*, London: Longmans.

Spencer, H. (1862) *First principles*, London: Williams and Norgate.

Spencer, H. (1864) *Principles of biology*, vol 1, London: Williams and Norgate.

Spencer, H. (1867*)* *Principles of biology*, vol 2, London: Williams and Norgate.

Spencer, H. (1870) *Principles of psychology*, vol 1 (2nd edn), London: Williams and Norgate.

Spencer, H. (1871) 'Specialized administration', *Fortnightly Review*, December, reprinted in H. Spencer, *Essays: Scientific, political and speculative*, vol III, 1901, London: Williams and Norgate, pp 401-44.

Spencer, H. (1872) *Principles of psychology*, vol 2 (2nd edn), London: Williams and Norgate.

Spencer, H. (1873) *The study of sociology*, London: King.

Spencer, H. (1876) *Principles of sociology*, vol 1, London: Williams and Norgate.

Spencer, H. (1880) *Principles of psychology* (3rd edn), 2 vols, London: Williams and Norgate.

Spencer, H. (1882) *Principles of sociology*, vol 2, London: Williams and Norgate.

Spencer, H. (1884) *The man versus the state*, reprinted in Offer (1994), pp 61-175.

Spencer, H. (1891a) *Principles of sociology*, vol 2, 2nd edn, New York: Appleton.

Spencer, H. (1891b) 'On the origin of music', *Mind*, vol 16, pp 535-7.

Spencer, H. (1892a) *Principles of ethics*, vol 1, London: Williams and Norgate.

Spencer, H. (1892b) *Social statics, abridged and revised: Together with the man versus the state*, London: Williams and Norgate.

Spencer, H. (1893a) *Principles of ethics*, vol 2, London: Williams and Norgate.

Spencer, H. (1893b) *Principles of sociology*, vol 1 (3rd edn), London: Williams and Norgate.

Spencer, H. (1896) *Principles of sociology*, vol 3, London: Williams and Norgate.

Spencer, H. (1897a) *Various fragments*, London: Williams and Norgate.

Spencer, H. (1897b) *Principles of sociology*, vol 3, London: Williams and Norgate.

Spencer, H. (1901) 'The social organism', in H. Spencer, *Essays*, London: Williams and Norgate, vol 1, pp 265-307.

Spencer, H. (1904a) 'Unpublished letters', *The Independent*, vol 56, pp 998-1005.

Spencer, H. (1904b) *An autobiography*, 2 vols, London: Williams and Norgate.

Spencer, H. (1910) *The principles of ethics*, 2 vols, New York: Appleton (first published 1892/3, London: Williams and Norgate).

Spencer, T. (1836) *The successful application of the new poor law to the parish of Hinton Charterhouse*, London: Ridgway.

Tame, C.R. (1980) 'The libertarian tradition no. 1: Auberon Herbert', *Free Life*, vol 1, no 2, pp 1-3.

Taylor, M.W. (1992) *Men versus the state: Herbert Spencer and late Victorian individualism*, Oxford: Oxford University Press.

Taylor, M.W. (ed) (1996) *Herbert Spencer and the limits of the state*, Bristol: Thoemmes.

Taylor-Gooby, P. and Dale, J. (1981) *Social theory and social welfare*, London: Edward Arnold.

Thane, P. (1984) 'The working class and state welfare in Britain 1880-1914', *Historical Journal*, vol 27, no 4, pp 877-900.

Thane, P. (1990) 'The debate on the declining birth-rate in Britain: the "menace" of an ageing population, 1920s-1950s', *Continuity and Change*, vol 5, no 2, pp 283-305.

Thane, P. (2000) *Old age in English history: Past experience, present issues*, Oxford: Oxford University Press.

Third Report (1836) *Third Report of the Commissioners for inquiring into the condition of the poorer classes in Ireland*, London: HMSO.

Titmuss, R.M. (1950) *Problems of social policy*, London: HMSO and Longmans Green.

Titmuss, R.M. (1958) *Essays on the welfare state*, London: Allen and Unwin.

Titmuss, R.M. (1962) *Income distribution and social change*, London: Allen and Unwin.

Titmuss, R.M. (1968) *Commitment to welfare*, London: Allen and Unwin.

Titmuss, R.M. (1970) *The gift relationship*, London: Allen and Unwin.

Titmuss, R.M. (1974) *Social policy*, London: Allen and Unwin.

Tönnies, F. (1887) *Gemeinschaft und Gesellschaft*, translated by C. P. Loomis (1955) as *Community and association*, London: Routledge and Kegan Paul.

Tönnies, F. (1889) 'Herbert Spencer's Sociologisches Werk', *Philosophischen_Monatshefte*, vol 25, pp 50-85.

Townsend, P. (1963) *The family life of old people*, Harmondsworth: Penguin (first published 1957).

Townsend, P. (1968) 'Welfare services and the family', in E. Shanas, P. Townsend, D. Wedderburn, H. Friis, P. Milhoj and J. Stehouwer *Old people in three industrial societies*, London: Routledge and Kegan Paul, pp 102-31.

Townsend, P. (1976) *Sociology and social policy*, Harmondsworth: Penguin.

Townsend, P. (1986) 'Paradigms of poverty: a comment', *Journal of Social Policy*, vol 15, no 4, pp 497-8.

Turner, J.H. (1985) *Herbert Spencer: a renewed appreciation*, Beverly Hills: Sage.

Twigg, J. (1994) 'Carers, families, relatives: socio-legal conceptions of caregiving relationships', *Journal of Social Welfare and Family Law*, vol 16, no 3, pp 279-98,

Twigg, J. and Atkin, K. (1994) *Carers perceived: Policy and practice in informal care*, Buckingham: Open University Press.

Ungerson, C. (1998) 'The informal sector', in P. Alcock, A. Erskine and M. May (eds) *The student's companion to social policy*, Oxford: Blackwell.

Veit-Wilson, J. (1986) 'Paradigms of poverty: a rehabilitation of B. S. Rowntree', *Journal of Social Policy*, vol 15, no 1, pp 69-99.

Vincent, A. W. (1984) 'The poor law report of 1909 and the social theory of the Charity Organisation Society', *Victorian Studies*, vol 27, pp 343-63.

Webb, B. (1926) *My apprenticeship*, London: Longmans Green.

Webb, B. (1948) *Our partnership*, London: Longmans Green.

Webb, S. and Webb, B. (1910) *English poor law policy*, London: Longmans Green.

Webb, S. and Webb, B. (1912) *The prevention of destitution*, London: special edition printed by the authors for the use of the trade unionists of the United Kingdom.

Webb. S. and Webb, B. (1935), *Soviet communism: A new civilisation?*, Special limited edition printed by the authors for the subscribing members of the London Teachers' Association.

Weinstein, D. (1998) *Equal freedom and utility: Herbert Spencer's Liberal utilitarianism*, Cambridge: Cambridge University Press.

Wells, H.G. (1914) *An Englishman looks at the world*, London: Cassell.

Welshman, J. (2003) 'The unknown Titmuss', *Journal of Social Policy*, vol 33, no 2, pp 225-47.

Whately, R. (1832) *Introductory lectures on political economy*, London: Fellowes.

Whelan, R. (1996) *The corrosion of charity*, London: Institute of Economic Affairs.

Wilding, P. (1983) 'The evolution of social administration', in P. Bean and S. McPherson (eds) *Approaches to Welfare*, London: Routledge and Kegan Paul, pp 1-15.

Williams, K. (1981) *From pauperism to poverty*, London, Boston and Henley: Routledge and Kegan Paul.

Wiltshire, D. (1978) *The social and political thought of Herbert Spencer*, Oxford: Oxford University Press.

Wolfenden Report (1978) *The future of voluntary organisation*, London: Croom Helm.

Young, R.M. (1970) *Mind, brain and adaptation in the nineteenth century* Oxford: Clarendon Press.

Index